Social Change

AN ASSESSMENT OF CURRENT TRENDS

W0009836

STAFF OF THE LUTHERAN CHURCH IN AMERICA
TASK GROUP FOR LONG-RANGE PLANNING

Harold E. Berg	Commission on Church Papers	1/1/66-3/31/68
Dana H. Johnson	Commission on Evangelism	1/1/66-3/31/68
Lois I. Leffler	Lutheran Church Women	1/1/66-3/31/68
Luther R. Livingston	Commission on Stewardship	1/1/66-6/30/66
John M. Mangum	Board of World Missions	1/1/66-7/31/67
Beryl B. Maurer	Board of American Missions	1/1/66-6/30/67
Lawrence E. Nelson	Commission on Youth Activities	11/1/66-1/31/67
Richard J. Niebanck	Board of Social Ministry	1/1/66-3/31/68
Marcus F. Otterbein	Board of Parish Education	1/1/66-3/31/68
Donald R. Pichaske	Board of Parish Education	1/1/66-3/31/68
Franklin H. Schott	Board of American Missions	7/1/67-2/29/68
Mrs. John P. Shannon	Commission on Youth Activities	10/1/67-1/31/68
Leonard A. Sibley	Board of Parish Education	1/1/66-3/31/68
Wilbur G. Volker	Board of Parish Education	1/1/66-3/31/68
William E. Wendt	Board of Parish Education	1/1/66-5/20/66
John J. Ziegler, Jr.	Commission on Youth Activities	1/1/66-10/31/66
	Edward W. Uthe, Director	

SOCIAL CHANGE
AN ASSESSMENT
OF CURRENT TRENDS

REPORT OF THE LUTHERAN CHURCH IN AMERICA
TASK GROUP FOR LONG-RANGE PLANNING

EDWARD W. UTHE, Director

FORTRESS PRESS   PHILADELPHIA

CONTENTS

Preface

In an attempt to prepare for the decade from 1970 to 1980 the Lutheran Church in America created a Task Group for Long-Range Planning to conduct a planning study. The task group was given the assignment of forecasting the shape of the society in which and to which the church will be ministering, assessing trends in theological thought, interpreting trends in the life and work of the church and, finally, suggesting the major issues with which the Lutheran Church in America should be concerned in the 1970's. Findings of the task group are intended to be used primarily by LCA boards and commissions as a guide to policy formulation and program development for the next decade.

A small mountain of working papers was produced by the task group. The ore has been mined and refined. It now exists chiefly in the form of a task-group report *Significant Issues for the 1970's* and in supporting documents such as the one you are now reading. The viewpoint that present and prospective changes in society have a powerful influence on the church and its view of its mission appear to be accepted by the initiators of this study and by virtually all consultants who were involved at various stages of the project. The function of the present document is to provide details about changes taking place in society. Thus material which contributed to the development of the task-group report is made available to supplement the report.

Three questions guided the investigation of various aspects of social change. They are:

1. What changes are likely to take place in society during the 1970's?

2. How will these changes affect patterns of living and thinking?

3. What implications do these changes have for the life and work of the church?

Identification of areas or topics to be included in the analysis of social change was the first step taken in the quest for answers. The functional relationships and interactions of many aspects of society were evident at that point and continued to be so. However, it is not possible to discuss every facet of society simultaneously. For purposes of analysis it is necessary to specify what the major components are and to give attention to each in turn, as in this document. The second step involved study of each major component by means of interviews with specialists in various disciplines and library research. Findings were crystallized in a review draft of a report on social change which was subjected to critical evaluation by forty-three specialists in various fields. Their comments were secured through correspondence, telephone conversations, and personal interviews. Reactions were also secured from a large number of LCA staff officials who attended briefing sessions making use of the review draft. Changes were made on the basis of these evaluations as the present volume was prepared. Extensive changes were made in some chapters, while changes in other chapters were minimal because reviewers had favorable reactions to their original content and form.

As you read this report, keep in mind the fact that it is intended to be primarily descriptive. The body of each chapter describes trends in society as they have been identified by many observers. The effort to describe trends in strictly neutral fashion, using the "implications" section of each chapter as the locus for expression of value judgments, has probably not been entirely successful. It is likely that value judgments are reflected to some degree in the handling of descriptive material; perhaps this is unavoidable. The discussion of the implications of major trends in each area of social change is intended to be illustrative and to stimulate further thought about implications for the church and its mission. Viewpoints expressed in this volume are solely those of the task group. The intention is to provoke thought about implications of social change for the church, not to determine policies or programs.

Several limitations inhere in any effort to describe the major dimensions of society and of social change in a volume of this size. It is necessary to be selective rather than attempt an exhaustive discussion of each area. Consequently each chapter delineates only the major dimensions of the topic in question. The emphasis is on fundamental trends rather than on specific events. Persons who desire additional information about developments taking place are encouraged to make use of the selected bibliography provided at the end of the volume. There is an element of forecasting in each of the chapters. The expected direction and pace of various trends are indicated. The time period used for a frame of reference is 1970-1980.

Clearly not all changes occur at the same rate in every community in North America. Some areas bloom as centers of new technology while others fade in importance. Life in a rural area is different from life in a metropolis. There are significant differences between Canada and the United States. Hawaii, Alaska, Puerto Rico, and other sections of the United States have distinctive characteristics not shared by other areas. Despite the existence of regional differences, there are broad trends of social change that affect to some degree nearly everyone living in North America. This report is concerned with continent-wide trends and characteristics. It is manifestly impossible and undoubtedly inappropriate to discuss conditions of specific localities and regions in a report of this nature. The study of local characteristics and trends can be carried on most fruitfully and accurately by local groups. Hopefully, this report can be used to elucidate the broad social setting of local conditions.

The Nature of Social Change

I. FACTORS INFLUENCING SOCIAL CHANGE

Three factors have shaped our present social-physical environment: demography, economic-technological resources, and belief and value systems. The demographic factor includes the size, distribution, characteristics, and movement of the population. The economic-technological factor considers the natural resource base, production techniques, and systems of communication, transportation, manufacturing, distribution, and finance. Belief and value systems take in such elements as a society's prevailing outlook on life, individual and group aspirations, economic and political ideologies.

These basic factors combine to influence and are in turn influenced by such functional social structures as government, the economy, and religious institutions. The form and function of particular social institutions are shaped by the demographic and economic-technological bases, and by beliefs and values of the past and present. Their fundamental function is to maintain sufficient social stability, combined with adaptation to new circumstances, so that persons may lead as satisfying a life as conditions permit.

The form and function of a given social institution is sometimes modified by forces that influence the institution. For example, responsibility for the economic and social welfare of the population was accepted by the United States government in spite of traditions of individualism and laissez-faire economics. Pressures that arise for change, whether outside or within a given social institution, originate in and have an effect on the three basic factors: demography, economic-technological resources, belief and value systems.

Unanticipated and unintended events sometimes have a dramatic impact on a society. Sharp declines in food production, destruction and waste of resources in war, nonuse of human and material resources in depressions, the unexpected discovery of new devices or resources, substantial advances in human rights or in international cooperation produce sudden and far-reaching changes in a society. Such events often come as surprises because factors contributing to their development go unrecognized or because few people recognize or admit the possibility of a radical departure from past patterns. When major events are unanticipated, people and institutions are seldom prepared to make reasoned responses to them. The events are dealt with on an emergency basis with responses that are limited in range and sometimes inappropriate in both quality and quantity.

In Western culture, since the end of the Middle Ages, both the demographic and the economic-technological factors have tended to move consistently and continuously in a single direction. The rate has fluctuated, but the overall movement shows an accelerating development. In the modern Western world there has been a relationship between the demographic and economic-technological factors. Increasing population and rising aspirations of the population have created pressure for greater development and wider use of technology. Technological advance has created conditions which encourage population increase and a rising standard of living. The functional social structures change in response to population and economic-technological change, although the response is frequently slow. The effect on living patterns of changes in communications, education, science, and medicine is more immediate and marked. The individual is faced with the necessity of adjusting to the changes and developing new patterns of living and thinking.

The value system factor derives its force from the strength of human aspirations and human needs. It has been responsible for such developments as wars (motivated by either political or religious ideology), enactment of measures providing welfare and education, and advances in recognizing human rights. Value systems affect the goals and methods of operation of social institutions from governments to voluntary associations. Beliefs and values sometimes generate unexpected events and sometimes guide the response which is made to unexpected events. The civil rights movement and responses to it exemplify this function.

Beliefs and values influence demographic and technological factors or, at the least, interpret developments in these spheres. The extent to which labor-saving devices are used is influenced by convictions about man and society as well as by economic considerations. On the other hand, value systems are affected as population and technological developments present new challenges and possibilities. The development of thermonuclear weaponry seems to have strengthened ideologies which oppose war as an instrument of national policy.

Agents of Social Change

Social changes made possible by the basic factors are implemented by means of new social inventions or the wider use of earlier social inventions and by means of new physical inventions or the wider use of existing physical inventions. The introduction of a new physical device, such as the automobile, is seldom accompanied by consideration of all the potential long-range consequences. The wide use of such inventions is dependent on the ability of an individual or group of individuals to produce and distribute the item and on the ability and desire of large numbers of people to acquire it. Usually little thought is given to the values which make the item desirable or to the influence it might have in modifying values.

A different situation prevails in the introduction of social inventions such as extension of voting rights or welfare services. The introduction of social inventions is often accompanied by consideration of both the short-term and the long-term consequences. Adoption of the invention is advocated by arguments based on the prevailing value system as well as on expected benefits. Adoption or wider use of a social invention depends on the ability of its advocates to influence the power structures of the society.

Three elements can be used as leverage to gain the adoption or extension of a social invention: occupying an established position in the power structure, gaining access to and influence with those who occupy established positions in the power structure, and using symbols which occupy a high position in the society's value system. Persons who occupy positions of power and responsibility tend, often unconsciously, to emphasize maintaining and perfecting the existing system and to slight the need for adaptation and innovation. The result is that adoption or extension of social inventions is seldom initiated by power-holders, although this generalization may be more true of the past than the present.

Advocates of change often must rely on the use of influence and valued symbols. Influence may take the form of persuasion, pressure, or conflict and is often a combination of forms. Slogans which use prestige words or which express highly valued ideals of a society harness the power of symbols in the service of the desired change.

In countries of the Western democratic tradition, there is a sharing of power between officeholders and the public. The public, in turn, is composed of a variety of groups with diverse interests and goals. Advocates of social change may succeed initially by gaining the support of either group, but the change will succeed in the long run only if it is accepted by both power-holders and the public. If the change requires legislation, it can be adopted only if effective influence is brought to bear on a majority of legislators. The legislation, however, will be unsuccessful unless it is at least passively accepted by the public or unless it is enforced with effective deterrent penalties. On the other hand, a change which is acceptable to the public can be enacted in legislation only if it is accepted by legislators or if they fear reprisals at the polls.

II. SOCIAL CHANGE IN THE UNITED STATES AND CANADA

North America has benefited from long-term favorable experience with the major factors which make social change possible. There has been a population-resource ratio that is favorable to social progress. Canada and the United States have been free from catastrophic random events which destroy a substantial portion of resources or create widespread social disorganization. Many features of North American life have created conditions conducive to the development of technology. And fundamental aspects of the North American value system have created a climate receptive to change and improvement. These circumstances have contributed to social progress throughout the history of the United States and Canada.

Factors inhibiting progress have existed, and as a result not all geographical regions or social groups have experienced the same rate of progress. From time to time some regions and groups have been adversely affected by certain aspects of the overall movement forward. Such pockets of neglect occur when the detailed effects of major changes are not anticipated or are felt to be relatively unimportant.

A favorable ratio between population and resources has provided a solid base for social and economic growth. Ability and willingness to devote a portion of production to capital investment and knowledge accumulation are prerequisites for social and economic development. As an example, food production must be sufficient to provide more than subsistence for the population and must be so organized as to free part of the population for other activities. The same principal applies to production of other goods and services which are needed to sustain a standard of living which a society, formally or informally, decides to maintain.

Education, research, and construction of production facilities are the three major recipients of resources set aside for the development process. The importance of production facilities has long been recognized; more recently greater recognition has been given to the role of education and research. Much research is now highly organized, so that new products and processes are often the result of a systematic search rather than being fortuitous discoveries or the result of one man's work. Raising the educational level of the population is currently thought to be one of the key factors necessary for progress in developing nations. Higher educational levels for the total population create a larger labor force with skills required by more advanced technology and make possible the identification of persons of high intelligence who are likely to make further technological and social progress possible. However, only a relatively advanced society can afford to provide a lengthy education for the majority of its members. Less developed societies are hard put to finance the direct costs (buildings, teachers, equipment) and to do without the labor of those who spend several years as students.

A favorable population-resource ratio has prevented any widespread or prolonged famine or shortage of other goods and services required by the society. There has been no decline of population or widespread destruction of resources. Until World War II only a small portion of the national product was expended for military purposes or aid to other nations. Substantial production not required to maintain society at a given level has been available for investment in development activities. Social or political upheavals have disrupted the organization of society and diminished the output of goods and services infrequently and for short periods of time.

Value Systems

Identification and description of value systems are often influenced by subjectivity and personal viewpoints. However, many historians, sociologists, and anthropologists have attempted the task with reasonable detachment. Although they differ in detail, there is considerable agreement among them concerning the substance and nature of the value system dominant in North America. Some of the characteristics and attributes which they have identified as being highly valued in the United States and Canada seem to be factors which contribute to social change.

The strength of the prevailing value system varies in population subgroups and in individuals. The prevailing system may be considered as characteristic for Canada and the United States insofar as it describes the dominant values which guide the behavior of most people. It even influences the behavior of groups and individuals who deviate from it, since it fixes norms for behavior. Persons who want to avoid the social penalties of deviant behavior will conform to the dominant value system, while those who want to secure the rewards of deviation use it as a foil.

The North American *perspective on time* has been identified as a distinctive characteristic with value implications. North Americans are oriented more toward the future than toward the past. Someone has pointed out that the "God-term" in contemporary discourse is "progress" or "change." It is no accident that advertisers feel there is a certain magic in the word "new" when they describe a product or a process. The current widespread interest in forecasting the future of American society is not a new field of interest. As long ago as the early 1800's publications gave prominence to this theme.

North American society may be more accurately described as a developing society than as a traditional society. Both elements, of course, are present. But the developing or change component is more highly valued here than in many other societies. Long experience with changes of various kinds has prepared North Americans to expect continued change. Political and economic institutions have undergone shifts in purpose and scope; social class structure has changed; standards of living have progressed steadily; availability of and expectations concerning services such as health, education, and welfare have been modified. Most of these changes have been in the direction of improvement, judged in terms of North American values.

This long-term experience of change in the direction of improvement may be the foundation for melioristic views about the future. There is confidence that any desired improvement is possible if enough effort is devoted to it. Poverty can be abolished; water and air pollution can be remedied; advances in space exploration are possible; critical problems in international affairs can be solved; manufacturing techniques can be improved; education can be made more efficient. *Optimism and confidence* occupy a role in the North American value system in contrast with attitudes of acceptance of the status quo and resignation in the face of problems in value systems of some other societies.

Meliorism has been tempered by the limited success of large-scale attempts to solve some social problems and by a greater awareness of the seriousness of some problems. Tangible problems, such as urban decay and environmental pollution, tax both ingenuity and resources for their solution. Metropolitan government and the war on poverty are the source of administrative problems which may not be solvable with existing skills. Community disorganization, racial tensions, family problems, emotional disorders, crime, and lowering of behavior standards may be the unintended and unanticipated consequences of social changes which have otherwise been regarded as progress.

Purposive problem-solving to make human life easier, healthier, and happier has come to be a characteristic of inhabitants of North America. Confidence in ability to solve problems leads Americans and Canadians to devote energy and resources to finding solutions to problems which are felt to be serious. This is made possible by the fact that the society possesses resources beyond those required to maintain a given standard of living. A systematic approach to the analysis and solution of problems has become part of life. It is applied informally and perhaps unconsciously to problems small in scope; research proposals are judged on the basis of the rigorousness with which they use scientific methods as well as on substance; sophisticated techniques of systems analysis are applied to large-scale scientific and industrial problems. Commitment to scientific method, to rational problem-solving techniques, has achieved the desired results. It has met the test which the American poses to any new idea, procedure, or device: Does it work?

Pragmatism, *basing value on performance,* has come to be one of the chief criteria used in the North American value system. It has several consequences. One is a skeptical attitude toward doctrinaire proposals—in fact if not in words. Political, economic, and social institutions have developed on the basis of their performance in relation to the needs and norms of society rather than being created *de novo* on the basis of political and economic theory. The pattern is evolutionary rather than revolutionary progress. When the system is not functioning satisfactorily or when new needs or norms emerge, the system is retained and modified rather than being replaced by an entirely new system. Emphasis on success and evidences of success are a consequence of pragmatism's influence on the value system. This may underlie the phenomenon of status-seeking: status is an evidence of success, and success is a dominant criterion in a pragmatic value system. There is a tendency to conform to this norm.

Canadians and Americans tend to assign *high value to items which can be measured with objectivity.* High value is attached to tangible, material aspects of life—health, comfort, devices to make work easier. There is a tendency to judge the worth of an enterprise by the number of people or the number of dollars involved. Work is a positive value: is can be judged on the basis of its output, its difficulty, or the amount of time devoted to it.

It has been pointed out that one of the newer status symbols may be having to work late or having to bring work home. The positive value assigned to work, whether it is physical or mental, contrasts with a relatively low value associated with such difficult-to-measure mental activities as contemplation or meditation. Even observable activities, such as various forms of interpersonal relationships, are not assigned high value unless they produce measurable results. Activities related to organizational structures and procedures or to time-scheduling are relatively intangible, but their measurable results possess a high positive value.

An attitude toward the world and man seems to underlie many of the value judgments which guide the decisions and actions of residents of the United States and Canada. This attitude implies that the *world exists for man,* that man has the right and obligation to utilize and exploit the world in order to make his life more comfortable and pleasant. Exploitation should be limited or controlled if it has undesirable effects.

Education is one of the intangibles which has always been held in high esteem in North America. The extent to which North Americans have been willing to devote energy and resources to education, from colonial times to the present, has no parallel. Emphasis was placed on education long before there was evidence to demonstrate its value to the economy. Education has consistently had a high positive valuation, whether for religious, political, or economic reasons.

A complex of *moral values* has been prominent in influencing the behavior of Americans and Canadians. Sometimes these have been expressed in doctrinaire fashion and sometimes they have been nearly inarticulated. They have influenced both individual actions and national policies. There is a tendency to make black-and-white moral judgments. Decisions, actions, motives, and results are easily labeled "good" or "bad."

Consequently, standards of behavior are clear-cut and definite.

Individuals knows what the standards are and approve of them as standards, even though they may not be governed by them in personal decisions and actions. Persons in positions of responsibility are judged on the basis of their conformity with the moral standards as well as on their occupational competence. A sense of responsibility to persons and to occupational demands is rather strongly developed. A sense of responsibility to others or a strain of humanitarianism lead to a sharing with others of medical, educational, and technological advances.

There is an emphasis on equality and individual freedom, which are to be guaranteed by law if necessary. Personal dignity is preserved by allowing as much individualism as is consistent with the dignity and freedom of others. The value of political democracy is assumed as a concomitant of equality and personal freedom. Freedom of individual thought and opinion is emphasized, but strong pressures are exerted to enforce conformity in external conduct. Pride of country is high, verging in the United States on an uncritical sense of superiority which regards the home country as a model to be imitated by all other countries of the world. This attitude is reinforced by unquestionable signs of material success and by an altruistic desire to achieve similar success for other countries.

North American Agents of Social Change

Social structures invariably become the focal points for change because they are the places where power is located, and they are instruments by means of which changes can be introduced. At one time religious institutions could effectively promote social change because they could exert strong influence on officeholders and because they wielded highly valued symbols. There is reason to believe that the leverage which could be brought to bear by the churches on these counts is diminishing. Churches must rely more now on reasoned persuasion than in the past. Prestige-based and symbol-based influences are stronger for scientific and educational organizations.

Conflict and pressure on officeholders as avenues for the promotion of social change were used in the past by farm groups and labor groups. Changing socio-economic conditions now tend to reduce the actual power of these groups. Civil rights groups and poverty groups may gain their ends by using similar tactics as well as by judicious use of persuasion and valued symbols. In each of these instances, groups penalized by the current political and economic organization of society use available avenues to influence government policies. Group solidarity and agreement on specific goals are essential elements contributing to their success.

Other special-interest groups are able to substitute economic power for the power of a voting block. Privileges granted to railroads by legislatures in the United States in the late nineteenth and early twentieth centuries were the result of such exercise of power. While such flagrant and extreme forms of special treatment seldom occur any longer, various industries do seek and receive such privileges as tax concessions and tariff protection for their own benefit, as well as for the best interests of the country as a whole. The nature of the advantages granted to a given industry determine whether the policy inhibits or encourages social change.

Since the United States has become a world power, accepting the responsibilities and risks that such status entails, military policy has become as significant as diplomatic policy. The size of the defense establishment, the allocation of huge annual financial outlays, and the political factors related to defense policy make it inevitable that decisions reached by the military sector will have substantial impact on society, the economy, and politics. There are evidences of continuing tension between judgments of military men and those of their civilian superiors. Whether or not one questions the size and composition of the defense establishment, the actual and potential impact of defense policies on society must be recognized.

The American economic system has functioned as a long-term

agent of social change. Industry has benefited by producing for a mass market. Some products satisfy an existing or latent demand; other products satisfy a market largely created by advertising. The quantity and variety of goods made available to North Americans in this way have played a major role in various social changes. The growth of the economy and the distribution of disposable income have been major influences in the shaping of modern society. Specific products such as the automobile and television have had far-reaching impact, both in making life more pleasant and in creating social problems.

Independent foundations are perhaps the only significant change agent in American society largely free of self-interest. They exert a substantial impact on society by their choice of projects for support. The scientific investigations they sponsor produce results which can change living patterns. The extensive studies of American education supported by foundations in the last twenty years may have been a significant factor in the creation of greater public interest in, and support of, education.

The comprehensive power structure of a society may be classified as monopolistic, competitive, or pluralistic. In a monopolistic power structure, one institution or group of individuals possesses exclusive control of the means of power. In a competitive structure, several groups with conflicting interests struggle for control. The winners gain and the losers suffer. A pluralistic power structure includes a variety of groups, each seeking its own ends. There are competitions between groups whose goals are mutually exclusive, alliances among groups whose goals are compatible, and simultaneous but unrelated efforts of groups seeking various goals. The pluralistic power structure which exists to a degree in the United States and Canada offers a reasonable possibility of insuring a recognition of the demands of all groups and of facilitating measures which will balance the interests of the majority and the rights of minorities.

Another way of analyzing power structure in free societies is to view it as a tension or balance between the interests of powerholders and the public. This analysis applies to both the political and economic realms. Political officeholders who do not provide governmental services which constituents want will be voted out of office, unless they are persuasive enough to change the minds of their constituents. Industries which do not provide goods and services which customers want will be voted out of office by lack of sales, unless they can persuade customers to want what is offered. In a system of this kind, persuasion works two ways— from powerholders to the public and from the public to powerholders. The ultimate decision and control lies in the hands of the public.

III. HUMAN REACTIONS TO SOCIAL CHANGE

Social change is the product of human effort, whether men initiate a desired change or react to changing circumstances in the environment. In either case, the activity related to change is usually prompted by the dominant value system and determined by the resources and abilities devoted to the activity. Factors which stimulate change are of many varieties. They include population density and distribution, the population-resource ratio, technological developments, shifts in value systems, contacts with other societies, changes in functions of various social institutions, and fortuitous events. The major factors contributing to social change in North America have been discussed above in conceptual terms. In the chapters that follow, the specific manifestations of these changes will be discussed in some detail.

In a time of social change, a nice balance is required between efforts devoted to effecting desired changes and improvements and efforts devoted to insuring stability by maintaining existing patterns and practices. When the balance tips toward the rapid introduction of new patterns and practices, strains and potential disruption of the system are introduced, if old patterns disintegrate before new patterns are well enough established to maintain the system. When the balance tips toward maintaining existing patterns and practices, introduction of desired improvements is delayed, perhaps indefinitely.

The necessary balance between maintenance and improvement efforts in a social system or institution has a counterpart in individuals. An individual is likely to oppose a change which he perceives to be in conflict with accustomed behavior patterns (ways of acting which in his experiences have produced desired results), or in conflict with the values to which he is explicitly or implicitly committed. In either case, he will view the change as a threat and will prevent it if he has the power to do so.

If he cannot prevent it, he may come to see that the change has desirable results and modify his outlook accordingly. On the other hand, he may continue to resist the change even though he has to live with it. In this case, inner feelings of conflict will arise. Such stresses occur in a society in which many changes are taking place, changes which are beyond the control of most individuals within the society and which call for the adoption of new patterns of behavior. The result is a feeling of alienation, normlessness, or futility and, in extreme cases, disruption of functions required for the maintenance of the social system.

Change is more acceptable in some areas of life than in others. A change is more acceptable if it is concerned with a way of doing things (a means) rather than with the goal of the activity (the end). A change is more likely to be accepted if it is seen as a more effective means of attaining a given end than if it is seen as the adoption of a new goal. Though a person will still feel threatened when his former mode of operation is replaced by something better, he is not required to modify his goals or value system. Rapid change is possible in such fields as economics and technology, because there is quick and clear evidence of the different results produced by new and old procedures. The chain of cause and effect is direct, easy to understand, measurable, and can be viewed as a means rather than an end.

On the other hand, in some areas of life the result of a new procedure may not be measured easily and the change may appear to be a change in end rather than in means. Resistance to change will consequently be greater and adoption of change slower. This is why change takes place slowly in social institutions such as political systems. Natural resistance to any change is compounded by feelings that values may be threatened and fears that the change may have unforeseen effects.

Rate of change also is affected by the degree of centralization and direct control which exist in the agency or institution where the change is to take place, and by the clarity with which the institution's goal is defined. A new industrial process or a new organizational system can be introduced relatively rapidly in a business enterprise because (a) decisions and control are centralized, with all units of the organization required to act in conformity with the decision, and (b) the organization's goal is clearly defined in measurable economic terms.

This contrasts with the relative slowness of changes introduced by means of political institutions. Often the goal is not clearly defined or is not easily measurable. Even when it is, action cannot be undertaken until a majority of the electorate is willing to accept it. The tardiness of government action in such fields as urban renewal and pollution control stems from the time required for the public to recognize the problem and to regard correction as a proper goal of government activity. Tardiness of government action in such fields may be contrasted with promptness of government action in fields where there is minimal disagreement about goals, such as defense measures in wartime. Lack of experience in dealing with some problems and questions about the best method of solving them is often a cause of delay.

A crucial question is how the inhabitants of North America can be expected to react to social changes that are anticipated in the next decade. The question is as complex as it is crucial. Reactions will vary among individuals and among population groupings. A given individual or population group will react differently to different changes, welcoming some and resisting others. It is beyond the scope of this report to consider all the possibilities. There is some value in considering the question in a more general way. What will be the typical response of the greater part of the population to the total complex of changes that are expected? An attempt is made to answer this question in the final chapter of this report.

IV. FORECASTING CONSIDERATIONS

Is it possible to forecast the future with any degree of confidence? Lists can be made of forecasts which have been supported by subsequent events and of forecasts which completely missed the mark. A few years ago it was possible to foresee that there would be an education explosion, that sincere and strenuous efforts would be made to minimize international conflict, that urban problems would require attention, that labor-management relations would tend to become more rational, that rapid population growth would take place, that television would gain a prominent place in mass communications. On the other hand, social scientists are rightly embarrassed by a multitude of political and economic forecasts which proved to be completely erroneous.

Forecasting must face honestly the limitations that inhere in the attempt. Time itself is a limitation. Despite some current attempts to guess at the conditions of life in the year 2000 and beyond, no one is likely to put money on the line in support of specific predictions that far in the future. There seems to be a consensus that fairly reliable forecasts may be made for a five-year period, but that even these must be subject to constant review and revision. A broad outline of future developments may be projected on a ten- to fifteen-year basis, provided that it is subject to review and revision.

One reason many forecasts have proved to be mistaken is that unforeseeable, fortuituous events do occur. Forecasts must recognize that unforeseen developments will alter expectations of the future. Events that are discontinuous with known streams of development insert unknown quantities into the equation. There may be specific events, such as the death of a president, an unexpected epidemic, an unprecedented new weapon. Or there may be intangibles, such as the climate of opinion at a given time in history. In 1929 the opinion climate changed from soaring optimism to bleak pessimism in a few months. The course of economic history may have been influenced more by the public's outlook than by more tangible factors. The way people feel affects what they do and has a strong influence on what happens in society. It affects also the way people perceive what the future holds; our view of the future is colored by our present experiences. While the fact is inescapable, our recognition of it will contribute to the development of a sounder perspective on the future.

Taking into account the limitations inherent in any forecasting attempt, what can be done to arrive at forecasts which are reasonably valid? Certain crescive trends can be discerned in the history of the past several centuries: for example, the extension of political freedom and national self-determination; man's expanding control over his natural environment to provide more comfort and convenience; weakening of barriers between social classes. Trends which have continued over a long period of time and have consistently moved in the same direction provide one dimension within which forecasts are to be made.

A second dimension is provided by enduring and consistent qualities of human nature. These qualities are probably produced by intrinsic biological, social, and theological needs. In a great variety of circumstances man has created, modified, and utilized institutions and situations in order that these needs might be met. The universal existence of some form of family life is an example. The form has varied in response to different physical and social circumstances, but the institution has persisted. In light of this fact, predictions that new conditions of life will render the family obsolete may be interpreted to mean that new forms and expressions of family life will emerge and that the institution will persist. Some social scientists feel that work is essential to an individual's feeling of worth, apart from any ethical or economic considerations. If this is the case, and if technology makes productive work in the traditional sense unnecessary, society may create new forms of work.

Crescive or long-term social trends and stable characteristics of human nature provide two dimensions of the frame within which forecasts are to be made. The third dimension is the introduction of new elements and the response they elicit. Possibilities of extending human life by replacing worn-out parts of the organism, of preserving human brains in functioning condition after the person dies, of manipulating genetic material to create offspring to meet specifications— such possibilities create a feeling of unease as well as raise a host of ethical and social problems. Perhaps society will choose not to use such frightening scientific advances, just as it has chosen not to use thermonuclear weapons since 1945. The response society makes to situations such as the developing world's water and food shortages will shape the future. Responses to new opportunities and situations are probably unforeseeable in essence.

It is likely, however, that responses will be made within the framework of long-term social trends and stable human characteristics. On the other hand, disruption may occur when technological developments make feasible the reversal of long-term trends. For example, developments in communications may render obsolete one of the traditional functions of the city as a center for exchange of information between persons.

Any attempt at forecasting must recognize both its assumptions and its limitations. The limitations have been indicated above. The assumptions are: (1) Future developments will be strongly influenced by crescive social trends and by stable characteristics of human nature. (2) The direction of future developments is likely to be indicated by frontier scientific discoveries, technological applications, and political-social-economic proposals. (3) While the direction and character of change can be anticipated with some degree of reliability, the exact degree and pace of change cannot be anticipated precisely. (4) Any forecast made on the basis of the best evidence available at a given time may be nullified by the introduction of truly novel elements and/or random developments. (5) Any given change may have differential effects on various geographical areas, population subgroups, and facets of an individual's life. (6) Change will be more rapid in the economic-technological areas than in functional social structures, with consequent social problems and stresses for society and individuals.

V. DIRECTION OF CURRENT SOCIAL TRENDS IN NORTH AMERICA

Chapters that follow discuss in detail current and anticipated developments in various segments of society. It may be helpful to have, as background for considering the specifics, an identification of major trends which have been pointed out by historians and sociologists. Each item listed below is discussed more fully in the remaining chapters of this volume. The forecasts are based on the extension of long-term trends and current developments.

North American population growth will continue, probably at a decelerating rate. Concentration of population in various age-groups will change according to a pattern indicated by present age-group concentrations and the effect of the passage of time on present concentrations. Continued migration to urban centers will produce increased population density in those centers and produce geographical spread of urbanization. Suburbanization will grow with urbanization, unless there is a shift away from widespread aspirations for home ownership. Urban and suburban problems are likely to increase accordingly.

Economic growth will produce a rising standard of living, reflected in increase in average real income per person, nearly universal access to necessities, and more widespread access to luxuries. There will be a sharp increase in families with annual income of more than $10,000 a year. The proportion of the population living below the poverty line will decrease. The effect on patterns of living may be a shift toward life styles of the more affluent segment of the population.

Improvements in living standards have produced changes in prevailing life styles and will continue to do so. Increases in real income may lead to a general upward shift in patterns of living, so that a smaller part of the population will follow living patterns of the lowest socio-economic groups and a larger part will adopt living patterns of the middle socio-economic groups. An increasing number of persons will be able to enjoy the amenities and engage in activities formerly reserved for those at the upper end of the social scale. An illustration of this is seen in the increased proportion of the population engaging in extended vacation travel and/or owning second homes.

Although there will be progress toward some form of guaranteed income, poverty will continue to be a problem. Affluence may create problems as it changes personal life styles. There will be a lessening personal emphasis on work and production and an increasing emphasis on enjoyment and consumption. Greatest employment increases will occur in government and the service industries, and a generally higher level of skills will be required of workers, creating employment problems for the undereducated.

Government's role in life will increase as it assumes larger and wider responsibilities for the well-being of the total population in response to popular expectations. Responsibility for financing government services and setting policies will rest chiefly with the federal government. The United States will move in the direction of broader social welfare benefits, such as those already provided in Canada. Increased government responsibility may require a larger proportion of personal and corporate income for taxes. Increase in bureaucratic organization and regulation will create annoyance and frustrations for individuals who must deal with the bureaucracy. Government will be charged with and will accept more extensive responsibility for protecting individual rights. Human services formerly supplied by voluntary agencies will tend to be provided by governmental agencies.

Education will absorb an increasing amount of national resources and schooling will occupy a more central place in the lives of most persons. Greater educational achievement will be reached at lower ages and an increasing proportion of the population will acquire more years of schooling. Attempts will be made to counter depersonalization caused by educational technology with more highly individualized instruction and explicit attention to human values as curriculum content. Accumulation of factual knowledge will be de-emphasized and development of high-level intellectual skills will be stressed. Increased prestige for intelligence and educational achievement may make them a larger cause of social class differentiation, even though efforts are made to counteract this tendency.

Continuing advances in physical and biological sciences and in technology will extend man's control over the physical world and his own body and mind. Science will make progress toward solving such problems as inadequate food supply, environmental pollution, decreasing resources, human disease.

New problems, however, now in the making because of current social trends may challenge scientific ingenuity. Advances in the space sciences will continue to raise certain theological questions, and increasing capability for biological and psychological manipulation will raise serious ethical problems. As the social sciences move toward greater precision and sophistication, developing more ability to channel and control social change, there will arise ethical questions concerning who is to decide desirable directions for social change and what criteria are to be used for making such decisions. Similar questions regarding the application of scientific findings capable of shaping individual behavior will arise.

Internationalism will be encouraged by the further development of a complex interdependent worldwide system of commerce and industry, by cultural exchange, and by tourism. The United States may continue to develop its sense of responsibility for world peace and economic growth. Attempts to discover goals and policies for meeting this responsibility may lead either to errors, disillusionment, and withdrawal, or to successes and the acceptance of greater responsibilities.

Recently there has been an emphasis on the need to develop relationships among various groups and persons within a given community. This type of horizontal social structure once was the prevailing mode of social organization for North American communities. It has eroded as people cultivate associations with persons of similar interests in other communities. A vertical structure has developed in which, for example, a physician or a plant manager tends to identify with his counterparts in other communities rather than with persons in his own community who have different interests. The extent to which either the horizontal or vertical structure influences the way people think of their relationships, and the way they identify with others, may have implications for ecclesiastical structures and relationships.

Changing social conditions will create stresses and tensions for individuals and for families as patterns of life and thought are reshaped. It is likely that a high value will continue to be placed on family life, at least formally, while various factors will tend to erode family stability. Nurturing affectional needs may come to be the chief social function of the family as organized society assumes a larger role in satisfying economic, educational, and other personal needs.

Shifting social patterns may require the discovery or invention of new sources for the development of friendships and emotionally satisfying personal relationships. The recent growth of "introduction services" and other social clubs for single persons may be symptomatic of the needs. The trend toward depersonalization in society may cause persons to become more acutely aware of their need for personal relationships even as circumstances create obstacles to developing them. Stresses introduced by social change, urbanization, and intricate social organization may contribute to an increase in emotional disorders.

The continuing shift from a moral to a causal interpretation of human behavior will probably minimize the assignment of moral blame, reducing the extent to which an individual may be held morally responsible for his actions. This will tend to make nonconforming personal behavior more readily acceptable. There is likely to be an increasing drift away from traditional norms of behavior in the direction of personal freedom, individualism, and even eccentricity. Relative ease in securing at least the necessities of human life will make possible authentic expressions of altruism and idealism for some, while others will go to extremes of hedonism or cynicism, with consequent anti-social behavior. Rejection of traditional forms and norms in much contemporary art and literature may presage a widespread acceptance of this approach to life.

Feelings of personal responsibility for the welfare of others may decline as government assumes responsibility for supporting or providing services formerly provided by voluntary organizations. Organized religion may decline as material progress appears to make the spiritual dimension irrelevant or even unnecessary. Emphasis on intellect and reason may incline others to bypass religion because of its nonrational elements. Still others will likely regard organized religion as outmoded because of its dependence on forms and practices inherited from the past. A great many people, however, will continue to sense a need for God and will find this need met through the traditional and innovative ministries of the church.

Greater concentrations of population, more complex social systems, and more sophisticated technology will lead to a high level of rational organization and interdependence in society. Widespread use of systems analysis, operations research, and advances in computer technology will contribute to a sophisticated and complex organization of society. There will of necessity be a high degree of specialization and division of labor. Interdependence and specialization will require a high-level performance conformity in occupational tasks.

Keeping the system running efficiently will permit little day-to-day improvisation or creativity. This will restrict the scope of individual decision-making in occupational responsibilities. More decisions will be made on the basis of computer analyses, sometimes without regard to qualitative factors and value implications which have not been identified with sufficient precision to be included in quantitative calculations. The possible effects of population concentration and a complex social organization on the individual lie in their potential for depersonalization as well as their potential for improving the quality of life. They may intensify personal anonymity and loss of identity even as they offer greater personal freedom and a higher material standard of living.

VI. SUMMARY AND IMPLICATIONS

A. Summary

1. Social change is the result of developments in and interactions among population, economic-technological resources, belief and value systems, functional social structures, and fortuitous events.

2. Decisions and actions which lead to social change are based on values implicitly or explicitly held. Such decisions often lead to unanticipated material and social consequences and contribute to unintended changes in the value system. Major social problems are often concomitants of unanticipated results.

3. Planned or purposeful social change occurs when the change agents occupy positions of power or influence powerholders and utilize symbols valued highly by the society. Symbolic values embodied in the scientific and academic communities currently tend to be powerful influences for change. What is not clear is the

extent to which general social change can be contolled without utilizing a highly centralized organization of society which places virtually unlimited power in the hands of a relatively few individuals.

4. Effective social progress requires a balance between introducing desired changes and maintaining sufficient stability to insure a functioning social organization. A similar pattern is required for adaptation to change by individuals.

5. Social change in the Western world since the Renaissance, particularly in North America, has been in the direction of material progress and upward social mobility for the population as a whole. The rate of change appears to be accelerating.

6. The direction of current trends in North American society holds promise for continued advance in the material aspects of human life if resources are devoted to solving environmental problems. Problems in the areas of personal adjustment and interpersonal and group relationships may become more serious.

7. Forecasts of social change can be made, subject to certain limitations, by identifying long-term trends, likely human reactions to possible changes, and frontier scientific and social inventions.

B. *Implications*

Major social trends are produced by extremely potent social factors. The church, particularly a single denomination, is unlikely to possess the measure of control of power, influence, or value symbols required for a significant impact on any major social trends. Any effort by the church to have an effect on major social developments must be coordinated with efforts of other groups or persons in order to utilize valued symbols, to exert influence, and to gain access to powerholders. Results will occur only as the consequence of consistent and persistent activity.

The direction of major social trends in North America indicate that three types of problems will continue and perhaps become more acute in the next decade: (1) problems related to the physical-social environment, (2) problems related to the well-being and human rights of various population subgroups, and (3) problems related to personal and family adjustment to social change.

The church should decide on priorities for allocating the use of its human and material resources to attempt solutions for these three types of problems and the specific problems within each category. It is unlikely that the Lutheran Church in America possesses resources sufficient to support significant attempts to find solutions to all existing and emerging problems.

Expected changes in patterns of living and thinking will create changes in the value large numbers of people consciously or unconsciously assign to the spiritual dimension of life and to their participation in religious institutions and activities. In order to reach such people the church will need to find ways to present the gospel meaningfully, new forms of institutional life, and new expressions of Christian discipleship. At the same time, a great many people will continue to find meaning and security in the more traditional formulations and expressions of Christian life and faith. The church must continue to serve these persons by maintaining and modifying, as necessary, its existing forms of ministry.

By identifying patterns of church life which are effective and appropriate in ministering to persons who are slightly above the current average socio-economic level, the church may prepare to minister to the larger numbers who are expected to reach this level as real income increases. Efforts to design patterns of church life and strategies for ministering to persons in the future should not detract from current efforts to minister to and improve living conditions for persons who now occupy the lowest socio-economic level.

It seems likely that in society at large both the horizontal and the vertical orientations will persist, each supplementing the other. Existence of national denominations and extensive inter-denominational activities at the local level would seem to be consonant with the dual vertical-horizontal orientation. The dual orientation does not, however, necessitate maintenance of all existing denominations. Horizontal and vertical perspectives can be preserved with a smaller number of denominations or even within a single unified church. There is every reason to believe that the vertical orientation will be maintained either in existing denominations or in mergers of denominations. The need for the near future is a strengthening of the horizontal orientation by cultivating more intensive and extensive cooperative activities at the local level.

2

The World Setting

I. INTRODUCTION

This chapter begins with a brief survey of present world conditions and continues with a more detailed discussion of those major world problems which seem most likely to affect and be affected by the church's ministry in the next decade. In the following chapter the North American scene will be considered in greater detail as the specific arena within the world scene in which and from which the Lutheran Church in America must operate. In the succeeding chapters specific areas and problems of national and personal life will be examined at greater length.

II. A BRIEF SURVEY OF WORLD CONDITIONS

The most important single factor in international relations is, without question, the cold war. Certainly the cold war has dominated and shaped United States foreign policy for the past twenty years. While Canadians have been less exercised by this contest between giants and the ideologies which motivate them, they have nevertheless been indirectly influenced by the cold war because of their proximity to its two major contenders.

The United States and Russia emerged from World War II as undisputed world leaders. But the alliance which brought them together during that war broke down over what each nation saw as the expansionist ambitions of the other. The United States reacted in two ways: by a policy of containment and by a program of massive economic assistance to non-Communist countries.

The containment policy called for the establishment of a network of treaty organizations (NATO, SEATO, etc.) which sought to surround and isolate the Communist bloc of nations. It also led to actual armed intervention in a number of internal foreign crises (Korea, Dominican Republic, Cuba, Vietnam) which appeared to be Communist-led or inspired. A strict policy of nonrecognition has been followed in the case of the People's Republic of China, together with a determined, though increasingly unpopular, policy of keeping her outside the United Nations. It should be noted here that Canada has consistently advocated a more open policy toward Red China and has actively sought a role as a third party in this and in other disputes between the United States and Communist nations.

The major share of United States economic assistance has been directed toward Europe. Much of that continent lay in ruins at the close of World War II. In the past two decades it has rebuilt its industry and economy until it is now able to declare its independence from the United States. England and Scandinavia are making overtures to the Common Market; they are moving slowly away from United States leadership. Continental Europe appears to be achieving greater internal unity and autonomy, and thereby also gaining greater freedom from what some Europeans see as an overdependence on the United States. By the same token, eastern Europe seems to be drawing away from Russian domination and toward its old neighbors in the West. Many observers see the emergence of a unified and independent Europe as a necessary "third force" between the United States and Russia.

The Alliance for Progress, which was to have been for Latin America what the Marshall Plan was for Europe, has never really got off the ground. This alliance grew out of fears that Latin America was to be the next focus for Communist expansion. The Cuban missile crisis made it clear that Russia had a firm foothold in the Western Hemisphere, one which the abortive Bay of Pigs invasion did not succeed in dislodging. Cuba was to be the headquarters for subversion throughout Latin America and a shining illustration of what Communism could do for the countries and peoples of that area. But after a number of years of very costly assistance from Russia, Cuba remains on the brink of bankruptcy. And while Communist subversion in a number of areas remains a threat, it has not yet proved to be the danger which many feared. Thus, for the time being, the Alliance for Progress has not received priority attention. Aid to Latin America has been channeled chiefly through the World Bank, reflecting a newer trend in United States foreign-aid strategy, by which aid is more often given indirectly rather than directly, and in a way which stimulates the greatest amount of self-help and the least amount of dependence. Nevertheless, the situation in South America remains volatile.

In Asia, Japan has emerged from the ashes of Hiroshima as Asia's most powerful industrial nation. South Korea has begun a program of renewal with massive American assistance. The Philippines have become increasingly prosperous, though still plagued by problems of internal corruption. A few other Asian nations such as Iran, Malaysia and Thailand, are enjoying greatly increased economic levels. But these bright spots cannot erase the grim specter of hunger and poverty which still haunts this densely-populated area of the earth. India has yet to fulfill the bright promise of her independence. Indonesia has only now begun a long upward climb after a bloody brush with Communism. Vietnam seems destined to suffer further hardships no matter how the conflict there is ended.

In the Middle East, Nasser's flirtation with Communism led him to over-optimism regarding the aid he might expect from Russia in his determination to defeat and destroy Israel. As a result, his influence within the Arab nations has been considerably reduced, giving rise to hopes for a more realistic policy in the Middle East.

Some troubled spots or at least question-mark areas are Nigeria, where a breakup into a number of pieces is possible; the "sword's point" relationship between the Somali Republic and French Somaliland; Ethiopia, with its explosive situation in Eritrea; the slaughter taking place between various tribes in the liberation movements in Aden and Yemen; the military dictatorship which has taken over in Greece; the still unsolved Cyprus situation; and the gap between the United Nations proposals for African republics and the political realities of Rhodesia, South Africa and South-West Africa.

Nevertheless, the cold war appears to be entering a new phase, with the renewal of ancient hostilities between Russia and Red China, and the emergence of a variety of differing ideologies in what once seemed a monolithic bloc of nations. The U.S.S.R. is not likely to abandon its dream of becoming a world-embracing power, but it does appear to be practicing a more realistic policy of peaceful coexistence. As a number of eastern European nations have reformed their economies and introduced market forces and profit motives, they have sought freedom for expanded trade with the West. The Soviet Union does not run these nations any longer, although it still dominates eastern European trade.

Throughout the world, nationalism is a strong force to be reckoned with. The great powers seem less and less able to exert control and influence, as independence is demanded not only by former colonies but by sectional or cultural groupings within countries, resulting in the subdivision of a number of nations. In addition to these strong national tendencies is an increasing number of regional economic alliances. Smaller nations tend to band together in order to offset the influence of larger nations and to achieve economic advantages which would not otherwise be possible. The nuclear stalemate between the United States and Russia has given these smaller nations greater freedom of movement than would otherwise be possible.

Another trend on the world scene has been the gradual dissolution of the British Empire. Economic pressure at home and political pressure from abroad has led to the withdrawal of British presence from many parts of the world. The vacuum created by this shrinkage of British influence is being filled only in part by expanding United States involvement.

As the ability of the great powers unilaterally to maintain world stability decreases, the United Nations take on added importance. But the UN, born in such great hope at the close of World War II, has not fulfilled the expectations which many held for such a world organization. The same resistance to change which marks individual foreign policies has also plagued the UN itself. Its charter needs revision to eliminate the veto privilege of the so-called great powers, to reconsider the place of the many smaller nations which have recently applied for admission, and to provide for properly financed peace-keeping machinery. But there is little likelihood such charter revisions will be undertaken unless there is a corresponding change in the foreign policies of its present and future members. This, in turn, can happen only if a climate of opinion is created which can make such changes possible.

Finally, a serious gap in United States foreign policy is the absence of any consistent opposition against non-Communist totalitarian regimes. The free world has thus been unable to move effectively against the governments of South Africa or Rhodesia, and has rested more comfortably with dictatorships in Spain, Greece, Portugal and Latin America than seems consistent with a genuine concern for human freedom and dignity. Thus encouraged, it is perhaps not surprising that Nazism is having something of a resurgence in West Germany, a development which will have to be watched carefully.

III. THREE MAJOR WORLD PROBLEMS

Of all the goals which seem likely to shape international relationships for the next several decades, three stand out as of major significance: peace, population control, and prosperity.

Peace

The search for peace is as old as the human race. It takes on added urgency in the decade ahead because of the proliferation of nuclear arms. Hopes for peace appear to lie in four major areas: the UN, the balance of power, arms control, and the development of programs of cultural and scientific exchange.

World War II had not yet ended when the nations of the world had already begun laying the foundations for the UN, which was envisioned as a means of establishing and maintaining world peace. Although initial hopes for the UN as a genuine world government were dampened by the insistence of the great powers on retaining the privilege of the veto, the UN nevertheless remains an important instrument for international debate and understanding, and thus the greatest single hope of mankind for peace. In instances where the UN has operated as an international police force (Korea, Congo), it has enjoyed a measure of success. It has also functioned as a forum for international debate in which international opinion can be brought to bear on national ambitions.

Nearly all the new nations have applied for UN membership immediately upon their creation and thus have been exposed to the thinking of the world community. While this influx of new nations has presented the UN with certain problems, the problems posed by their remaining outside would be far greater. Unfortunately, none of the divided nations are a part of the UN (Germany, Vietnam, Korea, China). As long as any significant segment of the human population remains unrepresented in the UN, that organization will continue to be thwarted in its quest for peace and understanding.

The UN has also been undermined and reduced in effectiveness by the tendency of the great powers, including the United States, to operate unilaterally. The United States has not been happy about the disproportionate share of the UN costs which it has been called upon to bear, and by the failure of other major powers (notably France and the Soviet Union) to pay their assessments for peace-keeping operations. However, expulsion or withdrawal from the UN appears to be a short-sighted solution to this problem. The UN is simply a recognition of the realities of our human situation—that we are, before everything else, part of one family, the human race, and that we all inhabit the same earth. Now that mankind possesses the ability to bring the human race, if not the earth itself, to an end, a world organization for peace seems the most necessary and logical goal for every nation, even in terms of pure self-interest.

It seems fair to point out that the United States has been more successful in achieving its aims when it has chosen to work within the framework of the UN (as in the case of Korea) than when it has by-passed the UN (as in Vietnam). A way must be found by which to balance the tension between national self-interest and the requirements of the international community of nations.

A significant development on the international scene has been the emerging of new nations. Colonial systems of all types are breaking down. National self-consciousness and national pride have given rise to an insistence upon self-determination on the part of formerly dependent nations and territories. Closely related to the rise of nationalism has been the rise of racial consciousness, as non-white people seek to free themselves from dependence upon and exploitation by whites.

While nationalism in itself is not necessarily a threat to world peace, rampant and uncontrolled nationalism, especially on the part of new nations without a tradition of self-government, could be a danger. This fact, coupled with the rivalry which exists between the great powers, could pose threats to world peace. A related threat to world peace is the relative instability of newer nations, and the tendency of the great powers to draw such nations to one side or the other.

It must also be noted that other smaller alliances will continue to be called for While it can be expected that the Atlantic alliance will become weaker as Europe becomes stronger, it seems certain that United States commitments and presence in the

Pacific will increase, and that America will slowly but surely become as much a Pacific nation as it is an Atlantic nation.

The next decade will probably see the emergence of a third bloc of nations which are not aligned with either the United States or Russia/Red China. The growing split between Russia and Red China will further distribute the balance of power between the nations. The nuclear deterrent capability possessed by the United States will no doubt continue to be an important factor in maintaining world peace and stability. But even this deterrent will ultimately be self-defeating if it succeeds only in imposing the framework of the cold war on newly-emerging nations.

There are growing signs that many smaller nations wish to be identified with neither side in this struggle. Because struggling underdeveloped nations pose a far greater threat to world peace than thriving, developing ones, this new reality in international relations calls for programs of economic assistance to developing nations which are not tied to attempts to maintain a spurious and tenuous balance of power.

The age-long dream of a world from which war has been eliminated was made more urgent by the discovery of the atomic formula and the successful creation of the first atomic weapons. Ever since the discovery of the atomic formula, the possession of nuclear arms has been the hallmark of a major nation. While the United States and the Soviet Union have sought to limit membership in the "nuclear club" largely out of self-preservation, a much stronger argument is the self-defeating nature of such weapons in the hands of smaller nations, and the tremendous cost of developing and maintaining them, a cost which is bound to distort seriously the economy of all but the wealthiest nations. This cost, more than any treaties, has limited membership in the nuclear club.

It is estimated that by 1975 fifteen to twenty-five nations will have sufficient resources to develop nuclear weapons of their own. In light of this, efforts will continue to be made to get nuclear non-proliferation treaties. A growing number of nations will possess the delivery systems by which to propel such weapons to any point on earth. This may make it possible to develop a more sober realization of the need for international understanding and cooperation. Or it may, on the other hand, simply open up new opportunities for national conquest. Not all experts agree that the fact of nuclear weapons is in itself a deterrent to war. As the United States discovered in Vietnam, a great power does not necessarily enjoy military superiority over a small and presumably weaker nation, since fear of escalation inhibits the larger nation from unleashing the greater part of its power. Thus, nuclear capability may prevent a major war only to encourage smaller brushfire wars. The great powers are reluctant to use such awesome weapons except in the most extreme emergency. This would seem to indicate, once again, the need for an international organization such as the UN in which such disputes can be arbitrated. A significant achievement, however, has been the completion of the treaty banning the use of nuclear weapons in outer space.

Not to be overlooked in the search for peace is international culture and educational exchange. The purpose of such exchange is to develop good will and mutual understanding. In the years ahead, the United States will have moved beyond the "information center" type of cultural exchange and will broaden areas of personal exchange and American-foreign study programs. Chairs, courses, and degrees devoted to American studies will need to be expanded in most European and some Asian countries. The White House Conference on International Cooperation Year suggested an increased flow into the United States of the world's creative talent and cultural products; encouraging tourism by dropping visitor visa requirements; lowering hotel and travel rates for foreign students; promoting United States music, theater and art festivals; developing international conferences and congresses in the United States; increasing funds for the United States Travel Service.

The increased importance of science will make international cooperation in the future highly desirable, or even essential. International scientific projects may develop atomic energy, biology, and world health centers staffed by people from all nations. There may also be a program through which an increasing number of scientists from advanced nations spend a year or more in undeveloped nations before settling down to a career.

A note of caution should be made here regarding the United States taking care that it does not encourage a "brain drain" into the United States for our permanent usage. The above suggestions refer to short-term exchange and visit programs.

International conferences of the various disciplines might deal with possible applications of approaches to world security and world problems. These would include scientific conferences and could be a means of bringing mainland China into disarmament negotiations. In the long-range future, scientists may even serve as advisors to political international conferences and be assigned to solve certain problems. Computers could be used to make world-wide inventories of resources or even to sample trends and attitudes of whole populations. International conferences may call attention to the need of solving problems of disease, exploiting subterranean areas, creating and distributing new food plants, rescuing arid lands, and making cheap atomic energy available to irrigate arid areas. Such conferences may also recommend machinery and programs to alleviate such problems.

Population

The UN's projections of world population for the year 2000 range from a low of 5.3 billion to a high of 7.4 billion. Currently about 125 million infants are born each year. In the same period about 55 million deaths occur. The difference between births and deaths (70 million) is the natural increase or growth in population. Continuation of present trends means world population would be increasing at the rate of 100 million annually by 1980 and 200 million annually by the year 2000.

Approximately 85 percent of population increase is estimated to take place in the developing countries of Asia, Africa, and Latin America. This continues a trend in evidence since 1900. At that time about two-thirds of the world's 1.6 billion inhabitants lived in Asia, Africa, and South America; roughly one-third lived in Europe and North America. By 1965 these proportions had shifted to three-fourths and one-fourth, respectively. Projections to the year 2000 based on current trends indicate that four-fifths of the world's people will be living in Asia, Africa, and South America, and one-fifth in Europe and North America.

The industrialized nations of Europe, North America, U.S.S.R., and Japan—nations which have made the "demographic transition" and control fertility—comprise a decreasing percentage of humanity. These nations have passed from an agrarian to an industrial culture and in so doing have learned to control first the death rate and then the birth rate. Growth rates have been reduced to below 1 percent in some nations of western Europe and below 2 percent in the United States and Soviet Union.

The developing nations, on the other hand, have achieved or are achieving control of their death rates, but have not yet learned how to control their birth rates. The combination of declining mortality and continuing high fertility results in annual growth rates of 2 to 4 percent. It is during the period of lag between the control of mortality and the control of fertility that growth rates usually soar to troublesome heights.

It is estimated that more than 2 billion of the world's people are still bound to traditional high-fertility patterns and do not realize that births may be controlled and limited. Lacking knowledge, they are largely without freedom of choice to determine the number of children they wish to bear and support. Acceleration of population can be checked effectively only by bringing births into balance with current low death rates. This requires widespread dissemination of contraceptive information and widespread acceptance of a smaller ideal family size. Even the most hopeful estimates of the widespread acceptance and use of contraceptives in the developing countries would not be able to limit the world's population growth to less than six billion by the year 2000.

Population control is part of a complex of factors involving nutrition, productivity, literacy, and other components of socioeconomic well-being. The rising hope of the developing nations and the desire to span the centuries and move headlong out of the primitive past into the cybernated future calls for a drastic overhauling of economic, social, political, and educational institutions which undoubtedly will be marked by confusion, crisis, and chaos as the struggle takes place. To provide guidance and assistance in the changeover, the development of natural and human resources and the building of new cities and culture in accord with rising hopes and desires will be one of the big challenges of the future.

Prosperity and Poverty

An even greater threat to peace than nuclear weapons is the growing living-standard disparity between the prosperous and the underdeveloped nations. The underdeveloped nations, including most of Asia, Africa, and Latin America, have a combined population of 2.5 billion, about three-fourths of the world's population. The population of these countries is growing at a much faster rate than that of the more industrialized nations.

Presently the developed nations possess about 45 percent of the world's arable land, and the developing nations about 55 percent. Compound the disproportionate distribution of land resources in relation to population with the relative stages of agricultural development, and a clearer picture of the nature and magnitude of the problem begins to emerge. Land availability is not only a question of land per se but the resources needed to make the land more productive.

Poverty reveals itself in a number of forms. The most basic is the amount of food available to sustain life. The average person in an underdeveloped nation has about two-thirds less food intake in terms of calories, protein, and other protective foods than a person in a more prosperous nation. Already malnutrition and even famine are present in some areas.

Prior to World War II the developing nations were exporters of some 11 million metric tons of corn, wheat, rice and other grains annually. From 1948 to 1952, the flow reversed. By 1964 imports amounted to 25 million tons per year and have continued to increase since then. Even this has not been enough to make up the steadily growing food deficits. By 1975 it is predicted that the food deficit in the developing nations will be approximately 42 million tons and 88 million by 1985. Some forecasts anticipate a world food deficit by 1985.

Poverty also reveals itself in disparity in levels of income. Average income per person in the United States exceeds $2,500 per year, while more than one-half the people of the world live in countries in which the average annual income is little more than $100. The most advanced nations account for 14 percent of the world's population and 55 percent of the world's income.

The entrance of these undeveloped nations into the world community by way of the UN and the vastly extended means of communication by which they are becoming aware of how the rest of the world lives results in dissatisfaction and unrest. The people of these lands have rising expectations and make strong demands for social and economic advancements. Their leaders will be expected to take measures to remedy the lack of food, medicine, and schools. The appeal of Communism and other forms of popular land reform and government ownership of industry will continue to be very strong in these countries. Although many nations will remain underdeveloped for years to come, some will offer an opportunity for the United States to show the advantages of free private enterprise.

Both national self-interest and humanitarian considerations would seem to indicate that the United States plans to continue and expand present policies of economic aid and technical assistance. Internal political pressures to reduce taxes by cutting back foreign aid may be short-sighted and ultimately uneconomic. If we do not feed and help these nations there will be chaos and perhaps even war. It is much cheaper in the long run to face countries which have been made prosperous by our help than to fight countries which have been impoverished by our neglect.

One problem in helping nations reach a higher standard of living is the problem of the tariff. In the 1970's the underdeveloped nations are likely to be just as hungry, poor, and undeveloped as they are today unless the developed nations willingly sponsor fair price structures for commodity markets and adjust tariff walls accordingly. The advanced nations must begin to see that the raising of living standards everywhere to a decent level is a collective moral problem and responsibility.

Developing nations could be helped by a pooling of resources on the part of advanced nations. International conferences to help developing nations may be held to deal with peaceful uses of atomic energy, conservation of natural resources, education, health, science, agriculture, and labor. These have and will continue to be sponsored by the UN.

Science and technology have brought prosperity to many nations. This provides an object lesson for the poor of the world. But no matter what technical tools are given to the developing nations, the applications of these tools will have to wait for certain economic and political changes. Increased production will be needed, yet the old traditions of culture, religion, and social customs may result in a fear of change. There will be an understandable tension between the desire for a better standard of living and a reluctance to forsake ancient ways of life.

Perhaps, then, countries such as the United States can best help through such multilateral approaches as the UN, the World Bank, and the Asian Development Bank. This will result in less direct aid or contact with governments themselves and more help through area banking institutions. The United States contribution to such development banks should be contingent on other nations contributing funds and/or providing manpower and resources.

IV. SUMMARY AND IMPLICATIONS

A. Summary

1. The United States-U.S.S.R. cold war may continue to moderate as each country sees its own self-interests served best through cooperation rather than competition. Some unforeseen event, however, could intensify tension.

2. The U.S.S.R.-China cold war may intensify as they differ over leadership, program, and objectives of world Communism. Much will depend on the leadership emerging after Mao dies; new leadership could lessen the differences between these two nations.

3. The United States-China cold war may intensify unless present policies are changed or common interests are found that can break down present barriers.

4. The United States will continue to base defense on military deterrents and will continue to work for a strong western Europe within the Atlantic community. The Atlantic nations will continue to strive for a sense of community among themselves. The United States and the Atlantic community will continue to work together both in and out of the UN and will continue economic and military cooperation. Western Europe could become more strongly integrated, with perhaps some political unification.

5. There may be an increase in international cooperation in areas of space, weather, science, and economics. Much of this will be sponsored through the UN. International scientific projects may develop in areas of atomic energy, biology, and world health centers staffed by international teams; research on possible application of scientific approaches to world security problems; attacking problems of disease; exploiting subterranean areas; creating and distributing new food plants; making economical atomic energy and bringing water to arid lands.

6. The UN will be active in resolving particular conflicts growing out of boundary and social disputes between and with a number of countries.

7. Increased communication will make it difficult for nations to isolate themselves from new political theories and implications which may develop within Marxist and non-Marxist nations.

8. Fifteen to twenty-five new nations may join the "nuclear club" by 1975 and some may have delivery systems. This may either lead to a more sober realization for the need of international cooperation and understanding or it may open up new opportunities for national conquest. It seems certain that many nations will increase the tempo of efforts for nuclear non-proliferation treaties.

9. The people in the underdeveloped nations will continue to see the wonders of science and technology, and their expectancies will rise; but no matter what technical tools are given to these nations, the application of the tools will have to wait for economic and political changes. Tension between the desire for a better life and the reluctance to forsake ancient ways of life will prevail for a time. The gap between developed and developing nations will continue to increase unless the advanced nations provide massive economic, technical, scientific, and food assistance. Anticipated population increases will counteract efforts to raise living standards in underdeveloped areas.

10. United States economic aid may be channeled through area development banks in which United States contributions are related to the funds, manpower, and resources of other countries.

B. *Implications*

Churches which seek to respond responsibly to changing world conditions will wish to sound a prophetic message which calls the world's attention to the truth that God has created and would redeem the whole world. This implies equitable provision for health, education, security, housing, and opportunity. It involves the constant restudy of the church's world-wide mission program so as to be sensitive to the needs and feelings of people in the various parts of the world where our missionaries are at work—to enable us to recognize and bear witness to the activity of God.

There is need for a diminution of national sovereignty on the basis of mutual concessions and equal rights, accompanied by a decrease in military and defense spending consistent with the realities of the world situation, which will permit greater investment on the part of developed nations in the underdeveloped areas of the world.

A deep concern for the human situation in a technological world, and sensitivity to the needs, feelings, and fears of all people should be cultivated among church members. This could lead to the expansion of church-assistance programs and the encouragement of church members to contribute generously through direct personal assistance and financial resources. The churches should seek to create additional avenues by which to cooperate with each other and with other agencies in an ecumenical attack upon human need.

Church efforts may contribute to the creation of a climate of opinion throughout the world in which respect for human life will be reflected in realistic methods of birth control and family planning. Such an emphasis may come to be regarded as a legitimate, if not essential, aspect of the church's work in the less developed nations.

3

The North American Setting

I. THE PATTERN OF HUMAN SETTLEMENT

Though the records of history reveal that man has lived in cities for over 5,000 years, only in the last century has the phenomenon of the metropolis appeared. The traditional pattern of a small urban minority residing within cities dependent upon surrounding self-sufficient agricultural villages persisted over the centuries until the time of the Industrial Revolution. With the application of scientific methods to the processes of production and distribution, radical changes began to evolve in the pattern of human settlement. The productive advances arising from specialization and division of labor called for greater interaction, cooperation, and interdependence within and between establishments. Related industrial activities concentrated in close proximity to one another. The presence of a specialized labor supply attracted additional industrial and commercial establishments which in turn attracted more workers and other industries. The process fed on itself and thus set in motion the great wave of migration from country to city that continues unabated to this day.

With the revolution of internal transportation, the city burst its bounds and overflowed into the surrounding countryside. Thus did the time-worn *polis* (city) begin its evolution into metropolis. Along with the bursting of its bounds and overflow into the surrounding countryside went its identity and human dimension. The inbound wave of country to city migration was now met by a new outbound wave of suburban migration. The result of the interaction of these two waves of migration is a completely new pattern of human settlement different in magnitude and form from anything previously experienced by man. Within the interior of the city, under the stimulus of high density interaction, are produced the forces of innovation which constantly generate and accelerate social and cultural change. Subsequent liberal applications of brick, mortar, asphalt, concrete, and steel over its years of development have further separated man from his natural environment and its basic rhythms, and intensified the dehumanizing influence.

For our purpose the term "metropolis" will be used to describe an area embracing 500,000 people or more within an hour's travel time from the center. In terms of surface space-time relationship this means from thirty to fifty miles. Transportation is the key. The essence and reason for the existence of the metropolis as for its *polis* predecessors is mutual accessibility, primarily of residence and place of work. The metropolis extends as far as widespread daily commuting extends, and no farther.

Under the predominant influence of individualized transportation of the age-old "foot and hoof" variety, time distances tended to be proportional to straight-line distances, and the resultant pattern of settlement tended to be circular. With the development of the steam locomotive a network of communities sprang up at intervals along the railroad right-of-way, dictated by the combination of train speed and "foot and hoof" travel. The network of communities were all oriented to the center of the metropolis through the transportation system. As the rapid-transit system supplanted the steam railway, with more frequent stops, the network of the communities fused into continuous corridors or fingers of built-up areas along the right-of-way, forming a pattern of alternate densely settled corridors interspersed with areas of open space, thus modifying the earlier circular pattern of individualized transportation. The transportation network (supplemented by the utility networks of electric, telephone, water, and sewage) has served as the skeleton around which the flesh of metropolitan growth has formed. The supplanting of the individualized "foot and hoof" mode of travel with the equally individualized automobile has resulted in the "filling in" of the interstices and obliteration of open space between the corridors in the areas nearer to the center of the city, and a tendency to return to the circular pattern of growth. The construction of major arterial limited-access expressways has also had the effect of developing additional corridors or fingers reaching out into the surrounding countryside.

While the metropolis exerts primary influence over the area circumscribed by its daily commuting distance, it also exerts a dominant influence over the surrounding region within two hours' travel time from its center. This secondary area of influence is the metropolitan region. Here are found the satellite towns growing and thriving because of their location within the orbit of the metropolitan center. In the satellites are found the industries, goods, services, and residences so located because they are readily accessible to the marketing and supply functions of the metropolitan center. In addition, within the region can be found the types of facilities—lakes, camps, parks, picnic grounds, ski slopes, scenic areas, second homes, motels, tourist attractions—to serve the rapidly growing leisure-recreation needs of the burgeoning metropolitan population. Each primary or major metropolis is developing its summer, winter, or recreational metropolis as an integral part of the total pattern of settlement.

Within the metropolitan region an interesting reversal of a traditional pattern is taking place. For centuries the countryside has been the main locus of production, while the city was essentially a place of consumption. Now all activities, even the extractive ones, have come under the influence of specialization and industrialization. Agriculture has been transformed from a subsistence type of endeavor characteristic of the majority of the residents of an agrarian nation into a highly specialized, sophisticated, food-producing industry in which a little over one million farmers feed the entire populace.

At the same time, into the "population vacuum" thus created in the productive countryside have swarmed the nonfarm residents aided and abetted by the dispersal of industry. The land is under invasion, if not seasonal inundation, by tourists, vacationers, second-home residents, the retired, the outdoor enthusiast, the sportsman and the multiplying throngs of the burgeoning leisure-recreation industry. The use of the countryside is being transformed from a predominantly productive function to an essentially recreative one.

At the nerve center of the metropolis, where the main lines of transportation converge providing maximum accessibility to all parts, are found the institutions of first-order magnitude which serve the entire metropolitan complex. Also located here are those types of activities which require a high degree of mutual contact. These two functions, plus the supportive eating, drinking, parking, hotel and related services, combine in high-intensity competitive use of limited space. Space-utilizing activities originally located in the center city such as manufacturing, warehouses, retail and consumer services, and residences have been displaced into the outlying areas where the required space is more readily available. This constitutes another reversal of the traditional city pattern and has been accompanied by the exodus of the industrial workers into the satellite cities and industrial-park communities of the metropolis and metropolitan region. Most of the labor force in the center city is in the white-collar office or service industries. Under the constantly changing and growing demands of business and industry, the nerve center is undergoing a continuous process of selective adaptation of those functions for which it is uniquely suited.

Displaced second-order functions of consumer, retail, business, office, and services soon develop and concentrate in second-order centers within the metropolis. Hence the metropolis consists of an intricate network of secondary and tertiary centers linked together around the central nerve center in a vast complex of relationships with the industrial centers and satellites of the metropolitan region as a part of one interrelated whole.

Where one metropolis is located sufficiently close to another metropolis (as is the case on the East and West coasts, Great Lakes region and elsewhere in the country), a blending of the metropolitan regions and a fusing together into greater complexes known as the megalopolis can be observed.

The observation that our cities must faithfully mirror our culture leads to the question of the kind of environment the new pattern of human settlement provides for modern man. The city's mushroom growth and expansion into the hinterland, its dominant transforming influence on all of society, and its projected growth in the near future into the universal or world-wide city, would seem to indicate its ability to provide the most desirable environment to meet the needs of man. The growth of metropolis-megalopolis is based on the provision of real values: choice, freedom, opportunity, culture, entertainment, stimulation, privacy, variety, innovation. The opportunity to get ahead—jobs, higher income and advancement; the wide variety and choice in modes of living styles and work; the rich variety and stimulation of sights, sounds, and human experience; cultural enlightenment and sophistication; educational opportunities in a climate conducive to innovation, creativity, and change; the continual emergence of new ideas and opportunities; the dynamics of growth and development; the sense of being in the center of things, where the action is, a part of something big, are all part of its massive drawing power for modern man. The eternal magnetism and lure of the city reaches its heights in the modern metropolis, and as its mass increases so does its attractive power.

Population Trends

The population of the United States is estimated to reach 220 million by 1975 and 235 million by 1980. (Estimated population was 200 million on November 20, 1967.) Population estimates for Canada are 23 million by 1971, 25 million by 1976, and 28 million by 1981. The present rate of growth, viewed favorably and arduously promoted by many, is looked upon with considerable alarm by others. Given the nature of domestic problems currently prominent on the American scene, questions are being raised concerning the point at which increasing quantity begins to adversely affect the quality of American life.

Currently, there is some evidence to suggest that a change in the ideal family size is taking place. In 1965, for the first time in twelve years, the annual number of births dropped below 4 million to 3.8 million, and a further decline has occurred since then. As a result, earlier population projections have been revised downward.

Observers point to the following as influential factors in this decline of the birth rate: (1) the economic factor, especially the rising costs of rearing and educating children through college; (2) an early marriage, with the wife working and tending to delay the time of arrival of the first child and spacing out others; and (3) some disenchantment with larger families. An April 1966 Gallup Poll and other studies also indicate a decline in expected family size. One authority has projected an average family size of 2.8 children for women born in the fifties. There is also evidence of a growing weariness with the population explosion and its crowded schools and colleges, snarled traffic, unemployment, and attendant problems.

The current high-school age group is composed completely of "baby boom" youngsters. Now at the 13 million mark, high-school enrollment is expected to exceed 15 million in the 1970's. As the bulge moves on into college, the Census Bureau estimates that college and professional school enrollment will increase from 4 milion in 1960 to 6 million in 1965, 8 million in 1970, 9 million in 1975, and 10 million in 1980.

Migration continues to be a major factor in the ebb and flow of population among mobile Americans: city to city, city to country, country to city, farm to farm, region to region, inner city to suburb, suburb to country, and back to the inner city again. It is the incessant motion of a people on the move, functioning in semi-nomadic style, while continuing to think in sedentary terms

51

with institutions organized accordingly. The freedom to move, to seek to better oneself, seems to be deeply imbedded in the American way of life.

The tie between economic fluctuation and population mobility is best illustrated in the 20-29 year age group where over 40 percent change their residence each year as they seek to establish economic footing. On the average, one out of every five Americans participates in the annual migration, the change of residence ritual.

A growing area of migration only beginning to be recognized in its entirety, increasingly characteristic of a more affluent society, is the seasonal flow of people to seacoasts and mountains, ski slopes and lakes, hunting and fishing areas, warm climates and resorts. Tourism and leisure-recreation activities in an expanding variety of forms have become one of the basic mainstays of the economy. About 5 percent of Americans are two-home families, another 10 percent are on the way to this goal, and about 50 percent have it high on their aspiration list. Mobility is one of the most significant characteristics of a growing American population, and the pattern and extent of migration are almost impossible to project.

The migration flow-pattern between regions of the country has not changed appreciably over the past decade. The major stream of immigration is still westward, with sizable exchanges between the North Central and South, and the Northeast and South. The flow continues from the country, villages, and small towns to metropolitan areas, and from low income to high income areas. People continue to follow jobs, and differential rates of growth characterize the country.

The most rapidly growing states are New Jersey, Delaware, Maryland, and Virginia along the East Coast; Michigan, Ohio, and Indiana in the North Central region; Florida and Texas in the South; Colorado, Montana, Utah, Nevada, Arizona, and New Mexico in the Rocky Mountains; California, Washington, and Oregon on the West Coast; and Alaska and Hawaii. In addition to the projected regional concentration of population growth among half of the states located primarily in the Far West, South, industrial Midwest, and East Coast, a steady increase in the concentration of population in metropolitan areas is projected. By 1985, 80 percent of the total population will be living in urban areas. The effect of the continuing concentration of population in metropolitan areas and the consequent expansion into the outlying hinterland is strikingly set forth in the estimate that by 1985 one-half of all Americans will be living in three super-cities: (1) Boston to Norfolk on the East Coast, (2) Buffalo to Milwaukee on the Great Lakes, and (3) San Francisco to San Diego on the West Coast—three vast megalopolitan complexes of commerce, industry, and mass humanity interlaced by communication networks of concrete, copper, aluminum and steel into one interrelated whole.

On the basis of the projection of current population trends into the future, America stands on the verge of amazing growth. If we accept the observation that the rate of acceleration in the numbers of people in the world is the real force behind the changes of the future, then population comes close to being the number one concern of the day.

A large increase in numbers of people forces changes in the way of doing things as old ways prove inadequate for the task. Hence, population growth is transformed from a quantitative to a qualitative force for change. An increase in the numbers of people not only forces the development of new technology, it raises new questions as to the quality and purpose of life. The numbers game becomes transformed into a search for new ethics, new philosophies, new moralities, and new religions.

Town and Country

For the purpose of this study we have defined "town and country" as all nonmetropolitan counties, excluding cities of more than 25,000 people. Thus 2,725 counties out of 3,071 counties in the United States are classified as town and country or rural

America. More than 90 percent of the land area of the country is nonmetropolitan.

The term "town and country" today has a somewhat different meaning than it did a generation or decade ago. At the turn of the twentieth century much of the land was wilderness and in the process of being settled. People settled tracts of land by either purchasing or homesteading. Distances traveled were small. Schools, churches, economic centers dotted the country, and were within easy reach of home. Comradeship was developed with relatively few people because of distance and lack of communicative devices. Since then, some town and country areas have deteriorated, others have improved; some have gained population, others lost. Consolidation of farms and mechanization of farm labor improved production but also eliminated jobs.

The town-and-country dilemma cannot be considered apart from its relationship to the metropolitan scene, yet there are emphases which require special attention. One of the primary factors is scientific development leading to better automation and production. Changes usually are gradual, making it possible for those responsible for the production methods to readjust to a different kind of life. Mechanization will continue to be a part of developing society, providing higher standards of living and a more bountiful life.

Mobility plagues town and country. When the first census was taken in 1790, one out of twenty Americans lived in an urban setting. Today fourteen out of twenty reside in the city. Seventy percent of the people live on less than 1 percent of the land. If the trend continues, 100,000,000 more individuals will be stacked upon the present 140,000,000 by the year 2000.

Among the reasons advanced for this traumatic change is the decline in the farmer's income. Qualifications of youth have equipped them for better jobs and salaries; modern machinery makes it possible for one to do the work required previously of several. The decline of farm prices makes competition so keen that the small farmer cannot stay in business. Decline in the need for tenant farmers and increased burden of real estate taxation adds to the dilemma.

Vital growth is taking place in many rural areas as manufacturing diversifies and moves into small towns, and as better and more rapid transportation systems provide an adequate way for man to live beyond the confines of the metropolitan area and yet meet the demands of his work. It is important not to equate the farm population with the rural population of which it is a part. One segment of the population in town and country is made up of rural nonfarm residents. Rural nonfarm people live in open country, villages, small towns, and along highways. They are blue- and white-collar workers, business and professional people, artists and industrialists, part-time employees and retirees. This segment of the population is growing rapidly. Urban congestion has led many to believe that the only solution may be in the direction of dispersal.

Technology is changing both urban and rural life. Many small communities have become captive pockets of poverty. Increasing in number are the unemployed in the fields of mining and agriculture. American affluence must face the acute poverty of the American Indian, Spanish-speaking Americans, Negro Americans, and the southern whites. When man does not have the opportunity to provide for himself and his family, there is a loss of dignity and a resignation to a second-class citizen status.

The very small communities are finding it difficult to exist. With the advent of good highways, effective transportation, easy access to communities, families will travel 25 to 50 miles to shop, visit the physician or dentist, and care for essential needs. The functional economic area takes in a much larger area than formerly. Old rivalries between villages and country are disappearing; functioning economic units develop. A functional economic area is that territory surrounding a city of approximately 25,000 population or larger, where there are many people who are dependent upon the city for employment and their major shopping center.

II. PHYSICAL ENVIRONMENT

Along with the attractiveness, allure, and opportunity of the metropolis, another picture emerges that is somewhat less enchanting. Men of vision point out that there is great disorder in metropolis. A 1966 Gallup Poll of residents in cities of 500,000 or more revealed that about one-half would prefer to move outside the city. An image increasingly portrayed of metropolis is that of a city into which people daily throng to work and from which they flee evenings and weekends and from which people move as soon as they can secure the necessary finances.

Increasing evidence indicates that the metropolis is deficient as a living environment for man: that is noisy and uncomfortable, crowded and congested; its continuing sprawl contributes to formlessness and *anomie*, restricts choice, impedes interaction, inhibits identification, is subject to paralysis from strikes and utility failures, and suffers from massive atmospheric pollution. The metropolis has suffered greatly from uncontrolled development, rapid growth and change, obsolescence and instability. Circulation is congested, accessibility is uneven, facilities are unbalanced, residential segregation is growing, and stratification deepening. The list of social ills of the metropolis dramatically reveals the intensity of its distress as a living environment for man: blight, dreariness, deterioration, incessant noise, congestion and crowding of traffic and people, pollution of air and water, dirt, litter, slums. The city seems to produce poverty, boredom, frustration, mental and emotional stress, alcoholism, drug addiction, disease and illness, delinquency, divorce, family breakdown, illegitimacy, venereal disease, crime, riots, racial tension.

Serious questions have been raised regarding the ability of narrowly conceived economic values and decisions to provide a desirable environment for man. The initial thrust for corrective action came from an alliance of those seeking reform and those seeking profit. The planners and advocates of public housing were trying to improve the environment, and the commercial and financial interests were trying to maintain the level of business and property values in downtown areas. Much has been accomplished in urban renewal by public and private interests alike, and more ambitious projects are in the works. Hartford's Constitution Plaza, Pittsburgh's Golden Triangle, Philadelphia's Penn Center and others are examples of what can be done in rebuilding the commercial core of a decayed city.

The federal government has responded to the distress cry of the cities. Currently more than 250 separate programs of federal aid addressed to the panoply of metropolitan problems are in operation for cities, states, and political subdivisions. The government also responded with the creation of the cabinet-level Department of Housing and Urban Development and followed through with the 1.26 billion dollar Demonstration Cities and Metropolitan Act of 1966. The Demonstration Cities Act, in which the Congress finds and declares that improving the quality of urban life is the most critical domestic problem facing the United States, provides up to 80 percent of the cost of developing comprehensive plans and the administration of development projects covering the gamut of metropolitan ills. Only a beginning, it is designed to stimulate the cooperative effort of all levels of government and the economy in convincing demonstrations of what can be done. Recent legislation has placed the federal government squarely in the business of rebuilding large sections of old cities, promoting new cities, and linking together metropolitan bodies that may, in time, supersede the city governments of today. The private sector of the economy also has initiated efforts to improve the urban environment.

With all the activity over the plight of metropolis and the action to correct its ills, two basic problems remain relatively untouched: (1) the question of the kind of environment to be created for modern and future man, and (2) a comprehensive plan to control the present megalopolitan sprawl and effect the desired pattern of human settlement. Thus far the corrective action taken is of the brushfire variety addressed to immediate

57

ills and not designed to deal with fundamental problems. In view of expected expenditures required for modernizing, extending, and building new rapid-transit facilities, and the proposed next phase of the federal highway program in and around metropolitan regions, a continuation of the present pattern of sprawling unbridled expansion of the metropolis, penetrating more deeply into the countryside, can be expected well into the future. Some expansion and modification of previous types of development will take place, but nothing in terms of comprehensively planned overall development can realistically be expected at this time. Estimates of the cost of making cities livable run as high as 1.1 trillion dollars for the next ten years and 2.1 trillion for the next twenty years.

The continuing trend toward the concentration of people in metropolitan areas clearly reveals the multiplicity of problems associated with a rising population density. In California, the most rapidly growing state in the union, over one-half of the population is concentrated within a sixty-mile radius of downtown Los Angeles. The assumption that economic motivation would produce an unplanned but functional beauty has been found to be sorely wanting. No longer can the practice of subordinating the environment to economics be tolerated. Questions of livability, health, and beauty must be raised from secondary to primary importance. While the nation stands today near the pinnacle of wealth and power, it is a land of vanishing beauty and growing ugliness, of shrinking open spaces, and an overall environment diminished daily by encroaching pollution, noise, and blight.

Another major thrust in the developing concern for the future of the American city comes from the modern-day heirs of Ebenezer Howard, the grandfather of town planning, who in 1898 first proposed to relieve the congestion of his native London by building a series of carefully planned "new towns" for people and industry in the neighboring countryside. Urban "newal" instead of "renewal" is the approach. Backed by the substantial resources of private corporations, something in the neighborhood of seventy large communities with at least passing claim to be new towns have got under way around the country.

A CROSS-COUNTRY SAMPLE OF NEW TOWNS

Name	Location	Projected Population
Lake Havasu	Lake Havasu, Arizona	60,000
Litchfield Park	Near Phoenix, Arizona	75,000
Valencia	Los Angeles County, California	200,000
Mission Viejo	Newport Beach, California	80,000
Irvine Ranch	Orange County, California	80,000
Laguna Niguel	Orange County, California	40,000
El Dorado Hills	Near Sacramento, California	75,000
Janss/Conejo	Ventura County, California	87,000
New Orleans East	New Orleans, Louisiana	175,000
Columbia	Howard County, Maryland	110,000
Clear Lake City	Houston, Texas	150,000
Reston	Fairfax County, Virginia	75,000

Incorporated in the thinking of the new town planners is the restoration of the city to the pedestrian, to place man once again within walking distance of schools, churches, business, industry, recreation, and his neighbor, and to restore contact with the natural environment. Human traffic is separated from vehicular traffic as much as possible. New town proponents consider their approach to the ills of metropolis to be an economical and feasible way to provide for the growing population, achieve a habitable environment, and stem the uncontrolled spread of the megalopolis.

There has been some negative reaction to new towns. "They were really very nice towns if you were docile and had no plans of your own and did not mind spending your life among others with no plans of their own." "If we can't organize and rebuild our existing cities, what guarantee is there that we can do any better with new ones?" "Beyond offering some amenities not otherwise available, new towns offer little." "The social goals implied in fully realized new towns are not shared by most potential buyers." "A glorified suburb." "The vast majority appear destined to become country club communities for upper-income families."

A somewhat different approach is contained in the modular city design of the National Land Development Policy Committee. This group proposes the construction of twenty-five new modular cities of 600,000 to 1,000,000 population to be built from scratch in sparsely settled areas across the country. Each module is to be a self-contained entity grouped in clusters of five cities at ten-mile intervals from a central city. Industry and transportation are to be located underground. As each module city reached 100,000 to 150,000 population, a new module would be developed ten miles away in a clockwise direction around the central city. The central city would contain large office buildings, computer centers, financial district, and major cultural activities, but no industry and few retail stores or residential units.

One of the outstanding voices seeking to evolve some semblance of direction out of the disorder of human settlement is the internationally known city planner Constantinos Doxiadis of Athens, Greece. Through his Center for Ekistics (the science of human settlements) Doxiadis strives to find a scientific system which will lead to workable conclusions for the problems of metropolis. His organization is dedicated to the understanding and construction of the city of the future whose goals are happiness and security for man. Starting with the five basic elements of the city (nature, man, society, structures, and networks), he begins with man and moves outward in ever increasing dimensions through room, building, groups of buildings, villages, towns, cities, metropolis to ecumenopolis and builds the ekistic grid by which he seeks to analyze and plan the development of a habitable pattern of settlement. Upon the grid so constructed he superimposes the dynamic influence of economic, social, political, technological, and cultural factors.

Seeking to restore the primacy of the human dimension to the planning of cities, Doxiadis compares the communications network to the nervous system and the transportation network to the circulatory system of the body. Too long has the transportation system been viewed as the skeleton determining the shape and spread of the city. When the transportation machine came between men, the human scale began to vanish. To restore the human scale, it is necessary that the transportation network be placed in its rightful role as the circulatory system, underground, out of sight as the blood circulatory system in the human body, readily accessible, functioning automatically, able to move the individual wherever he desires in a maximum of ten minutes— supportive of the human scale, not disruptive.

Some of the most significant developments in the understanding of the pattern of human settlement of modern man across the countryside have come from the hands of Hugh Denney of the University of Missouri and Karl Fox of Iowa State University. Fox's concept of the Functional Economic Area as developed in Iowa, and Denney's Growth-Service Center concept developed in Missouri, provide long-needed working tools. While Fox restricted his efforts to Iowa, Denney has delineated a network of growth-service center areas stretching throughout the nation. Using the same time-space relation of an hour's traveling time applied to the delineation of the metropolis, and dependent upon the transportation network provided by the automobile, growth-service centers and their tributary areas have been identified as a pattern of human settlement within which man can generally satisfy all his needs. Within the growth-service center area is found residence, work, consumer goods, medical, hospital, recreational, educational, religious, and other services. The growth-service center area includes the major center or cluster of centers plus the satellite villages, towns, hamlets, and open-country residents in the area. The population of these areas, bound together in a geographical community of interest, vary in size from 25,000 up to the 500,000 level of metropolis. In most cases they disregard established political boundaries of municipalities, townships, counties, and states. The approximate bounds established geometrically are subject to the natural variation of the terrain. The radius and shape of the area may vary from 50 to 60 or more miles depending upon the lie of the land and prevailing travel speed. In heavily congested areas the distance between centers is significantly shortened because of choked traffic flow. In each case the boundary approximations are subject to empirical verification and adjustment on the part of local residents with allowance for overlap in the border areas. Within the areas social organization increasingly reflects the ongoing development of the area.

The growth-service center area, like metropolis, is a living organism undergoing varying degrees of change. In more rapidly growing areas new centers will have a tendency to appear at the borders of two or more areas when the population growth and other social forces at work make them feasible. Likewise, in declining areas centers will drop by the wayside when the population base no longer justifies their existence, with functions being transferred to neighboring centers.

Transportation

Choked by traffic congestion and the inadequacy of expensive expressways to alleviate the hopelessly mired daily rush-hour convulsion, and faced with the impending crisis of additional population pressure, major cities are turning once again to a long-neglected and almost forgotten former servant—mass rapid transit, the modern version of the old traction industry. Spurred by the Mass Transportation Act of 1964, which authorized the expenditure of 375 million dollars for capital improvements of mass transit facilities over a period of three years, cities are vying for approval of projects calling for up to two-thirds federal funding. It is estimated that total spending for mass transit will reach 12 billion dollars in the next ten years. This contrasts with a total of only one billion dollars spent for mass transit in the past twenty years.

It is far cheaper to spend money on an adequate transit system than to spend millions on costly freeways which become inadequate almost as soon as they are built. With modern equipment a single track of rapid-transit service can move upwards of 40,000 passengers per hour. By contrast, the capacity of one freeway lane is an estimated 2,000 to 2,500 people per hour.

The impact upon cities of the expansion and rejuvenation of existing rapid-transit systems and the construction of new systems will be far-reaching. The renewal of downtown areas and the build-up of apartments and office buildings along transit routes are part of the changes foreseen. At the same time metropolitan areas will be extended farther out as the new transit systems provide quick and efficient service to the central city. In the words of one observer, the federal mass-transit money "disbursed with wisdom" can help buy the American city what may be one of its last chances to reshape itself into a decent environment, and help expand these cities into functioning metropolitan districts.

On a family availability basis 74 percent of all families owned one or more autos in 1959. By 1976 this proportion is expected to rise to 85 percent. On the basis of adults (sixteen years and over) per car, the ratio in 1959 was 2.4 adults per car; by 1976 this is expected to be 1.7 adults. Annual expenditures for the purchase and operation of passenger cars alone currently absorbs about 10 percent of the nation's income.

The vast network of highways, roads, streets, bridges, and tunnels interlacing the communities of the United States stretches some 3,500,000 miles throughout the country. The most recent major development, the 41,000-mile interstate highway system initiated in 1956, is more than half completed. The pace of car-buying continues to outstrip roadbuilding. In recognition of this, a new program of highway construction to build a network of suburban arterial belt and connecting highways designed to speed the flow of traffic and provide better movement through the megalopolis is scheduled to begin in 1974. Also in the works is a plan to use land more efficiently in densely settled areas by purchasing entire city blocks instead of strips through them. This will enable the construction of freeways, office buildings, apartments, and parks as a total planned complex.

As in the case of rapid transit, the influence of the network of suburban arterial highways will exert a major influence on the cities and towns throughout the megalopolis. Extension of the sprawl, relocation, rebuilding and renewal, new centers of business, industry, and population, parks and open space will be part and parcel of the dynamic response of the shifting mass of human settlements to the invigorating increase in the circulatory flow of its traffic lifeblood.

Few early twentieth-century visionaries could have foreseen the influence of the automobile on the "American way of life." Some observers have attributed the undermining of the traditional American family to the automobile which produced restlessness and rootlessness, thus making the home a temporary dwelling place, cutting the individual adrift from his family environment to the point where he no longer feels an obligation to live by its accepted standards. Given a sense of freedom and autonomy never known before, coupled with the feeling of acceleration and exhilaration the powerful machine provides, young people develop value systems in conflict with those of their parents. Today, atmospheric pollution from the gasoline-driven automobile has reached the point where the California State Department of Public Health has stated that between now and 1980 the gasoline-powered engine must be phased out. "The only realistic way to bring about this historic kind of changeover on schedule is to demand it by law in the public interest; that is, to serve legal notice that after 1980, no gasoline-powered motor vehicles will be permitted to operate in California."

Perhaps nowhere are the rapid changes in transportation more dramatically portrayed than in the railroads. Only a century ago the iron horse roared across the countryside in an unchallenged display of power, stirring the hearts of young and old alike, and was hailed as the decisive link in the forging of a new nation. By 1965 passenger travel (exclusive of commuter trains) had dropped to the lowest point recorded in any single year going back to 1890 when comparable records began. Eclipsed by the automobile and airplane, intercity rail passenger travel has almost been relegated to the domain of tourist and scenic railroads and railroad museums as a passing part of vanishing Americana. American intercity rail transportation has all but abdicated its passenger service in favor of exclusive concentration and specialization on freight. As a result, new attention is being given to the development of high-speed rail service between cities from 200 to 500 miles apart.

In terms of passenger-miles traveled on domestic lines, air travel has jumped thirty-fold during the two decades 1940-1960, reflecting the major revolution taking place in transportation. Total domestic inter-city travel volume continues to expand at a healthy rate of nearly 5 percent per year. Air travel moved from a position of 3 percent of the volume in 1940 to 44 percent in 1960, and is expected to account for 80 percent by 1976. Domestic air travel totaled 8 billion passenger miles in 1950, 30 billion in 1960, and is estimated to exceed 150 billion by 1976.

III. CRITICAL COMMUNITY SOCIAL ISSUES

Community Life and Community Organization

Factors which tend to create a sense of community and whose failure results in community breakdown are similar activities and the development of similar values, attitudes and beliefs; dependence on common activities for protection against such disasters as crime and fire; dependence on common sources of supply. A small village with a volunteer fire company is more likely to develop a sense of community than a larger town with a paid department. One reason for the breakdown in community life which is characteristic of the urbanized-technological society lies in its great diversity and mobility. One consequence of locality specialization and the mobility it implies is a decrease in the importance of local institutions. Churches in particular have always been at the core of community organization. They have played such an important part that many conflicts in communities have essentially been conflicts between two church-groups in the community. But there is evidence that the typical residential-parish type of congregation no longer fulfills this function.

One of the major factors in community disorganization is locality specialization: communities which daily export or import workers, communities which import people for leisure or education, and communities which appeal to special age or economic groups. The government itself may unwittingly encourage disorganization through such policies as FHA mortgaging which makes the purchase of new homes much easier than the purchase of older homes.

Strenuous efforts to counteract community disorganization have been made by a growing number of community and neighborhood organizations. While such community groups differ widely both in philosophy and program, they have in common a concern for the livability of the city and a determination to return control over community environment to those who actually reside there. This has resulted in a confrontation between the metropolitan "power structures" and the residents of the inner city. The "war on poverty" has attempted to give some voice and representation to those most intimately affected by community planning, resulting again in some opposition from entrenched power structures which fear such a move as a threat to their own interests. By giving financial assistance to Saul Alinsky-type groups, and by actively cooperating with certain aspects of the war on poverty, the churches have attempted to align themselves with the inner-city resident rather than the non-resident representatives of the power structure. This in turn has created tension within the churches, which depend for much of their strength on the suburban middle class. As an agent of reconciliation, the churches have sought to bring together these two opposing forces and stimulate dialog between them, enabling each to see the problems of the community from the other's point of view. While it is too early yet to know how successful such attempts will be in reorganizing the community, enough progress has been made by groups such as the Urban Training Center in Chicago to give hope that the church may be able to lead the way and thus recapture its earlier role as a focal point of community organization.

Race

Among the racial minorities in the United States are Negroes, Chinese, Japanese, Filipinos, and American Indians. To these groups may also be added Puerto Ricans and Mexicans who are not racially distinct from the white majority, but are nevertheless subject to minority treatment. About 10 percent of the total American population is Negro. About one-half live in the South; most of the rest are to be found in the major metropolitan areas of the North. Puerto Ricans and other Latin Americans are found mostly on the Eastern seaboard, especially in New York City. Mexicans and Japanese are mostly in the Southwest, while the Chinese and Indians are scattered throughout the country.

Relations between the white majority and the minority groups are marked by various forms of discrimination. Discrimination may be economic, barring minority groups from certain jobs and offering lower wages for those which are open to them; legal, aimed at preventing the minorities from voting in substantial numbers or from receiving equal treatment at the hands of the courts; political, aimed at denying them representation in government; and social, aimed at maintaining separation between the races in housing and in other forms of social intercourse.

The result of such discrimination has been to insure that racial minorities enjoy fewer of the benefits of American affluence and suffer more of the hardships of American poverty. Racial minorities, especially Negroes, have become increasingly restless and vocal. Under pressure from Negroes and white liberals, Congress has enacted a number of far-reaching pieces of legislation aimed at giving the minorities equal treatment under the law and equal access to economic and social opportunities. But, important and effective as such legislation has been, it has not yet resulted in a substantial change in the basic relationship between the races, with the result that in the summer of 1966 there were 36 riots which were racial in character, and in the summer of 1967 there were 66 such riots.

Specifically, it appears that racial minorities are trapped in a vicious circle from which they cannot escape without help from the white majority, which has not been disposed to come to their aid. The child born into a minority family has about two-thirds as much chance of completing high school as his white counterpart, and about one-fifth the chance of completing college. Furthermore, the schooling which he does receive is substantially inferior at every level. As a result, he will have about one-half the possibility of getting a job upon completion of his education, and his earning potential will be about one-fifth that of his white counterpart. This means, in turn, that the chances are only one in ten that he will escape from the environment in which he grew up, so that his children will repeat his cycle of learning and earning. It is understandable that any human being caught in a trap not of his own making will sooner or later rebel. The major effects of racial discrimination in America are slums, unemployment, poor schools, broken homes, and crime.

The attack upon racial discrimination must take several forms. The legal battle has been virtually won. The only major area in which adequate law does not exist is in the matter of open housing. But the legislative battle is only the beginning. Now must come the struggle to bring equality to the schools, to eradicate the slums, to bring equal employment opportunities. The educational problem will be discussed in the chapter on that topic. We take up here, briefly, the housing and unemployment situations.

The direction which the racial revolution will take in the future depends largely on the reaction of the majority of Americans.

If the majority continues to resist changes in the relationships between the races to accept them only reluctantly when forced by law to do so, bitterness and cynicism will harden the racial minorities, and the stage will be set for full-scale riots between the races. Extremists and agitators on both sides will exploit such riots for their own ends and to enhance their own positions of leadership. But there is little evidence that more than a few members of any minorities or a few die-hard racists desire such an outcome. What is more likely to happen is a consolidation of political forces under the black-power umbrella as the minority groups acquire political sophistication. While the words "black power" may have an ominous sound, they are well within the tradition of American political reality, and therefore represent a positive rather than a negative development, provided sound leadership is encouraged.

Housing

To meet the needs of an increasing population as many new structures will have to be built as have been built since the earliest immigrants first moved out of sod huts and log cabins. There is every reason to believe that the trend towards urbanization will also continue. As more and more people move into the metropolitan regions, the competition for land will stiffen, and the general problems of getting around, finding a bit of open space, will become widespread and urgent problems.

There are those who look upon the old central city as *passé* and who would let it die. But the urban civilization for which the United States and Canada are destined requires that the central city play a part. Our central cities are the core of our new urban civilization, the core around which the suburban and rural communities will be centered. These cities will educate and shape the future recruits for the suburbs. Many cities, however, will undergo major racial and social changes. Disorder and insecurity as well as economic considerations will not only speed white emigration to the fringes, but industrial emigration as well. Already the loss of the city's more affluent taxpayers has made the cost of municipal servicing nearly impossible to bear. A generation ago, municipalities were collecting more taxes than the state and national governments combined; by 1962 their total had dropped from 52 percent to 7.3 percent of the total.

At the present moment one-fourth of all the people in the United States live in slums. A slum prevents the functioning of decent family life. A room occupied by a whole family in a New York City sixth-floor tenement may have a worse impact on family life than a one-room house in a squatter community in Venezuela. It is the impact on the people that should in all cases be the measure of a slum's banefulness.

If public financing is a problem for the inner city, personal financing is equally so. One of the main troubles with our mortgage system has been that its opportunities have been withheld from America's poor. They have not only been looked upon as bad risks, but the fiction has been created that they deserve only tenancy in a public housing project. A Philadelphia study showed that thousands of row houses could be purchased at $1,500 to $5,000 per house and carried at as little as $40 to $60 a month. All that was needed was a mortgage fund to facilitate purchases. Such a program would be far less costly than public housing; it would reduce vandalism, give a stake to many families in their community, and give them the opportunity to become members of the next generation's middle class. However, past government policy discouraged such financing and perpetuated housing inequities by indirectly subsidizing suburban families, without a corresponding subsidy for lower financial groups.

An *apartheid* threatens the United States, and unless this country acts now the split may be irreparable by the end of the century. If current trends continue, Negroes by the year 2000 will outnumber whites in eight of the nation's ten largest cities. Until 1950, exclusion of minorities from neighborhoods was not only sanctioned by federal manuals and judicial decisions, but was encouraged by officialdom. Withdrawal of government mortgage assistance was threatened unless exclusion was practiced. While such restrictive contracts have now been struck down by the courts, the public attitudes that gave them support survive. There are already signs that this is happening. California adopted its celebrated anti-open housing Proposition 14 by a margin of 4.5 to 2.4 millions.

Unemployment

Since the end of World War II both the United States and Canada have enjoyed the longest sustained period of prosperity in their respective histories. But this prosperity has not been evenly distributed among the population. Pockets of poverty have been created among racial minorities and in depressed rural areas. Along with disparity in income has come an advance in technology which has left millions of unskilled farm workers and mine workers unemployed. These unemployed workers and their families have either drifted into the major metropolitan areas in search of work, or have remained in abject poverty in isolated rural areas, where they tend to be forgotten and by-passed.

The unemployment situation in the inner city is particularly acute. While the rate of unemployment for the population as a whole has fallen below the 4 percent mark, it soars to as high as 30 percent in ghetto populations. The existence of large numbers of unemployed (and in some cases, unemployable) persons in deteriorating center-city ghettos has set the stage for riot conditions. American society has proved to be more adept at putting down riots than in preventing them, and less tolerant of riots than of the conditions which create them. The result is a not surprising breakdown in respect for law and the enforcement of law. Crime rates, especially among young people, have increased spectacularly in the past decade. No doubt there is a direct relationship between such delinquency and the abnormally high rates of unemployment among the young in the same areas.

IV. SUMMARY AND IMPLICATIONS

A. *Summary*

1. Technological advances have produced increases in size and complexity of cities by introducing changes in the nature and functions of the economic system. Consequences of these changes have been largely unanticipated, and city planning has had limited success in coping with them. The result is an erosion of the quality of life in the urban environment. While corrective measures are being attempted and efforts made to attend to future needs, achievements up to the present are not encouraging.

2. Expected increases in the size of the population of North America provide one base for predictions of continued economic growth. On the other hand, increases in population density in metropolitan areas will continue to intensify already existing city problems. For the immediate future it is expected that a higher proportion of the population will be in the youngest and oldest age brackets, the age groups that require the greatest amount of public services.

3. Region-to-region and country-to-country migration may be expected to follow the patterns which have been observed in the past. Seasonal migration connected with long vacations and higher standards of living will probably increase.

4. Qualitative changes may be expected in rural areas as the farm population continues to decline and older economic patterns become less viable. Efforts will be made to utilize the potential which rural areas offer for recreation and population dispersion.

5. Erosion of the physical environment of cities has been accompanied by many forms of community and social disorganization. This is most apparent in slum and ghetto areas. Among the several efforts being made to remedy the situation, the more promising seem to be community action groups, compensatory education, special employment provisions for those who are marginally employable, and rehabilitation of existing housing, accompanied by measures which facilitate home ownership.

6. The race issue has come to be recognized as a central problem for American society as greater concentrations of Negroes have developed within the cities. It is unavoidably clear that equal rights must be provided in political power, economic status, education, housing, and social acceptance.

B. *Implications*

The breakdown of community life in the urbanized-technological society of our time has affected the life of the church and its members. A congregation is essentially a locality-oriented organization, and locality-oriented organizations have become less important and meaningful in a society characterized by mobility and differentiation. There are indications that cohesiveness in at least some congregations is based on common interests of members rather than on geographical location. Further consideration needs to be given to developing strategies and structures which can best fulfill the church's mission in the metropolitan areas of population concentrations. This will necessarily include identification of values and merits of contemporary urban life, development of a variety of experimental ministries, efforts to help persons cope with the complexities of an urbanized-technological society, and dissemination of information about major issues and significant trends in society.

By becoming aware of the likely consequences of population increases and migration the church can develop a basis for attempts to influence public policy and decisions made by its constituents. Population trends lead to both quantitative and qualitative changes in society. New questions are raised about the quality and purpose of life; a search emerges for new ethics, new philosophies, new moralities, new religions. If our goals are optimal and equal conditions of life for all, the question must be raised about how large a population the nation (or a community) can properly support. It is necessary to give consideration to population stabilization as a goal and to acceptable means of achieving the goal. More specifically, population projections provide the church with data as to which population groups are likely to increase in size, and for which strategies and programs should be devised. In the 1970's there will be substantial increases in the number of people under 35 and over 60. A larger portion of the population will have the benefits of higher education.

Critical community issues of the present promise to remain critical for several years and demand the attention of the church. By means of policy decisions, educational efforts, and action programs the church should direct its attention to correcting community and social disorganization. This would involve participation in community action groups, creation of constructive attitudes and actions designed to combat racial discrimination in all forms, support of efforts of others aimed toward equal opportuntiy in education, employment, housing, and possession of political and economic power.

4

Government and Politics

I. THE STRUCTURE OF AMERICAN POLITICS

Three characteristics of the American political system are basic and will continue to be influential in the future.

The first and perhaps most significant of these is the two-party system. This system will remain because the electoral laws, organization of parties, campaign practices and social customs make it difficult for a third party to rise to major status. Third parties will continue to serve as outlets for dissent and will have an impact in particular elections and regions, but because they serve rather narrow interests they will not emerge into permanent major parties.

A second feature of American politics is the absence of a clear-cut party line. Many programs and political beliefs (and even voters) overlap the two parties. Both major parties endeavor to develop programs with as wide an appeal as possible. They also try to relate to and identify with every economic, social, racial, or religious group. These practices will no doubt continue into the future.

A third characteristic of the American political system is the decentralization of authority within the two political parties. Each state party is independent and self-sustaining. Each state party is decentralized down to county, city, town, and precinct levels. Thus there is normally a lack of effective discipline in many levels of party organization. A national party exists only when a national committee is brought into being every four years. The national nominating convention is most often controlled by those who hold power within the state and local party machines.

Local committees stay in power even if their party loses a national election, a fact which tends to preserve the two-party system.

Some observers feel that this type of political system is too fragmented for effective policy-making in a rapidly changing society. They point out that in some respects we have not a two-party system, but actually a four-party system—the Democrats and the Republicans having both a liberal and a congressional conservative wing. Such a system has tended to react to change rather than to dominate it.

The American voter tends to cross party lines, to split his ticket, and to change his mind. It is estimated that only 60 percent of the American electorate is regularly partisan in voting habits. While the number of persons voting in national elections is increasing, the percentage is still in the 60 to 70 percent range. This drops below 50 percent in off-year elections. This is partly due to apathy. The American citizen does not feel an obligation to vote in off-year elections. Many citizens see no real difference between the two parties; politics and politicians are low on the value scale of many Americans, and local registration laws keep many persons from voting. The federal government may establish national standards for registration requirements and election procedures. In an age when people move frequently, shorter residence requirements are desirable.

The function of American political parties is to give direction and responsible control to the struggle for power. They bring the struggle for power under control by institutionalizing it. The functions of the parties which are vital to a democracy and which will continue on into the future are selecting nominees for public office; making known the issues of an election, the qualification of the nominee and his promises in campaigns; manning the polls and counting the ballots in elections, and finding qualified persons for appointive office.

The function of the winning party is to form policy and to organize the legislative and executive branches of government. The function of the losing party is to engage in responsible opposition, offering alternate programs and watching the conduct and execution of the majority party's program. The minority party also organizes its legislative members in order to keep a check on the majority party organization. These roles will not change in the foreseeable future.

The politicizing process starts early. In America it begins about age three and is basically completed by age thirteen. It usually remains stable, at least in terms of party loyalty, for life. This would suggest the strength of family influence on political behavior. Political choice has a psychological side. There is usually a choice between alternatives. The "for-and-against" and the "ins-and-the-outs" psychology is at work. Sociologically speaking, third parties, generally radical, go against the grain of American life. The bounty of the economy and a unity of principle among Americans militates against radical movements.

Four features of our constitutional system have a polarizing effect: the single-member legislative district, the division of power between nation and state, the method of electing a president, and the presidency itself. State politics serves as a safety valve for special pleading and eccentricity. The general ticket (winner-take-all) system tyrannizes the presidential politics of each state and forces all politicians to think in terms of building a majority. The American system of elections (electoral laws, campaign practices, social customs) is loaded against the rise of minority parties. Third parties may serve as outlets for dissent and as symbols of our tolerance.

Possible Trends in American Politics

There does seem to be evidence that one-party sections of the nation will give way to two-party systems, that there will be less class-oriented party membership, that Americans will be more attracted to a party offering a creative program than to a party which opposes change. If a third party does arise it will be from one or more of the following groups: the South (white); the non-Communist left; the ultra-conservative right.

American politics will not be vastly different ten to twenty years from now unless revolutionary changes occur in our national character, constitution, or society. There will be changes, but they will be reforms, not revolutions. The political scene in the future will look much the same as it does today. The basic principles of the Constitution determine that there be a separation of powers, a certain system of national elections and a federal system headed by a President. No doubt the political parties will continue to be decentralized in structure and have as their main goal the majority rule at the next election.

Although extremism may not be manifested in organized political parties, it will continue to have an influence in domestic politics. Extremism is often supported by those who hold a "rule or ruin" attitude. The extremist attacks to destroy and generally has no positive program to improve conditions. The extremist does not respond to an appeal to reason, but rather relies to a large extent on hate and fear. He sees the world as a simple place and everything wrong with it as caused by a conspiracy directed by his "enemy" (such as capitalism, communism, Vatican, Jew). He desires radical, violent change rather than working cautiously with workable changes. He does not think in terms of practicality or compromise, in democratic diversity, and plays no constructive role in domestic affairs; he cannot really accept the results of an election where he "loses."

II. NATIONAL AND LOCAL GOVERNMENT

The federal government will expand as the dominant force for social change because major social problems will be encountered more and more on a national scale. The major areas of federal influence and concern will be the problems of unemployment (wages, retraining, and relocation programs); public-work programs (national parks, slum areas) designed especially for unskilled young people; application of science and technology to pursuits of national goals; organization of manpower, work methods, and administration so that goals can be reached via the most efficient means.

Under "creative federalism" the power of states and local governments will increase as well as the power of private organizations. The federal government will become a partner with states, private industry, universities and local governments. Money will continue to flow from Washington, but more decisions will be made by the people closest to the problem.

Creative federalism means a cooperative relation between a central power and powers independent of it. For example, federal funds may be given to a local school district in order to enrich the educational program, but the decision of what courses to teach and who will teach is determined by the local school board. Another example of creative federalism is the Appalachia Act which provides federal funds to be used in areas to promote future growth. The location of areas and selection of programs are determined by the governors of the states involved. A community addresses its needs and program suggestions to its state governor, not to an agency in Washington, D.C.

This could lead to an increase in "regional authorities" as neighboring states are drawn into federal programs assisting a given area. Three levels of government might exist—states, regional authorities, and the federal government.

Today the President is the central figure in the legislative process, for his programs occupy the dominant place on the congressional agenda. Most major laws are drafted in the President's office, and the budget is put together there for presentation to Congress. But Congress asserts its power through a series of investigations purportedly for the purpose of legislative needs. Often, however, the investigation is for the purpose of harassment or placing pressure upon government officials.

Another power center is in the major departments of the executive branch. (The Defense Department, especially, has been able to influence government policies). Some civil servants within the vast bureaucracy have closer ties to key members of congress than to their department heads or even to the President. Independent regulatory commissions have more recently arrived on the scene, exercising power that is executive, legislative, and judicial, yet not clearly belonging to any of those three branches of government. These commissions developed in response to needs never foreseen by the drafters of the Constitution.

Local Government

Most of the large cities of today are trying to solve mounting modern-day problems with outdated structures. The population has expanded beyond the old city limits, forming many separate governmental units around the metropolitan core. Many city planners see the need to organize larger geographical areas so that there can be an administrative integration of a total metropolitan area. This would allow for unified planning, coordination, and administration. It would also be necessary to have smaller units of local government to perform functions best administered by smaller municipal organizations.

There are many who feel the metropolitan area will need new governmental structures in the future. The large number of governmental units, the imbalance in local financial resources, the complex system of roads and transportation facilities cannot be handled through independent jurisdictions. Even a single "metro" unit would not be adequate. These voices call for area-wide governmental units or activities. Some responsibility would be assigned to the federal government, some to state government, and some to local authorities (such as transportation, sewage, water).

The future may see the creation of a department of local affairs on the state level with independent "desks" for each major metropolitan area within the state. Also, a reconstruction of county government may occur, so that the county can become the metropolitan government of its area. There might also develop a new limited-purpose metropolitan service agency with power to expand its function, finance, and representation, or the creation of a new layer of local government (e.g., "metropolitan council") above existing localities and below the state. The experience of some Canadian cities (e.g., Toronto) may suggest fruitful patterns of operation.

III. SIGNIFICANT AREAS OF GOVERNMENTAL ACTIVITY

Civil Rights

No discussion of government and politics would be adequate if it omitted the area of human equality, civil rights, welfare, and social needs. There is a greater awareness of human equality and inequality today. Formerly, only the rich could afford lawyers, and so the rich had lawyers and the poor did not. Today we are aware of the injustice involved and feel a need to provide legal help for all who need it but are unable to afford it.

There is also a growing awareness of the urgency to do something about the great social needs of our times. For example, the war on proverty will continue in the future. Thirty million people live below the poverty line in the United States; this is about 15 percent of the population. Although the number of persons living below the poverty line will lessen, there is a growing concern to do something about those who remain in poverty. This interest will be accompanied by public concern over better methods of doing welfare work.

Pressures on authority will continue and will take new forms. The formal demonstrations, marches or sit-ins are accompanied by organized economic pressures and community-action organizations. The tenement union (an organization of tenants of apartments located in low-income areas) is gaining momentum. The impetus for such unions has often come from labor unions, churches, university faculty members, and civil rights leaders. Such tenement unions pressure landlords to comply with all housing laws and building codes and set forth specific requirements on painting, lighting, pest control, custodial care, maintenance, and garbage disposal. "Stewards" also aid the tenant in seeing how to improve his own living conditions in the apartment.

It might be that poverty and other areas of social concern and need (education, housing, nutrition, health) will no longer be debated as issues but will be seen as problems to be solved by the mid 1970's. The federal government's civil rights progress has not always been matched by state and local governments or the business and labor community. If all levels of government, as well as the private sector and its institutions, would unite their efforts it would give greater impetus to the movement to provide justice for all.

It is difficult to predict which direction black power may take. Some leaders plead for black power as the only way to end the Negro's sense of inferiority and as the means to political power wherever Negroes are in a majority, organizing economic boycotts or creating all-Negro commercial institutions.

Overall public opinion will continue to be ambivalent with respect to civil rights. Anyone running for national office on a "states' rights" platform will get votes from all sections of the nation even though the total vote will not be of large proportions. Backlash voting will continue to develop in certain urban areas.

The courts will continue to be one of the principal instruments for progress in civil rights. Court decisions seem to insure protection against those who attack or intimidate civil rights workers. Laws that would eliminate discriminatory jury selection have also been asked for. Perhaps the most controversial aspect of civil rights proposals is that which requires that discrimination in housing sales and rentals be prohibited by law. Even though this remains a controversial issue, it is one that must be solved if we are to achieve genuine integration. Thus we may look for an increase in both federal and local laws necessary to insure civil rights.

What might be called the "Kentucky Plan" could indicate the type of progress in civil rights legislation in the future. Kentucky opened to Negroes businesses serving the public and guaranteed fair employment standards to the labor force working for businesses employing eight or more persons. This was the first state south of the Ohio River to enact such a law. Increased federal funds attached to public health programs will increase the pressure on hospitals to practice complete integration.

Government and the Economic System

Economic planning will continue to be necessary. Private business and its decisions are influenced by government controls, federal budget, the banking system, securities market, taxation, labor laws, anti-trust laws, and public and private spending. The federal government will continue to assume responsibility for regulation in order to effectively protect and promote the needs and concerns of both consumers and producers.

The free enterprise system does not automatically assure full employment; public and private spending can result in fluctuations in production and employment. The government can provide balance through fiscal and monetary action. The government needs to see that spending is high enough to assure full employment but not so high as to produce uncontrolled inflation. More and more the national government is taking responsibility for adjusting factors in the economic system so as to insure a smoothly developing economy.

Government policies in Canada and the United States demonstrate a concern with human welfare. The government commits itself to goals of economic development, full employment, equal opportunity for all, social security. Minimum standards are set for income, nutrition, housing, health, and education. This means that planning is very important. The most difficult problem is keeping government administration simple and efficient. Planning also means the government is prepared to use even novel policy measures in order to keep the labor force employed.

IV. CHURCH AND STATE

There are basically three views of the relationship of church and state. One sees Americans as a religious people whose institutions presuppose a Supreme Being. These people believe government should aid religion as long as it does not favor a particular group. A second view sees society as completely secular, and they favor a strict separation of church and state and require all public institutions to be secular down to the last detail. A third view is that government should be neutral toward religion, between sects and between believers and non-believers. This neutrality principle seems to predominate now and probably will continue to guide Supreme Court decisions.

Sunday closing laws provide an example of the neutrality principle. Supreme Court decisions state that Sunday closing laws are valid if they can be interpreted as directed primarily to a non-religious end such as the provision of a uniform day of rest and recreation. Merchants who close their places of business on Saturday as a matter of religious duty need not be exempt from a Sunday closing requirement. However, if they are granted such exemption this does not make the legislation invalid as a law respecting an establishment of religion.

Some take exception to this by saying the Sunday laws are legitimate as an expression of the religious tradition of the Christian majority and as an effort to support and maintain that tradition. This view does not see minorities as being forced to do anything affirmative and believes the minorities should be tolerant of the majority and not ask the majority to give up its Christian heritage and tradition.

Some question whether a religious tradition should be maintained by the force of the state. Justice Douglas says that Sunday laws are indefensible and that it is a subterfuge to interpret such laws as secular regulations. The majority, however, tolerate incidental aids which accrue to religion from measures designed to serve other purposes. The neutrality principle recognizes the

state as secular, but a secular state which does not give preference to secularism and is actively concerned for religious
freedom.

Neutrality not only permits but requires the recognition of
religion and has an active concern for religious freedom. Neutrality would not forbid rules excusing persons of particular
faiths from school attendance on certain religious holidays or
considering changing extra-curricular school activities so as
not to conflict unduly with programs of church groups.

As far as public education is concerned, the neutrality principle means that it is not the function of the public school to
inculcate religious belief or habits of worship. The exclusion, however, of the subject of religion from a program of general education would not be neutral, for such exclusion would imply that
religion is unimportant. Objective teaching, at various age levels,
about religious beliefs and practices as part of our culture and
history may be included.

In regard to released or dismissed time for religious instruction
the Supreme Court has made the location of classes the critical
issue. If the religion classes are held in the school there would
seem to be more direct promotion of attendance and even
financial support. The future will bring this problem more out
in the open. Many parents do not favor separate schools and yet
they feel Sunday church school is not enough and that it implies
religion is a "weekend" extra.

Numerous questions in regard to aid to education for private
and public schools will continue to be asked in the future. Is
the aid to the child? To the school? Is it welfare help such as
lunch or transportation? Recently the New York Supreme Court
ruled that anything given to the private school child is given
to the school for the child as a part of the school. Aid for transportation, lunches, texts, relieves the school budget and thus
gives aid to the private school.

Questions have been raised by some regarding the tax exemption of church-owned properties. Others have pointed out that

the taxes lost through such exemptions are more than equaled by the educational and welfare services given by the church to society. Key issues are whether the property is used primarily for religious activities and whether churches ought to make voluntary payments for public services.

V. SUMMARY AND IMPLICATIONS

A. Summary

1. The two-party system will continue, with a gradual erosion of one-party sections of the country and less class-oriented party membership. Although third parties and political extremism will have an impact in certain areas and specific elections, the two major parties will continue to provide the functional aspects of political life.

2. Decentralized party leadership will continue, with coalition, compromise, lack of party discipline, and continued penetration of parties by lobby and interest groups.

3. The American voter will become decreasingly party-conscious, more independent and less partisan, giving support to the party of creative programs rather than the party of conservatism.

4. Parties may cooperate in designing educational programs aimed at increasing the quantity and quality of voting. Some efforts may be made to secure national control of registration requirements and procedures for national elections, and to provide a broader base for financing election campaigns.

5. The federal government will continue to expand as the dominant agent for social control and change as society becomes more complex, and as major social issues become more numerous and are seen as national problems requiring national solutions.

6. Economic planning will continue to be a major function of the federal government in order to insure full employment, equal opportunity, social security, minimum living standards.

7. The federal government will enter more and more areas formerly the responsibility of religious and private groups, such as hospitals and welfare institutions. As the cost of such operations goes up, federal grants or loans to welfare programs operated by religious groups will be defended on the grounds that payments are being made for secular services.

8. Additional regional authorities will be developed among adjacent states. City governments may be expanded into metropolitan areas, and their authority reorganized to provide more unified planning and administration, and to enable city government to cope with increasing urban problems.

9. The executive branch of government will become stronger as the locus of basic policy decisions and judgments.

10. The neutrality principle will continue to be the determining criterion for relations between church and state. This view will allow for the consideration of religious groups and their needs when necessary for the good of the whole, permit the use of religious symbols in civic ceremonies rooted in history, allow religion to be included as a subject for study in a program of general education.

11. Along with a growing awareness of the need for human equality will come a crisis in authority. Formal protest will become more highly organized into economic pressure and community action. There will be a growing evidence of dissent from authority in all areas of life—church, government, home, and school.

B. *Implications*

The church will undoubtedly continue to regard the nation and its communities as the arena in which God's justice and love are to be expressed. This concern of the church can be expressed in two forms: through actions taken by the church as a corporate body and through the actions of its members as individuals. Both forms of action require programs of education and interpretation which will help members of the church become aware of the changing nature and function of politics and government in an era of social and economic change. Cultivation of knowledge about the empirical functioning of government should be accompanied by cultivation of theological interpretations of the nature of government and the cultivation of attitudes which engender positive and constructive action in public affairs.

One facet of the involvement of the church and its members in public affairs concerns the increasingly important role which government seems destined to play and the widening scope of its responsibilities and activities. Increasingly, government will be called upon to protect and provide for the well-being of the populace. Both the positive values and the potential dangers of this trend must be recognized. Church members can be helped to recognize the intentions of radicals and reactionaries at the extremes of political thought and at the same time to recognize frequent discrepancy between goals and the means advocated to attain the goals.

As the government's role in public welfare becomes greater, the church may wish to re-examine its policies relating to welfare institutions. It may wish to address itself anew to questions of its welfare function, the nature of its welfare services, the support and quality of the services it sponsors. Relationships between church welfare programs and the government may undergo change because of future changes in government policies and in church policies.

The evolving church-state relationship of institutional separation and functional interaction seems to hold promise for the future. It is within this framework that specific issues (such as taxation of church property and public aid for church-related schools) may profitably be discussed. It also suggests the possibility of examining and comparing governmental structures and church polity in a search for ways in which the church can embody procedures which can stimulate creative modification of governmental structure.

5

Economic Trends

I. ECONOMIC GROWTH

The most conspicious feature of the economies of the developed nations is continuing and accelerating economic growth. While factors such as resource base, population base, and social values may underlie economic growth, its observable manifestation is increased productivity—an increase in value of goods and services produced which exceeds the increase in man-hours expended for production. In the period from 1953 to 1964, for example, the gross national product of the United States rose by about 40 percent while the employment index rose only 12 percent. The difference between these two figures indicates the magnitude of the ten-year productivity increase.

Between 1910 and 1945 productivity (output per man-hour) rose an average of 2 percent per year in the private sector of the United States economy. Since 1947 the average rate of increase has exceeded 3 percent. A careful study completed by the National Industrial Conference Board in 1964 estimated that there would be a net (constant dollar) increase of 60 percent by 1975 in gross national product. A twenty-year projection by the National Commission on Technology, Automation, and Economic Progress forecasts productivity gains of 82 percent during that period. Taken entirely in personal income, this would be an 82 percent increase in earnings. Taken in time, it would mean full-time employment of 27 weeks per year to maintain the 1965 living standard.

The extent to which productivity increases are reflected in disposable income is dependent on changes in the length of the work week, the proportion of corporate earnings that are distrib-

uted to employees, and the tax structure. The NICB estimate
is that between 1963 and 1975 total personal income after taxes
(but not adjusted for inflation) will increase by nearly 100
percent. This does not mean per capita increase of 100 percent;
the population increase will reduce the per capita increase.

Anticipated change in family income is as striking as estimates
of increases in gross national product. The following table
indicates the change expected by 1975 in terms of constant
dollars.

Income per Family	Percent of Population	
	1963	1957
Under $5,000	36.0	21.5
$5,000-$14,999	58.5	58.0
$15,000 and over	5.5	20.5

Note that the upward financial mobility characteristic of the
twentieth century is expected to continue. Families will move
out of the lowest income group into the middle income group,
and from the middle income group into the highest income group.
The result is that a smaller proportion of the population will be in
the lowest income group, about the same proportion will be in
the middle group, and the percentage of those in the highest
income group will be almost four times as great. The anticipated
upward economic mobility of the population as a whole is a
continuation of a long-term trend.

Increases in personal income will increase the amount of
money people have available for purchase of optional or luxury
goods and services. As living standards rise there will be a tendency for some items currently considered luxuries to become
necessities. People may not feel that they are any better off than
they were, however, for they will compare their own living
standards with the rising standards of the entire population.
Those at the bottom of the income scale will feel even more
disadvantaged and probably more discontented.

It is expected that between 1963 and 1975 there will be a

doubling of business investment and a 118 percent increase in after-tax profits.

Currently the economy is expanding at a more rapid rate than predicted by the NICB study—a rate significantly higher than the historical experience of the United States. There are high rates of savings and investment and rapid expansion of industries normally subject to cyclical economic fluctuations. There is increase in the durable goods component of the economy as well as the personal services component. It is expected that the present relationship between public and private economic activity will undergo minimal changes during the next several years. Demand for increased governmental services may require increases in the level of taxation, although it is possible that application of present rates to increased personal income will produce ample government revenues.

Although forecasts of economic trends tend to be optimistic for the long term, they acknowledge the real possibility of temporary interruptions caused either by rapid inflation or by periods of economic recession. Furthermore, they are made on the basis of assumptions, such as the absence of widespread and large-scale war, a fair degree of international monetary stability, and an ability to avoid extreme fluctuations within the domestic economy. If any of the assumptions prove to be unjustified, the forecast is likely to be inaccurate.

The trend toward the professionalization of the managerial group will continue, along with the separation of ownership and management functions in large corporations. While corporations will continue to be operated for profit, they will expand their concept of themselves as having responsibility for the welfare of the public. Consequently, many corporations will support or engage in activities which would be difficult to justify using financial profit as the sole criterion. Because of this shift and of expanding government regulation, the private enterprise aspect of corporations will become less prominent, and their semi-public nature will become more evident.

II. EMPLOYMENT AND UNEMPLOYMENT

The economy of the United States will face a labor-force increase of nearly unprecedented proportions as the high birthrates of the postwar years introduce persons into the labor market in the 1970's. The strikingly rapid growth of the labor force will pose one of the principal economic and social challenges of the next decade. The increase in labor force will not come from immigration, as was the case in some earlier eras, but from the coming to maturity of children and young people who were born between 1945 and 1955. Providing jobs for new entrants to the job market and providing the education and training to fulfill job requirements may challenge our ingenuity.

The working-age population will probably rise faster than the nonworking-age population (children and the aged). This will be a reversal of the "support ratio" changes that have occurred in recent years. A larger number of (potential) workers in relation to the total population is one basis for anticipating the possibility of rapid increase in gross national product and consequent rises in living standards.

In the past decade the annual growth of the labor force has been about 1.2 percent. In the period from 1963 to 1975 it is expected to be about 1.8 percent per year. The 1975 work force is projected at 91.4 million, with 88.7 million actually employed and 2.7 million in the armed forces (assuming a return to the 1964 level). There will be a decrease of one million farm jobs and an increase of 19 million non-farm jobs during the 1963-1975 period. Manufacturing employment, increasing by only 14 percent, will decline in relative importance. There will be larger increases in trade and commerce (33 percent), service industries (43 percent), and government employment (54 percent).

Distribution of the work force in various employment categories will change considerably during the next ten years, if past and present trends continue, as in all probability they will. Agricultural employment will continue to decline. In 1947 it accounted for 14 percent of the work force; in 1966, 5 percent; and in 1975 it is expected to account for only 4 percent. It was about 1955 when white-collar workers outnumbered blue-collar workers for the first time. By 1975 it is expected that there will be a 3 to 2 ratio of white-collar to blue-collar workers. The category in which the largest increase is expected is technical and management personnel; this group is expected to increase by 45 percent. In contrast, blue-collar employees are expected to increase by 14 percent, and among them unskilled workers by only 2 percent.

A slight decline in the average number of hours worked per week is expected. The 1964 average of 38 hours will decline to 36.7 hours in 1975, with a more rapid decline occurring for agricultural workers. These figures take into account paid vacations and holidays. It is expected that most of the decline in average hours worked per week will be the result of longer vacations and increased holidays rather than a reduction in the daily work schedule.

If trends of the recent past are followed in the future, the 1970's will witness a decline in the proportion of employed persons over 65. The employment rate for this age group dropped from 48 percent in 1947 to 28 percent in 1965. The same period witnessed a similar but smaller decline in the proportion of employed persons in the 55-64 age bracket—from 90 percent to 85 percent. Declines in self-employment and farming, coupled with improved Social Security and pension-plan benefits probably have contributed to these changes and may be expected to do so in the future.

There have been age and sex shifts in the composition of the work force. Again, trends which have been noted in recent years are expected to continue. As higher education becomes more common, proportionately fewer persons under 21 will be in the work force. The labor market's proportion of women continues to grow, from 31 percent in 1947 to 38 percent in 1965. (The 1944 wartime high was 37 percent.) The most radical change has been in employment of women in the 40-59 age group. Less than a third of the women in this age group in 1947 were in the labor force, but currently more than one-half are. Several forces seem to be contributing to a definite trend toward remunerative employment for married women as well as single women.

Changes in the volume of employment are governed by three fundamental factors: (1) size of the labor force, (2) changes in output per man-hour, and (3) changes in the total demand for goods and services. High unemployment rates of the late 1950's and early 1960's were caused by rapid increases in the size of the labor force and output per man-hour, accompanied by unusually slow growth in demand for goods and services. Increases in demand since then have decreased unemployment from more than 7 percent to less than 4 percent (2 percent for married men). Many economists feel that proper management of the economic system, by creating conditions which raise or lower demand for goods and services, can stabilize unemployment at about 3 percent of the labor force. At this level, the unemployed are chiefly workers who are changing jobs, those displaced by economic relocations or adjustments, and school dropouts who are not old enough to secure employment which sets a minimum age limit of 18.

Current unemployment is not evenly distributed among all groups in the population. Highest rates occur among Negroes, school dropouts, ghetto residents, and inhabitants of depressed rural areas. Despite governmental efforts and, more recently, efforts of private industry to provide jobs for Negroes, the Negro unemployment rate remains twice the unemployment rate for whites. It has been predicted that by 1975 the unemployment rate for Negroes will be more than five times that for the labor force as a whole, if nonwhites continue to hold the same proportion of jobs in each occupational category that they did in 1964.

The key to maintaining full employment lies in maintaining a balance among three basic factors: size of labor force, productivity changes, and demand for goods and services. Aggregate demand can be influenced by federal fiscal and monetary policies —by increasing or decreasing the supply of credit and currency, lowering or raising taxes, changing tariff restrictions and trade policies, and by other actions. There has been increasing acceptance of the idea that the government has a responsibility to stimulate demand when there is a downturn in economic conditions and to dampen demand when it threatens to cause uncontrolled inflation. In addition to attempting to maintain unemployment at a low level through these measures, the government has directly attacked the problem of unemployment in depressed areas by programs designed to stimulate economic development of those areas. Similar direct attacks on the problem of unemployment among Negroes have been made through training programs, laws prohibiting discriminatory hiring practices, and other measures.

There has been widespread discussion of the effect of automation on unemployment, with some social scientists taking an extremely pessimistic view that automation has been responsible for high unemployment levels in the past and will create massive unemployment in the future. In contrast, many economists and businessmen expect a future labor scarcity even when maximum advantage is taken of foreseeable technological improvements. There is agreement that technological advance often creates job displacement and temporary unemployment. Lack of agreement about its effect on the general employment level may stem from different assumptions about the other two factors that influence employment: demand for goods and services and labor force size.

It is possible to support both contentions by selective use of historical examples. There have been times when introduction of more efficient production machinery has been accompanied by increases in unemployment. There have also been times when introduction of new and more efficient processes has been accompanied by increases in employment. This is true for the economy as a whole and for particular industries within the economy. A possible explanation of this apparent paradox lies in the strength of demand for goods and services at various times. When demand is slack, employment decreases; if productivity also rises it probably decreases more rapidly. When demand is heavy, employment increases; productivity gains help prevent a scarcity of goods and services.

During the last few years demand has been stimulated by substantial federal defense expenditures related to Vietnam. Shortages of investment capital and inflationary pressures are indications that the economy has been overstimulated. If economic activity fell below acceptable levels without such defense expenditures, other federally-funded programs could be used to restore the proper balance.

In any event, limitations of human and material resources will make it impossible to automate all production processes overnight. Speed of introduction is limited by the long-range planning it requires, the huge investment involved, and a severe shortage of technical manpower. Introduction of new processes is related to the type of industry. In some industries, such as oil refining, it would be impossible for human beings to perform functions with the required precision. On the other hand, some industries have found it more expensive to use automated processes than to use more conventional assembly-line techniques.

By the operation of the marketplace, manpower will flow to those processes in which human productivity is high in comparison to the productivity of machines. It is felt that symbol-manipulating functions performed by the brain will be automated more rapidly and more economically than functions requiring complex eye-brain-hand sequences. Many clerical functions and low-level management "handbook" decisions will be automated before the job of the janitor becomes obsolete.

There are differences of opinion about the type of human skills that will be required in a more highly automated industrial system. Some feel that more education will be a necessary prerequisite for employment; others contend that industrial requirements will be adapted to available skills and educational levels. The first point of view probably describes conditions in a time of labor surplus, and the second illustrates those in a time of labor scarcity.

The United States National Commission on Automation, Technology, and Economic Progress found it useful to view the labor force as "queued" in order of relative attractiveness to employers. In a slack labor market employers often use educational attainment as a convenient screening criterion regardless of its direct relevance to the job. This makes it possible to handle large numbers of applicants economically. As economic demand rises and labor shortages develop, employers tend to look for anyone who can meet the functional requirements of the job in question, regardless of educational attainment. When there is a surplus of engineers, some engineers are employed in high-level draftsman functions. When there is a scarcity of engineers, some draftsmen are employed in low-level engineering functions. In a time of labor scarcity anyone who is functionally literate and able to learn to drive an automobile will have or can acquire employable skills. This can be seen in some current efforts of employers to upgrade workers and to provide training programs for persons who would be considered unemployable in a time of labor surplus.

In the future the economy will probably follow past precedents by adapting job requirements to available human skills. If available resources are of high quality, the market will make use of their potential. If quality is low methods will be developed to use the resources that are available. Japan and western Europe operate sophisticated industrial economies with educational population profiles inferior to that of the United States, at least in terms of average numbers of years of formal education completed. It seems reasonable to believe that a highly automated economy could be and would be engineered to fit a variety of educational backgrounds.

III. ROLE OF GOVERNMENT

Perhaps the most significant development in the economic system has been the tendency for government to play a larger role in regulating the economy, both by introducing incentives during slack periods and by establishing curbs during periods of too rapid expansion. Increasing size, complexity, and interdependence of the economic system have made necessary at least minimal central control and have led to an increasing acceptance of such control by industry and the public.

There is nearly unanimous agreement that the government must assume some responsibility for the health of the economy as a whole, with particular attention to hardships caused by unemployment and poverty. Some of the devices by which the government attempts to regulate the economy are increasing or decreasing the supply of credit and currency, lowering or raising taxes, changing tariff restrictions and trade policies, changing government spending, cooperating with corporations in meeting defense requirements, and assisting in the solution of labor disputes.

According to many economists in both government and private financial circles, inflation can be controlled by public fiscal and monetary policies. Fiscal control is achieved by manipulating spending and taxation. Increases in spending and reductions in taxes are utilized to increase total demand in the economy. Conversely, tax increases and reduced government spending are used as deflationary measures. The Federal Reserve Banking System changes the supply of available money as part of the total effort to achieve economic stability and growth. By raising or lowering rediscount rates, changing reserve requirements for member banks, buying or selling government securities on the open market, the Federal Reserve System can regulate the amount of credit available.

The scope of government activity is large. It includes measures and policies designed to insure economic stability and growth;

programs designed to alleviate poverty and unemployment; consumer protection through measures such as those requiring automobile safety devices and "truth-in-packaging." The extension of governmental activity in relation to the economy in the past and proposals which are made for the future suggest that government will play an increasing role. Three key recommendations of the Commission on Technology, Automation, and Economic Progress may indicate directions for the future.

First, measures which encourage the development of an adaptable labor force are proposed. These measures deal chiefly with educational opportunities and include free compulsory education through high school; post-high school vocational training and free public education for two years beyond high school; access to university education for all qualified students; and availability of continuing education and retraining for all individuals throughout their lives.

Second, the Commission called for governmental creation of job opportunities for all persons otherwise unable to secure employment. The government would become the "employer of last resort." Jobs to be provided by the government would improve the American environment in such areas as education, health, transportation, and pollution control. State and local governments and some types of nonprofit institutions would submit proposals for new programs which would use available labor and would not reduce existing levels of employment. The federal government would provide financial subsidies for such programs. It is estimated that over 5 million useful jobs calling for manual and subprofessional workers could be created in this manner.

Third, the Commission recommended that a system of income maintenance be established to guarantee a minimum income for persons who are unable to take part in the job economy. Existing welfare policies, which do not provide any benefits for a segment of the poverty population, would be supplemented or supplanted by new programs. The "negative income tax" concept might be used. It has received support from Barry Goldwater's

1964 economic advisor, the president of the Ford Motor Company, and other sources.

International monetary developments affect the economies of virtually all countries. Disruptions of the international monetary system can cause severe dislocations which can trigger curtailments in world trade and cause internal economic recession. Efforts being made to maintain international monetary stability have secured the cooperation of most nations of the West. Informal cooperation is supplemented by international financial institutions such as the World Bank, the International Monetary Fund, and the Inter-American Development Bank, and other agencies of the UN. Recent events have demonstrated both the desire for cooperative efforts to maintain stability and the difficulties which such efforts encounter.

IV. SUMMARY AND IMPLICATIONS

A. *Summary*

1. Productivity increases will provide a basis for continuing increases in living standards and per capita income. A higher proportion of the population will be in the middle income group and smaller percentages in the highest and lowest income groups.

2. While frictional and structural unemployment will continue to be a problem, and there is a possibility of high short-term unemployment caused by recessions, most forecasts anticipate a low unemployment rate for the 1970's and envision the possibility of labor shortages.

3. Public policy commitments to maintain economic stability and growth, combined with availability of techniques which can be used to achieve this objective, seem to promise long-term economic progress. Within this long-term trend some fluctuations will undoubtedly occur.

4. Technological advances will continue to change employment categories and the number of jobs available in each

category. Employment is expected to rise most sharply in the government and personal service sectors of the economy. Level of education completed will place a ceiling on occupational status for most individuals. It will be impossible for the disadvantaged to work their way out of poverty; large-scale programs designed to help them do so will be required if any substantial progress is to be made. The proportion of women in the labor force will continue to increase.

5. The average number of hours in the work week will continue to decrease slowly during the next decade and will be chiefly reflected in more paid holidays and longer vacations. Improved retirement provisions will encouarge more workers to retire earlier.

6. There will be increasing acceptance of the concept that the government has a responsibility for the economic growth of the nation and the economic well-being of the population. This concept, coupled with the complex nature of the modern economic system, will tend to enlarge the role that government plays in the functioning of the system.

7. The success of current efforts to achieve stability in the international monetary system will depend on the willingness of national governments to permit a measure of internationalized control. Progress has been made in this direction, and there are hopeful signs that such progress will continue. Even so, there is the possibility that concern for national interests will create obstacles that block measures needed to insure stability.

B. *Implications*

Understanding the operation of a complex economic system and accepting its necessities is no easy task for most of the population. Yet participating constructively in the system depends in some measure on such understanding and acceptance. Possibly the church in its teachings which relate to work and society can and should facilitate personal adjustment to an increasingly complex and impersonal economic system. Attention might be given to necessary and desirable changes in the relationship between government, business, and labor; to our nation's role in international trade and in aid to the developing nations; to how the operation of the economic system affects various groups in the population.

Increases in productivity and in the standard of living are likely to intensify value changes which are already evident. The "work and save" ethic is yielding to a "consumer's ethic." Employment opportunities related to producing material goods will be fewer than employment opportunities related to providing services to others. There are signs that a corresponding shift in values is taking place. The church is challenged to use these new categories in its formulation and teaching of personal and social ethics. As life styles of the population are increasingly influenced by affluence and leisure, the church is challenged to discover Christian life styles which are appropriate to the changing economic setting.

The persistent problem of poverty in North America will not be solved by 1980, and the church will undoubtedly continue to feel a responsibility to contribute to its solution. Since government provision of welfare services is likely to expand, there may be less of a need for church-sponsored and supported welfare services. There may well be an extension of the "partnership" arrangement, which provides public funds for welfare programs operated by churches or other private groups. Church resources might well be used for pioneering projects. Undoubtedly the church will continue other approaches designed to improve the lives of the poor: community organization, direct political action, and influences on the business community. There is a growing recognition that patterns of middle-class religious life are of limited value for the poor and that indigenous Christian life styles are appropriate for subcultures within the North American population as well as for Christians of non-Western cultures.

Changing employment patterns have implications for the organized life of congregations. More holidays, longer vacations, and earlier retirement make more time available for church activities. At the same time, greater affluence and opportunities for using time in a variety of ways present strong competition. If the church develops programs which are genuinely meaningful for people, it will secure responses from them. The gradually but steadily increasing proportion of women in the labor force will undoubtedly cause changes in the role women play in the church. Increases in personal disposable income may increase the potential financial base of the church—if income rises faster than the cost of desired living standards and if church-related experiences are meaningful enough to secure genuine involvement.

6

Natural Science

I. SCIENCE AND SOCIETY

Science and technology have become important features of our society. Since the end of World War II a three-way partnership in science has emerged between government, the universities and industry. This has produced the era of "Big Science." Federal funds are being used to enable science to serve areas of national interest such as space and ocean exploration, medical research, and the development of military hardware and weapons. Federal funds also support basic and applied scientific research.

Lack of an overall planned program of national scientific goals, and a competition for funds has caused debate about the advisability of creating a department of science and technology. Such a department would be headed by a cabinet secretary and would be responsible for the broad range of government science and technical activities including such existing programs as weather, standards, water, and geological survey. There is general agreement as to the need for some kind of government office for science and technology; such an office may be created in the next few years. National science goals could be established by asking individual scientists in universities and industry to prepare plans and priorities for their programs along with the nuclear, defense, and civil scientists in government. A United States Department of Science and Technology could then submit such a program to Congress for approval.

The lapse in time between discovery and application is shortening, the number of scientists is increasing, and the amount of money for scientific research is at an all-time high. As the individual scientist becomes more aware of the possible ethical and moral implications of his discoveries, he is more likely to become involved in the political direction of science, helping to establish national goals, priorities, and projects.

Federal funds to universities for scientific research will continue to grow, although the rate of growth is slowing down. Universities must provide liberal education for many and not just science education for the few. This will be a growing concern, as large federal science research grants dwarf grants for programs in the humanities. This could change the nature of our colleges and universities. Many scientists see the need for keeping science closely related to the humanities to provide interplay between science and other disciplines. Universities must provide a background of liberal education for scientists as well as helping all students understand the nature of science.

The current emphasis on peaceful uses of atomic energy will increase in the future. More international conferences will be held on how science research can solve world health and agricultural problems. There is currently a rather strong push for a science advisor section in the United Nations. A long-range forecast would include the possibilities of a World Academy of Science made up of an international team of scientists. One important task of such an academy would be a world inventory of natural resources, both present and anticipated.

Legal, ethical, and moral problems will arise in the future as man applies his scientific knowledge to the control of reproduction and evolution. Do parents have an absolute right to reproduce if they have defects that would produce a genetic fault in their child or if they are unable to support and care for a child? Are there other values besides physical fitness? Genetic clinics may be available in from 5 to 15 years. At these clinics prospective parents can be examined in order to detect possible hereditary disorders. This is being done at the present time in several university research centers. When genetic clinics become more numerous, will couples go voluntarily? Will advice be backed up with the power of law?

An even larger question will be raised by man's control of his biological evolution. Biology, especially biomedicine, biochemistry, and molecular biology will produce many challenges to our society. If the theory of evolution disturbed many people, what will be the effect of creating a low-grade form of life in laboratories? What will happen when parents are able to predetermine the sex and traits of their children? Some will say this is an interference with nature. Others will say it is no more an interference with nature to correct a genetic fault in an unborn child than to perform an operation on a child born with a deformity. Who will make such decisions? Will government be asked to stand over all in order to serve the needs of society?

Some of man's basic needs are food, adequate warmth and shelter, and health. Science will soon be in a position to fill many of these needs for most of the human race. The uses of science will need to be examined with extreme care if science is to be the servant of society. We can get information but not moral judgments from research and computers. All mankind will need to understand Albert Einstein's statement: "It is easier to denature plutonium than to denature the evil spirit in man."

II. LIFE SCIENCES

The "Life Code"

Only recently have we come to learn that there is a particular molecule in all living things that controls and gives direction to the growth of the cells. This molecule is known as DNA. In living organisms DNA contains a "code" which is passed on to each daughter cell as it divides and grows. The code is applied through messengers which are called RNA. The RNA messengers carry the information needed to develop specialized parts of the organism such as arms, legs, brain, skin, feathers, bones, scales. DNA also produces enzymes which direct the flow of the genetic message. Sometimes these enzymes fail and a deformity occurs in the growing organism—perhaps a physical deformity or mental retardation. Just as DNA determines the color of skin and eye and the shape of the ear, it also determines the physical make-up of the brain and the processes of mental activity of the brain.

Current studies are now centering around how one cell can grow into a complex organism such as man. It appears that cells are "told" when to start and when to shut off. When cells grow into what they are programmed to be (such as a liver, a heart, an eyeball) there is a feedback device which turns off that part of the DNA in the cell that started the action. Scientists are trying to discover what substance starts, stops, and regulates cell growth. As we learn more about cells, viruses, and immunology, we shall find ways to transplant organs without having the host body reject it as a foreign substance.

The Brain

The human brain is also under intensive study. Present research indicates that learning and memory are related to RNA molecules in the brain. This new theory is based on the knowledge that the genetic code which determines the shape and function of every living cell is stored in the DNA molecule in chemical code. The code is carried by RNA messengers. In the development of an organism different genes are turned on and off according to the DNA "program." The brain is a network of about ten billion nerve cells (neurons) each acting somewhat like a computer—each with its own "memory bank" and its own electrochemical device for fast "read out" of the memory. This is similar to blood cells being immunized and then "remembering" what germs to attack. Some brain neurons control muscles, some control functions such as sensing light and heat. These specialized neurons are interconnected by interneurons so the brain can function as a unit. The operation of the neuron is both chemical and electrical.

Memory once was thought to be entirely electrical, with impulses from the senses opening up "memory paths" that were established by either strong impression or repetition. These "circuits" could then be opened for recall purposes. This theory has been largely disproved on the basis of experiments in which animals taught new tasks remembered the tasks even when given shock or drugs to stop all electrical activity.

A new theory suggests that there are various levels of memory: short-term memory, medium-term memory, and long-term memory. "Shortness" does not refer to the duration of the signal presented, but to the time lapse before memory is consolidated into long-term memory. This is variously quoted as from seconds (in shock-avoidance experience) to thirty to forty minutes (considered more or less standard). The role of attentiveness, awareness, and orientation is important to permanent memory. Also, activity of particular regions in the brain (such as the hippocampus) seems to be required. The hippocampus (a ridge along the descending horn of each lateral ventricle of the brain, consisting of gray matter covered on the ventricular surface with white matter) says: "Now print this." An animal given a strong shock right after learning a new task will forget it. If the shock comes a half-hour later the memory is impaired. After twenty-four hours the shock would have no effect on the memory.

This theory believes that the short- and medium-term memories are electrical and that long-term memory takes a physical form, is spread throughout the entire brain, and is chemically coded and stored in the brain's molecules. This leads to the view that specific molecules are shaped by the DNA-RNA code and act as the medium for carrying out all higher brain functions such as memory and learning.

Some experiments show that when the brain of an animal is stimulated by some form of learning, RNA production goes up and is different in its composition than RNA found in the brain neurons of unstimulated animals. The RNA composition is different also in the early learning stages when compared with a later learning stage. This seems to say that RNA molecules store the learning for recall.

The human brain has ten billion neurons. They die at high rates, possibly as many as 100,000 a day, as part of the aging process. If a compound could be found to stimulate the declining production of RNA, man's mental ability and productivity could extend well into old age. It may be possible in the future to learn how to encourage controlled replacement of worn-out brain cells.

Research indicates a disease such as Parkinson's is linked to a chemical deficit in the brain. There is hope that drugs or enzymes can be found to compensate for such deficiencies. Some studies also indicate that certain types of behavior faults (e.g., rape) may be caused by brain lesions. Knowledge of the brain's molecular composition can also revolutionize treatment of mental retardation and various mental diseases.

Another area of brain research that will lead to a better understanding of the learning process deals with the relation of stimulation (environmental and sensory) and intelligent behavior. Sensory enrichment increases intelligent behavior and also slightly increases the weight of the brain by stimulating the proliferation of glial cells. Rats exposed to environmental stimulation become better problem solvers than rats experiencing environmental or sensory deprivation.

Experiments indicate that proper nutrition, in addition to stimulation, is also necessary to develop the brain more fully. When neurons are deprived of nutrition or lack stimulating learning experience they fail to develop RNA content capable of making adequate connections between the neurons and tend to atrophy. Stimulating educational programs introduced at early life could raise the general I.Q. ten to twenty points. The level could go higher through the use of drugs which stimulate mental activity.

Other Developments

New developments in molecular genetics which may appear to be "way out" and yet which raise hosts of legal, moral, and ethical questions are:

— The possibility of developing, in the embryonic stage, larger brains with a greater number of neurons.

— The possibility that man's brain can be extended through extrasensory equipment such as microwave receiver and transmitter devices to extend our range of communication and put man in more direct connection with computers.

— Fixing, resetting, reordering desired gene combinations in culture tissue and growing them either for transplants or as whole organisms—making an exact copy of a man by manipulating his cells in culture and allowing a set of chromosomes to grow and develop within an egg cell.

— Taking cells from human and animal sources and making a hybrid cell and growing sub-human or super-human creatures.

Some authorities believe that modern brain research is likely to have more impact than the artificial creation of life or some other new development. They indicate two reasons for believing this. First, modern brain research and its discoveries would have the effect of revolutionizing our understanding of brain function and this would revolutionize science and society. Second, new concepts of the mind may challenge theological concepts such as "spirit" and "soul."

III. ECOLOGICAL SCIENCES

There are two unifying principles of modern biology. One can be thought of as vertical and the other as horizontal. The vertical is the continuity of life through the study of heredity and evolution. The horizontal is the study of the unique properties evident at each level of biological organization.

Ecology is the study of the horizontal, i.e., the interrelation of all living things and their environment. It embraces nearly every type of science (physical, natural, social), for all of them deal with man's surroundings and their influence and impact on man. Because ecology covers the interrelation of living things and environment, it must embrace wide areas such as space, atmosphere, weather, water, land. Human geography is the study of human settlements in their relation to environment. It includes the study of the human race (size, distribution, varieties), the occupation and use of land, and the use of natural resources. It is important to note that in the past few years ecologists have become more involved in environmental issues. New terms such as "human geography" and "environmental science" have come into use. An Environmental Science Services Administration has been created within the United States Department of Commerce (largely because the Weather Bureau was its nucleus).

It will be increasingly necessary in the future to consider the total physical environment in relation to human well-being. Urban planning will have to consider the effect on health of all aspects of the physical environment. These include both natural and man-made conditions affecting physical and mental health and safety.

One reason for the increased concern over environment is that the physical problems of an increasingly urban society grow at a faster rate than the human population. As the population increases there are more people to use the things manufactured out of natural resources. Disposing of unwanted items and waste becomes a problem.

Problems related to waste management in urban centers take three major forms—air pollution, water pollution, and the disposal of solid wastes. The major hindrance to finding solutions to waste management problems is not technological as much as public policy. Often political boundaries do not correspond to natural watersheds. Air and water pollution cross city and state lines. Although the federal government is taking more initiative in research on pollution and the development of solutions to the problems, the public must demand action in order to stimulate authorities to move more quickly.

To help solve the problems involved in man's relationship to his environment and to determine the best use of land and other resources, norms or standards of measurement must be established. Such norms might be found by studying the complex pattern of interrelationships evident in undisturbed natural communities. Man can learn much through the study of animals and their environmental relationships.

A Senate bill is pending that would enable the federal government, through the Department of the Interior, to support ecological research in order to provide: (1) an inventory and evaluation of development projects that might modify environments; (2) studies of natural environmental systems; (3) special ecological preserves on federal, state, and private lands for scientific research on representative natural environments.

Oceanography

Oceanography is just beginning to get serious attention, and the tempo is accelerating rapidly. There is excellent reason to believe that research into "inner" space will hold more practical helps for man than research into "outer" space. Over six hundred companies are involved currently in probing the ocean's riches which include billions of tons of minerals (such as magnesium, boron, uranium, copper, gold, and silver) plus large stores of oil and food. Oceanography is already a part of the curriculum in the new Long Beach High School in California. Nearby water areas will be used as laboratories for the study of marine and plant life. Exploration and undersea research is also receiving increased attention from the federal government and the United States Navy. Anti-submarine warfare possibilities have caused the Navy to study how to live and survive in undersea living quarters. Three current areas of study which may lead to new discoveries:

Project Mohole. Although now abandoned because of a lack of funds, this project envisioned an attempt to drill six miles through the floor of the ocean to the mantle of the earth. The immediate purpose was to gather fossil-bearing sediment, meteorite debris, and rare mineral deposits. The Soviet Union is now engaged in plans for a nine-mile hole in the Murmansk region. The findings of such projects will help us know more about the nature and history of the earth and the formation of the earth's crust and continents.

Usages of Water. Desalinization of seawater is already well under way so that usable water can be available everywhere in unlimited amounts. Many areas of the world do not have a water shortage, but lack fresh or usable water. It is likely that economically feasible desalting plants will be available throughout the world in the near future, making possible the development of the west and southwest parts of the United States into arable and livable land.

These developments will create new physical and economic resources of whole populations and result in a better standard of living. They will encourage development of coastal resorts and seaports, supply industry with a vast amount of reusable water, free fresh water for human needs, and possibly result in population shifts as new land areas are opened.

Water as a Source of Food. There is good reason to believe that in the future a large addition to man's food supply may come from food available in the ocean. "Farming" of the ocean may produce inexpensive and highly nutritious food in the form of plankton and fish meal. Fish "herds" and plankton could be raised in offshore pens. Ocean research could open up new sources of protein and could well have global implications which raise the question of possible UN ownership of the ocean floor. Weather and climate could be controlled by warming and cooling the ocean, and it may be that the UN will have to have surveillance of such climate control experiments.

IV. SPACE SCIENCES

There are several theories as to the origin and destination of the universe. According to the "Big Bang" theory the universe evolved from a primary atomic blast and then through a series of smaller bursts. The "Steady State" theory suggests that there was no particular beginning nor will there be a particular ending of the universe, but rather that there is a continual birth of new stars as old ones die out. The "Pulsating Universe" theory maintains that the universe alternately expands and contracts. This theory is based on recent observations that the universe may be expanding less rapidly now than a billion years ago. Perhaps there were atomic blasts in the past (and there may be more in the future), but the galaxies now flying apart from a previous bang may be slowing down and may someday start falling back together again. But another atomic blast could start it all over again. This theory would see the universe as "closed" and having an outer "edge." It contrasts with theories of an "open" universe which expands indefinitely.

Scientists are attempting to find out whether the expansion of the universe is speeding up or slowing down and by how much. The discovery of quasars in 1960 was thought to be able to shed light on this question. In 1963 a distant radio source was discovered which appeared to be four billion light years away. In 1965 one was located apparently nine billion light years away. If true, this means we are seeing nine billion years back to what would be the early birth of our universe. Comparing these quasar speeds with those of nearby galaxies, we may be able to determine whether the universe's speed of expansion is changing and by how much. Quasar studies thus far appear to support a closed or finite view of the universe.

Quasars pose many difficulties. They give off a power equal to all the stars in our galaxy but are not of the size necessary to produce such power. Further study hints that they may not be what we first thought they were, but rather were ejected from a gravitational collapse at the center of our own galaxy perhaps only five million years ago, and their great energy power is due to high-speed passage through intergalactic gases. Whatever quasars are, a fuller understanding of them in the years ahead will definitely change our understanding of the universe.

Further research will include a NASA launch of an orbiting astronomical observatory to analyze ultraviolet light from the stars. This will help test current theories about the origin, shape, and destiny of the universe. It will help us know if the universe is finite or infinite, whether space is curved or stretches out in all directions. Future quasar research will indicate if the Russian scientist Nicolai Kardashev is right in his view that quasars are monstrously powerful and intelligently controlled beacons. We may hear some talk about "God" as "closed spacetime."

Man in Space

Already man has walked in space and we have seen close-up pictures of the moon and Mars taken by Ranger and Mariner fly-bys. We have also been able to make soft landings on the moon, taking very close photos of the moon surface. What we will be doing in space in the future depends on the priorities we select and the money we are willing to spend. Although the military implications of space are soft-pedaled, they will certainly be a major factor in establishing priorities.

One basic factor to keep in mind is that any space probe is useful only to the degree the craft can send back signals of its position and data discovered. Radar waves have been deflected from eight hundred million miles away (Jupiter) and by 1978 it is hoped a radar beam can be deflected from an object four billion miles away (Pluto).

The future in space may follow this approximate timetable:

1970—Manned flight to the moon.
1980—Manned moon base in operation.
1985—Manned flight from moon to Mars (possible fly-bys of Venus and Mercury).

1995—Permanent Martian base.

2000—Probes to every planet in our solar system (results will be delayed because of the years it will take to complete the trip). The year 2000 might also see landings on asteroids and using them "piggy back" for years of observation before returning to home base.

2100—Man may set foot on Pluto. More distant space travel seems unlikely, although space probes may investigate other solar systems.

Space explorations will be able to further test the Einstein theory which states that all internal motion slows down in objects moving at great speeds away from earth. If true, astronauts would live and age more slowly, reaching a star in five years of their time but one hundred years of earth time. Otherwise, generations of men and women may be born, live, and die aboard a star ship. Space exploration will require international cooperation in space probes, explorations, and discoveries. This will lead to new laws, treaties, agreements, and ownership arrangements. Space probes do not at present seem to hold much practical help for man.

Life on Other Planets

Present knowledge of the universe indicates the possibility that life exists on other planets. The sun has supported life on earth for several billions of years. Our sun is an average star; we can assume that there are similar stars that could support life on planets having earthlike atmosphere and conditions. Galaxies appear to be scattering, and so it may be assumed they were formerly in a more concentrated system. It is possible that all came from a primary atomic blast, in which case many of them would be quite similar. When stars and planets are born, changes occur which produce chemical, physical, and climatic conditions suitable for life. There may be as many as ten billion planets in such suitable relation to a star as to have conditions suitable for life. Since the number of stars is unlimited (our galaxy alone may have as many as one hundred billion similar stars), it seems plausible that life may exist on other planets.

In our own solar system Mars is the only other planet which appears to have the ability to support some kind of life. Current theories suggest that Mars and earth had similar primitive conditions. Life on Mars could have existed also. Does it? Chances are slim, but the odds are certainly not zero.

NASA is planning instruments to detect any microbe life on Mars. Other instruments are being designed to detect any photosynthesis on Mars, for if there is Martian life it would have to include some kind of surface-living photosynthetic species. Instruments to answer the question of life on Mars should be available within the next ten years. Martian samples taken by these instruments can be studied to see if there is life on Mars, and if there is, what kind of life it is. Would life on Mars be made up of the same building blocks as life on earth? All earth life is made up of the same acids and chemicals. Whether Martian life is made of the same material can be determined by an examination of Martian samples.

Mars and moon probes will be of value even if no life is found, for they may yield fossils and organic chemicals which, upon study, would add important knowledge to our understanding of the origin of the universe and of life itself.

V. SUMMARY AND IMPLICATIONS

A. *Summary*

1. Large-scale governmental support for scientific research will continue to stimulate scientific progress. A federal department of science and technology may be created and given responsibility for establishing national science goals as well as for coordinating research and other scientific programs. Individual scientists will continue to become involved in the political

direction of science, serving as advisors to the executive branch and to legislative committees.

2. International cooperation in science may increase in the form of specific projects and permanent agencies.

3. Great advances will be made during the next decade in understanding the genetic code, and there will be progress in techniques by which genetic material may be modified in order to correct hereditary defects.

4. New knowledge of the living cell will contribute to more effective treatment for many diseases which cannot be satisfactorily controlled at present.

5. The creation of simple forms of life in laboratories may become common.

6. Brain research promises to uncover techniques which can heighten intellectual activity, improve learning, and treat emotional disorders more effectively.

7. Ecological sciences will receive greater emphasis as efforts are made to improve the environment. Techniques of climate control may improve in their capacity for transforming areas which are currently uninviting into comfortable and productive environments.

8. World water and food supplies will be increased by means of new technologies such as desalinization, reuse of water, improved agricultural techniques.

9. Progress in space exploration will be accompanied by an improved understanding of the origin and nature of the universe.

B. Implications

Scientific advances involve an increased understanding of the physical world and its inhabitants. They lead to capacity for more effective control. Participation in such advances is in harmony with the theological viewpoint that God has given man dominion over his earthly environment. Dramatic advances in man's ability to control and modify both his environment and the human organism point to a need for an emphasis on man's responsibility to God as he exercises dominion over the earth. Increased understandings of the interdependence between man and the various aspects of his environment may strengthen the sense that it is man's destiny not only to control his environment but also to live in harmony with it.

The sharp conflict between science and religion that existed in previous generations has for the most part disappeared. For most people it probably has been replaced by a compartmentalization rather than by serious reflection upon possible relationships between scientific discoveries and religious beliefs. While many theologians and scientists have formulated promising approaches to this topic, it is likely that the majority of church members are unaware of them. Because a worldview based on procedures and discoveries of science is likely to become ever more pervasive, the church should assist its members to find ways of integrating Christian teachings and insights derived from science.

Theological issues may be raised by advances in the space sciences and in sciences which can modify personality and behavior. Members of the church may experience conflict as discoveries of science appear to contradict what they have accepted as Christian teachings. Other persons, unaware of the theological implications of scientific discoveries, may unreflectingly move toward scientism as a worldview. The church must assist its members to develop viewpoints which realistically take into account scientific insights and which make distinctions between the discoveries of science on the one hand and philosophies derived from science on the other.

Serious ethical issues are raised by current developments in science. Among them are the artificial prolongation of life, modification of brain function, and genetic manipulation. The church should continue its efforts to develop an ethical stance on such issues by means of dialogue with scientists and policy-makers. The ethics of devoting resources to various types of scientific investigations should receive the attention of the church, both in public pronouncements and in the education of its members. Questions may be raised about allocating extremely large amounts of money for scientific research which promises only marginal human benefits while large portions of the population have serious unmet needs. Criteria are needed to guide decisions for allocation of resources that are available.

7

Health and Medicine

I. MEDICINE AND SOCIETY

Historically the philosophy of medical practice has been relatively simple: the alleviation of symptoms and the community prevention of disease. Helping the sick is the most ancient responsibility of medicine, symbolized in the Greco-Roman world by the cult of Aesculapius. In this tradition the first duty of the physician is to do all within his power for his patient's welfare. In another tradition which can be traced to the cult of Hygeia in Athens and to the Mosaic sanitary regulations for camp life, the physician is concerned with the health of the community as a whole.

Changes in medical practices have occurred rather slowly in the past, and thus have rarely caused serious disturbances in the medical and social structure. Now medical research is proceeding at such an accelerated pace that the very pattern of medical thought and practice is being torn apart. The rapid increase in the number and effectiveness of therapeutic and prophylactic methods available to physicians is creating problems for which neither medicine nor society is prepared. These problems will likely soon compel a reformulation of medical philosophy. Medical research has shown that the relatively simple assumptions of symptom control of past generations are no longer valid. Increasing understanding of cellular chemistry has shown the complexity of the human organism. Systems are delicately interlocking and side effects of treatments can be more serious than ever before dreamed. Paradoxically, this new knowledge makes the diagnosis and treatment of disease more tentative and experimental today than it was thought to be a generation ago.

A further complication is the fear that in the future rapid technological innovation will create new health problems at such a rate that the task of developing methods of control will impose scientific and economic burdens far heavier than those encountered in the past. To meet the situation it will be necessary to reorient medical practice and research, keeping in mind the wide range of adaptive potentialities the human body possesses. These potentialities are called into play less and less in the modern world because man has created a protective, sheltered environment. Yet man may require a new kind of adaptiveness in order to function effectively under conditions created by modern technology. Physicians will need to collaborate with engineers and other scientists to help man effectively adapt to his ever-changing environment.

It is not for physicians, of course, to decide what modern life should be like, because this choice involves value judgments which transcend medical evaluation. But the final decision should be conditioned by a kind of biological wisdom that only medicine can provide. Thus, whether he wants it or not, the physician will be compelled by the very power of the means at his command to accept increasingly larger social responsibilities. He will have to take into consideration not only the welfare of the patient but also the interests of the community and the future of the human race. When theoretical physics became an instrument of political power after Hiroshima, many physicists became acutely aware of their political responsibility. Likewise, the power of physicians over life and death has become so great that medicine can no longer be considered apart from social philosophy.

The United States government grasped this social understanding of community health earlier than the medical establishment. A prime example is Medicare, providing government health insurance for citizens 65 and over. It is likely that additional legislation will extend Medicare to children of needy families and totally disabled persons under 65. Proposals have been made to include dental care under a similar legislative program. A likely future step is to include under Medicare all persons living in families with an income considered to be substandard. There is motion toward providing free or low-cost health services for the entire population. Some physicians expect this to occur within fifteen years.

In the opinion of many experts, providing low cost medical services will place serious stress on practicing physicians and hospitals. Persons who now, for financial reasons, ignore minor symptoms will seek medical advice and treatment for relatively simple complaints. This coupled with a shortage of doctors and increase of population augers a future crisis for America's medical services.

Life, Health, and Ethics

The most objective evidence of medical progress is the fact that life expectancy at birth is increasing steadily. This is due in large part to the control of infant mortality and also to the development of many techniques for postponing death caused by almost any type of disease. This increased power of medicine has large social implications. To save the life of a child suffering from some hereditary defect is a humane act and the source of professional gratification, but the long-range consequences of this achievement may magnify medical problems for following generations. Likewise, prolonging the life of an aged and ailing person must be weighed against the consequences this entails for the individual himself and even more for the community of which he is a part. These ethical difficulties are not new, of course, but in the past they rarely presented issues to the medical conscience because the scope of the physician's action was limited. Soon, however, ethical difficulties are bound to become larger as the physician becomes better able to prolong biological life in individuals who cannot derive either profit or pleasure from existence and whose survival creates painful burdens for the community.

The problems posed by the prolongation of life have their counterpart with regard to the prevention of disease. Three examples will serve to illustrate how the decision to adopt certain public-health policies, which appear justified from the scientific point of view, has to be weighed against social and economic consequences.

The recent uproar over the chemical contamination of cranberry products provides an example of countless similar problems in the modern world. Substances used in agricultural and food technology may have deleterious long-range effects. On the other hand, it is impossible to carry out the complicated tests required for the evaluation of chronic toxicity for all these substances. It would soon paralyze progress in food production if all substances which have not received a verdict of absolute safety were to be declared unusable. Tentative decisions must be reached and policies adopted on the basis of available knowledge and medical judgment.

Various forms of air pollutants can be serious threats to human health. Several of the most dangerous pollutants have been identified, and it is known that certain changes in the design of automobiles and industrial equipment would go far toward alleviating the worst aspects of air pollution. But here again, it will take much wisdom to decide how far industrial practices and automobile traffic should be controlled in order to minimize the incidence of respiratory diseases related to air pollution.

Vaccination against viral diseases will soon present another test for medical wisdom. Techniques can now be developed for producing and purifying almost any kind of virus, thus making possible effective vaccines for viral diseases. But clearly there are both biologic and economic limitations to the numbers of vaccines that can be used in practice. Therefore, the question is no longer the technical one of developing methods of vaccination, but rather the ethical one of deciding against which diseases to provide protection. The decision involves social as well as medical factors.

II. MEDICAL MANAGEMENT

In the future a majority of people will consult a physician for reasons identical to those for which many persons see their doctors now, but such consultations will be met with new techniques of examination. Enlightened appraisal by the general public of the value of the early recognition and treatment of disease will lead to a demand for the screening of apparently well persons by tests which can easily and reliably detect treatable conditions—those which may kill or seriously impair enjoyment of life. Specialized techniques will be used for the diagnosis of life-threatening disease or injury requiring full hospital investigation and treatment; disabilities calling for some form of surgery or prosthesis; symptoms requiring reassurance and/or domiciliary treatment; and socially dangerous conditions requiring special action, such as insanity and certain types of infectious disease.

From such a formulation two key processes emerge. First, the determination of medical need and the decision as to the type of management called for—what may be called the function of the doctor of first contact. Second, the application of scientifically based medicine to the relief of the patient's condition, already largely—and in the future probably wholly—the function of the hospital.

The "doctor of first contact" (a term preferred over general practitioner because the doctor of first contact will have a very different range of skills and activities from those of the traditional general practitioner) will decide when a condition that calls for hospitalization is present and will direct the patient to where his needs can best be met. Many developments in medicine suggest that the doctor of first contact will have little responsibility for hospital treatment. Essentially he will be a wise counselor with ability to understand his patient holistically, and will have a wide range of social, psychological, and medical expertise.

This doctor of first contact will be responsible for those forms of manipulation and treatment that can be effectively handled outside the hospital environment and for which satisfactory control is possible without specialized tests. The number of such activities may well increase steadily with the stabilization of medical knowledge. Once adequate clinical research has laid down the potentialities and limitations of some new procedure, it usually moves from the hospital to the doctor of first contact.

Patients will be referred to hospitals by the doctor of first contact either for treatment which he is incapable of providing or for further tests. The characteristic feature of the hospital in the foreseeable future will be the progressive transfer of decision-making to data-processing machines and various types of computers. If judgment is to be based on experience, there is no escape from the contention that a machine which can give accurate weight to all the relevant information and express the judgment in terms of quantitive probability can provide accurate diagnosis. It will still be necessary for the physician to recommend treatment by interpreting the data produced by the machine, in the knowledge that all the measurable data have been given due weight. His decision as to appropriate action may still be shown by the outcome to have been right or wrong.

In addition to the need for a way to assess accurately the totality of information probabilities that go into diagnosis, computers are needed because of the rapid increase in the number of laboratory procedures. Several clinical laboratories have recently reported that their work loads have been doubling every five years. Computers will also speed the turnover of patients because of time saved in gathering information and reaching clinical conclusions—an important factor in the future because of the potentially large numbers of persons requiring admission to hospitals.

When the output from automatic analysis machines can be fed directly into a computer, nearly all the manual steps are eliminated. Once data are in a general-purpose computer, great flexibility of handling is possible. This feature, combined with compact storage of information and great speed of operation, makes the computer a very important tool for the future of pathology. A computer will lessen the clerical work in the laboratory, bring about faster reporting, eliminate errors due to incorrect transcriptions, poor legibility, and poor arithmetic, and improve the quality of the work by carrying out more compatibility and statistical checks than are currently possible with present methods.

When results are stored by a computer, their analysis for administrative and research purposes becomes much easier. This last point is most important, because at the present time the vast majority of pathologists find themselves quite unable to answer factually such elementary questions as what is the normal range found in their own laboratory for a particular investigation on patient of specific age or sex.

Another use of the computer is its "on-line" function. It is already possible in an intensive care unit to monitor continuously and take measurements directly from the acutely ill patient (e.g., blood sugar, heart action, respiration rates). It may even be possible to program an on-line computer to operate suitable devices which will automatically dispense appropriate treatment in certain situations, eliminating even the slight delay in treatment now caused by the lag between the time the doctor or nurse is alerted to a problem and the time action can be taken. It is certain that machines will be increasingly used to monitor vital functions during surgery.

Without attempting to proceed further in spelling out the hospital situation of the future, we can see that the requirements for hospital medicine are going to be quite different from those needed by the doctor of first contact. Logically, quite different approaches will be required for professional medical education. There will be the need for a generalized preparation of the doctor of first contact. This function requires persons with the basic medical knowledge and skills needed for disease detection combined with an ability to apply common sense, courage, and compassion in handling all human difficulties. An increasing number of hospital technicians and medical specialists will be required. Forward-looking medical schools are already appraising the needs for medical education in the light of these harbingers of the future.

As desirable as this future management of disease appears because of its promise of thoroughness, three factors will work to delay progress. First, sufficient funds will be lacking to provide research and the development of new medical technologies. Private sources simply cannot provide the financial resources required; and as long as the government spends huge sums on national defense on the one hand, and on the other, invests its medical resources primarily to pay for treatment of patients, hope is dim for significant governmental investment in research and development. Second, doctors and hospital administrators often do not react kindly to direction. It is almost inevitable that for utmost efficiency and reliability central computer banks will be required with stations in individual hospitals (just as airlines store reservation information in a central computer with stations at ticket counters across the country). Third, there likely will be a lag in recruiting and training procedures necessary to staff hospitals desiring to use new aids to diagnose and treat illnesses.

Even this general overview of the prospects of automatic diagnosis and treatment for the patient raises the specter of impersonal treatment of persons during crisis times in their lives. The problem is accentuated not only by the mechanization of hospital procedures, where technicians are trained to operate machines rather than care for patients, but also by the loss of the direct personal ministration of the doctor of first contact once the patient leaves his care and enters the hospital.

III. DISEASE CONTROL

Circulatory Diseases

At the present time approximately 55 percent of all deaths in the United States are caused by cardiovascular diseases, and 45 percent occur from all other causes. As further progress is made in eliminating infant and childhood illness, and as treatment and cure are found for other death-causing diseases among adults, more and more people will live longer; they will thus become subject to degenerative diseases, chief of which are cardiovascular, that accompany old age. It is likely, therefore, that in spite of programs to prevent cardiovascular disease and new techniques for early diagnosis and treatment, diseases of this nature will continue to increase.

Stroke is the third largest cause of death in the United States. In the older age group it is one of the leading causes of long-term illness and dependency. Each year 400,000 people are stricken by the disorder, and there are about 200,000 deaths. It is estimated that there are two million victims of stroke alive today, about one-third of whom were wage earners made unemployable by the residual effects of the disease.

Stroke has been a neglected disease for many years. At the root of this neglect are the misconceptions that it is inevitable and that efforts to prevent it or treat it are without hope of success. Several facts make it clear that stroke is neither inevitable nor irremediable. First, many strokes are preceded by warning symptoms, such as brief periods of loss of speech, weakness of limbs, or loss of consciousness. Second, intensive modern medical and surgical therapy can restore as many as 80 percent of stroke survivors to relatively active and productive living. Third, a highly coordinated research attack, spearheaded by the joint efforts of the National Institute of Neurological Diseases and Blindness and the National Heart Institute, is opening up new possibilities in stroke prevention and treatment. Research points to future progress in the following areas:

—rapid survey methods which can uncover factors suspected of contributing to stroke proneness;

—new blood-flow study techniques to gain further basic knowledge of the dynamics of circulation, the mechanisms that promote and retard clotting, why clotting occurs within the closed vascular system of a previously normal person;

—the restitution of function in stroke patients;

—training for research in cerebrovascular disease;

—educational campaigns, conducted broadly for the general information of the population and conducted individually by the family doctor for the prevention of cerebrovascular diseases;

—new techniques to speed recovery and eliminate discomfort of patients suffering from cerebrovascular accidents.

Many heart debilities are caused by congenital defects and viral attacks on portions of the heart. Progress in the management of viral attacks will reduce damage from this source. Improvement of surgical techniques will continue, allowing increased safety in heart surgery and making possible surgical correction of additional defects.

The major danger for the population as a whole is atherosclerosis and coronary heart disease. Atherosclerosis, the clogging of the arteries, is a natural result of aging. It is also caused by a build-up inside the arteries of fatty substances thought to be related to the amount of cholesterol in the blood. This in turn is related to the dietary habits. A large proportion of heart attacks is caused by interruption of the blood flow to a portion of the heart muscle, often by a small blood clot becoming caught in the coronary artery or one of its branches inside the heart (myocardial infarction). If the flow of blood is not quickly restored, the portion of the heart muscle normally supplied with blood by the affected artery "dies" and is replaced by scar tissue. The heart muscle is, however, extremely strong and can continue to function to supply blood to the rest of the body if the affected portion of the muscle is relatively small. The amount of disability is dependent upon the ability of the remaining healthy muscle tissue to continue to function. If it is seriously weakened, it is subject to overwork and failure.

Available therapeutic techniques have increased survival among heart-attack victims, and continued progress will reduce risks of recurrent attacks. Even so, mortality from first heart attacks is still appallingly high. Despite the improvement in the medical management of myocardial infarction, once the heart muscle is damaged, the heart is forever weakened. The greatest hope for reducing the death toll from coronary heart disease lies in devising effective means of preventing that first heart attack.

There are presently no cures for atherosclerosis and coronary heart disease. However, there is reason to hope that the disease process is reversible and that therapeutic agents will eventually be found that will cause regression of established atherosclerotic lesions and restore health to diseased arteries. Meanwhile, with existing therapeutic measures it may be possible to halt or slow down the progress of the disease and thus avert or delay the onset of disabling or deadly heart attacks. For heart-attack victims the outlook for immediate and long-term survival has been improved by new concepts of intensive medical care, improved resuscitative measures, and anticoagulant therapy. Clot-dissolving agents may provide still other powerful weapons against coronary thrombosis and other thromboembolic complications of atherosclerosis. But our greater hope for substantially reducing mortality from coronary heart disease lies in devising effective means of prevention.

Cancer

In 1965 an estimated 295,000 Americans died of cancer; in 1964 it was 290,000; in 1963, 285,326 cancer deaths were reported by the National Vital Statistics Division. This year about 300,000 will die of the disease. Of every six deaths from all causes in the United States, one is from cancer.

There was a steady rise in the national death rate (age-adjusted) until 1950; since 1950 it has leveled off. In 1930 the number of cancer deaths per 100,000 population (age-adjusted) was 112; in 1940 it was 120; by 1950 it had risen to 125; and in 1963 the number was 127. Except for cancer of the lung and pancreas, and leukemia, age-adjusted cancer death rates in general are leveling and, in some cases, dropping.

In the early 1900's few cancer patients had any hope of cure. In the late 1930's fewer than one in five was being saved—that is, alive five years after first being treated. Ten years later one in four was being saved. Today better than one in three is being saved; the gain currently amounts to some 47,000 patients each year. Of every six persons who develop cancer today, two will be saved and four will die. Numbers 1 and 2 will be saved. Number 3 will die but might have been saved had proper treatment been received in time. Numbers 4, 5, and 6 will die of cancers which cannot yet be controlled. This means that about half of those who get cancer could and should be saved by early diagnosis and prompt treatment. Thus the immediate goal of cancer control in this country is the annual saving of 285,000 lives, or half of those who develop cancer each year.

The great hope for cancer control lies in basic or fundamental research. It often is in areas which seem far afield from human health problems. For the last two decades both the National Cancer Institute and the American Cancer Society have put considerable emphasis on basic research. From these projects and fundamental studies financed by other agencies a torrent of information has cascaded into scientific journals, into the proceedings of thousands of great and small scientific meetings, and now into the capacious receptacles of information storage and retrieval devices—or electronic brains.

Some of the most innocent-appearing wisps of knowledge could have important implications for cancer prevention and treatment. Some years ago, for instance, two scientists reported that rat liver cancer cells took up a normal nucleic acid constituent called uracil, while normal liver cells did not—the normal cells used their own uracil. The experimenters fed rats a synthetic uracil containing sulfur. This "food additive" selectively sought out pre-cancerous and cancer cells, blocked their use of essential and natural uracil, and poisoned them.

One of the most fertile fields of fundamental biological investigation is immunity. Science knows that the system produces a number of proteins which protect man from infections. The proteins stick viruses together in an inert mass, rupture and destroy bacteria and other invading cells, and chemically treat these parasites, wastes, and debris so that they can be eaten by scavenger cells and eliminated from the body. A number of other mechanisms of body defense, including some which produce germ-destroying fevers, also are known. Immunity mechanisms, however, are not fully understood.

For many reasons a growing number of cancer researchers have been drawn into the field of immunity. In this field lie the secrets of spontaneous regression—the rare "miracles" by which patients sometimes dying of hopelessly advanced cancers suddenly recover. Herein are the unknown reasons why so many cancer patients lose their resistance to a variety of infections. In this area is the mystery of how the cancer cell escapes the fate of other predators—death under assault by antibodies and the other known and unknown body police forces. In immunology lies the hope of producing drugs and vaccines which will prevent cancer from arising and, when it establishes a beachhead in the body, beating it back and destroying it.

Mental Health

Mental health is of concern to every person. All suffer from periods of depression, tension, and indecision. When these conditions become either chronic or acute, they create a mental health problem. For many in the population these problems become overwhelming. In serious stages these persons become a threat to themselves, their families, and society in general. These problems, coupled with senility and congenital problems associated with brain damage or retardation, make mental health one of the serious problems of society today. More hospital beds are used by patients suffering from mental illness than for all of the physical illnesses combined. This is a function of the number of persons affected by mental illness and of the longer average time needed for hospitalization for mental illness.

On the basis of the present impact of treatment trends, population trends, and scientific knowledge now on the horizon, we can make conjectures about mental health in the future. The incidence of mental illness is likely to increase, particularly forms of disturbances related to the emotional and physical impact of aging and those related to increasing leisure time. Steps must be taken to fortify the resiliency and inner resourcefulness of youth; and unless there are serious efforts toward helping children find more consistent and adequate opportunities of developing patterns of identification, they are in danger of being lost in tomorrow's world.

According to current estimates one person out of twelve living in urban America will be hospitalized for mental illness at some time during his life. The proportion is much higher for those who live much beyond age 70. Attempts to compare the frequency of mental illness in different time periods and in different cultures encounter many problems of definition and availability of data. There is, however, little evidence to suggest that the frequency of mental illness varies greatly at different time periods or in different cultures. There is evidence that chronology and culture influence to some extent the forms which mental illness most frequently takes. Similarly, differences in frequency of occurrence in different social classes are minimal, although forms of illness, availability of treatment, and response to treatment do vary.

The outlook for the treatment of persons who become mentally ill is encouraging (except for the mental illness characteristic of old age). The number of first admissions to mental hospitals has continued to rise each year, but the resident population of these hospitals has declined each year since 1955. Elderly patients account for the great majority of long-term resident patients. Increases in the discharge rate and in the proportion of persons who can be treated as outpatients rather than hospital residents are usually attributed to the wide and effective use of tranquilizing drugs as well as to improvements in the social climate of mental hospitals and improved patterns of patient care.

Observable occurrences of mental illness are produced by highly complex and variable relationships among underlying causes, contributing causes, and precipitating causes. Forms of treatment vary according to the theoretical framework used by the practitioner. There seems to be a tendency to regard mental illness as a functional disability and to determine treatment on the basis of the characteristics and potentialities of the individual patient.

While public attitudes toward mental illness have not progressed to the point of regarding this as illness which the individual cannot prevent or treat by himself, greater public discussion has lessened to some extent the strong stigma formerly attached to it. There seems to be some increase in the extent to which persons are willing to use facilities available for treatment.

As the extent of occurrence of mental illness has become clear to both professionals and the public, attention has been directed to preventive measures. The most successful have been efforts to insure early recognition of maladjustment and provision of public services to limit the severity and duration of the illness. School counseling services and community mental health clinics serve this function to the extent that resources permit. More fundamental preventive measures would require extensive educational efforts together with amelioration of societal and interpersonal factors which play a role in mental illness.

IV. SUMMARY AND IMPLICATIONS

A. *Summary*

1. It will be more fully recognized that medicine is one principal field of application of all the basic sciences, among which the behavioral sciences will have come to assume relatively a much more prominent place. Especially in research, but also in practice, the medical man will have to collaborate much more closely with a wide range of nonmedical scientific experts.

2. The social organization of health services will become increasingly complex. This again will involve the collaboration of physicians with many categories of nonmedical personnel, a decreasing proportion of which will be "auxiliary"—it will be a collaborative rather than a "line" type of organization. There will develop a distinction of functions between the screening done by the doctor of first contact and the treatment of serious illness by teams of specialists. The role of computers as diagnostic and monitoring instruments will grow.

3. The traditional physician-patient relationship will be altered. More attention will be paid to the personal problems of the patient on a professional basis grounded in scientific knowledge.

4. The treatment of what used to be the greatest scourges of mankind, the epidemic infectious diseases and the endemic nutritional deficiencies, offer no comparable challenge now. These maladies have been virtually vanquished by medical progress.

5. Health services will come to be regarded less as areas of private practice and more as part of the government's responsibility to the population. Public financing of health-care costs will continue to be extended to additional segments of the population during the next decade.

6. There will be continued progress in the understanding and control of disease. Basic research designed to uncover causes and cures of diseases accounting for the largest mortality rates

will lead to greater control over circulatory diseases, cancer, and mental illness.

7. It seems likely that increased demands for health services will create a scarcity of medical personnel and resources.

8. Increasingly there will be an effort to assess the effect of man's changing physical and social environment upon his physical and emotional health. Efforts will be made to improve the environment when existing conditions cause serious health problems (as in the case of air pollution).

B. *Implications*

Medical advances in some areas will pose issues to those who are sensitive to ethical values. Examples of such areas are therapeutic abortion, organ transplants, and prolongation of life by artificial means. As effective procedures become standardized and more widely available, increasing numbers of persons will be exposed to them and will have to deal with the ethical issues they raise. The church should continue the efforts it has initiated to address itself to this problem. Through dialogue with persons in the field of medicine the church may develop viewpoints consonant with both Christian teaching and medical practice. These viewpoints can then be used in an educational program that the church provides for its members.

The tendency for health care to become part of the public domain and to be removed from the realm of "private practice" should be recognized by the church. If it is felt to be a desirable development, the church may consider supporting legislation which furthers it. In this event the church should issue clear statements as to the reasons underlying such support and should attempt to inform medical professionals, legislators, and its own constituents of these reasons. In earlier centuries the church regarded provision of medical care as part of its own responsibilities to society. A contemporary form of fulfilling this responsibility may be the encouragement of more extensive health-care services financed in some way by the government.

8

Education

I. SCHOOL AND SOCIETY

Preparing young people to play a constructive role in society is a major responsibility of the school. This responsibility includes preparing them to live with change and to contribute to constructive change. As technology and social organization become more complex, increasing responsibility rests on the school as a transmitter of basic skills and as an agent of socialization.

Six primary factors influence the content and procedures of American education at any given time and provide a basis for forecasting the directions in which education is likely to move in the future. The factors are (1) size, concentration, and characteristics of the student population; (2) public and private resources available for the support of education; (3) democratic ideals of equality and upward social mobility; (4) expressed and unexpressed concepts of national goals; (5) explicit and implicit concepts of the contribution education can make to the accomplishment of national goals; (6) the American educational tradition that associates elementary and secondary education with preparation for college and the concomitant emphasis on the school as an institution for transmitting the heritage of organized knowledge.

Since colonial times these forces have operated to shape and modify the American educational system. The schools have reflected the characteristics of each era. In the early years of the United States the school-age population was small and scattered.

Education

Limited transportation facilities made anything like consolidated schools impossible. The one-room school was a way of providing education for all the children of the community in a day when communities could not spare enough resources to provide facilities and teachers for small graded classes. Increase in population density and a shortage of qualified teachers led to the creation of graded schools with fairly large classes and to the development of teacher training institutions. As national wealth has increased it has been possible to increase the per pupil expenditure and to move toward greater individualization of instruction by providing more teachers and better facilities and equipment. Increased national wealth has permitted, and in a sense made necessary, an increase in the number of years each person could be spared from work for education.

The high value Americans have always placed on education is reflected in provisions for free and compulsory education, starting with the 1647 law of the Massachusetts Bay Colony requiring each community of one hundred inhabitants to establish and support a school. The operation of the schools and the content of instruction have been responsive to shifts in the national mood. A religious orientation and emphasis marked the common schools from their beginnings throughout the nineteenth century. In the late 1800's a new emphasis was added: the schools were to serve as an instrument to Americanize the masses of new immigrants. More recently, in the age of the cold war and the space race, the schools of the nation were expected to provide rigorous mathematical and scientific training and to produce an abundant supply of science and engineering candidates for the universities.

From its beginnings one of its primary purposes has been the preparation of students for admission to college. The goal of college entrance, sometimes acknowledged and sometimes not, has been one of the dominant influences on the curriculum of the elementary and secondary schools. Despite valiant efforts of many schoolmen, terminal secondary education has not received attention equal to that given to the college preparatory course.

Social values have also influenced the development of American education. The conviction that the community has responsibility to provide schools for all children of all the people stems from the democratic ideal of equality. Equality of treatment for boys and girls stems from the American conviction that equal opportunity should be given to both sexes. Recent awareness of the implications of the ideal of equality in the field of race relations has produced efforts to abolish racial inequalities in education.

Current Trends

The six factors which influence American education have converged to create two dominant emphases today: equality and excellence. Each corresponds to one facet of the national mood and is expressed in various ways in the educational enterprise.

The emphasis on excellence in education pertains to both what is offered to the student and what is expected of him. It can be seen in such features as the introduction of advanced placement courses in high schools, experimental ventures which stress cognitive learnings in pre-school education, increasingly rigorous standards of academic performance in high schools, and the lowering of grade placement for various types of material. The current emphasis on excellence apparently was initiated in the late 1950's and early 1960's by the Sputnik scare and widespread public discussion of the relative merits of the American and European educational systems. The mood motivating increased financial resources for education is implicit in the title of the 1958 legislation that first made substantial federal aid available on a wide scale: the National Defense Education Act. In response to the national mood, university scholars became deeply involved in curriculum improvement projects, and public school leaders initiated various efforts to upgrade education.

Efforts to provide equal educational opportunities to racial minorities and the economically deprived express the desire to apply the democratic ideal of equality to education. The concern for equality also motivates efforts to develop the maximum potential of each individual through special educational programs for both the gifted and the handicapped. It underlies efforts to provide college scholarships or other financial aid to qualified students with limited financial resources. It provides a philosophic base for procedures which introduce a greater measure of individualized instruction for all students.

Overcoming educational inequalities associated with race or poverty has come to be one of the chief concerns of American education. In spite of resistance, policies leading to either *de jure* or *de facto* segregation are being replaced with policies designed to foster integration and to provide compensatory education for the poor. Some studies seem to suggest that the simple physical fact of racial balance in a school may contribute to higher achievement levels for members of minority groups. School policies which include the broad social goal of racial integration and equality as well as strictly educational goals have produced proposals for widespread bussing, creation of educational parks and middle schools, and exchange of pupils between city and suburban school districts. There seems to be increasing support for the concept that equal education must be integrated education.

Progress has been and will probably continue to be slow because of the stubborn fact that segregation in housing creates serious logistic problems for any attempt to create racial balance in every school. Racial balance on a school-by-school basis can be achieved in the near future only by significant geographical relocation of substantial numbers of pupils for the in-school part of their lives. The problems of such a program provide an easy target for criticism from both those who feel major geographical relocation has a deleterious effect on a child's educational experiences and those who resist all attempts to promote integration.

Compensatory education is the second major thrust in the

effort to provide equality in education for the underprivileged. Its goal is quite specific: to provide the poor with experiences which will be the educational equivalent of experiences which come as a matter of course to children of more economically privileged families. The hoped-for result is an equalization of educational achievement at a given age. Examples of programs of compensatory education are Get Set, Head Start, Higher Horizons, and other provisions for extra personnel and resources and special programs for slum schools. Outcomes of some of the experiments provide reason for encouragement, but many have had only limited success in achieving their goals. Again, experience gained from present programs should make possible the creation of quite effective programs of compensatory education by 1980.

Future Enrollment

Population projections which provide the basis for estimating future school enrollments vary depending on the birthrate and enrollment assumptions which are used. Minimum and maximum projections made in May 1967 by the United States Census Bureau are given below. Minimum projections assume a slight continuing decline from present birthrate levels.

		Kindergarten-Grade 8	Grades 9-12	College
1965		35,120,000	12,975,000	5,675,000
1970		36,471,000	15,005,000	7,424,000
1975	Minimum	33,573,000	15,903,000	8,565,000
	Maximum	36,088,000	16,310,000	9,459,000
1980	Minimum	32,233,000	15,099,000	9,718,000
	Maximum	40,684,000	15,706,000	11,181,000
1985	Minimum	35,404,000	13,781,000	9,695,000
	Maximum	47,675,000	17,345,000	11,846,000

Maximum estimates for elementary school enrollments indicate a fairly constant level for the 1965-75 period, with increases after 1975. Minimum estimates, which may be more likely in view of recent birthrate trends, suggest a decreasing elementary school enrollment in the 1970-80 period, followed by a moderate increase. Estimated secondary school enrollments show a similar but smaller fluctuation for the period in question. College enrollments are expected to climb in the seventies, but at a slower rate than in the sixties.

Expected regional and community variations do not show in estimates of total school enrollment. Regional variations in school enrollments are likely to follow patterns of regional migration described in Chapter 3, with school enrollments of regions with large net in-migrations increasing most rapidly. If the population movement from city to suburbs continues as anticipated, suburban school enrollments may be expected to increase more rapidly than enrollments in other types of communities. In the cities, loss of children to suburban areas will be counter-balanced by migration to the cities and perhaps by continued high birth-rates for low-income city dwellers. Enrollment declines can be expected in most rural areas. Patterns of population migration and differential white and nonwhite birthrates are likely to create even greater difficulties for efforts to achieve racial balance in city schools.

Change in educational attainment or average number of years spent in school affects enrollments, just as the size and age-distribution of the population does. There has been a long-term increase in the educational attainment of the United States' population. Figures given below show the nature of that increase over a recent twenty-year period, in terms of the percent of the 25-29 year-old age group which had completed high school or college in 1947, 1957, and 1966. Figures in parentheses are percentages for the nonwhite population.

Ages 25-29

	Completed High School	Completed College
1947	51.4% (22.3%)	5.6% (2.8%)
1957	60.2% (31.6%)	10.4% (4.1%)
1966	71.0% (50.4%)	14.0% (8.3%)

Socio-economic subcultures within the total population are likely to continue in the 1970's and to influence the type of schooling offered in particular areas. The strong college-entrance orientation of the suburbs is likely to continue to exert a strong influence on suburban school programs. Although some erosion of traditional middle-class moral values is likely, suburban schools can be expected to give them formal assent and support. Programs of urban schools are likely to take more account of value systems and life styles that are characteristic of the poor and may evolve new educational patterns appropriate for this subculture. The question of appropriate patterns for schools which include children from more than one subculture will be difficult to resolve.

If minimum population projections anticipate the future accurately, the problem of teacher supply will become less acute at the elementary and secondary levels for the nation as a whole, although there are likely to be shortages in some geographical areas, grade levels, and subjects. There will be a severe faculty shortage in higher education. Present trends of recruiting high-quality teachers and of professional negotiation by teachers suggest that teachers' salaries will continue to increase. In certification procedures there is a movement toward reciprocity among states and a continuation of the trend toward placing more emphasis on academic subject matter requirements in teacher education. Conant's suggestion for using "master teachers" in connection with practice teaching or internship programs may become more widespread. There may be a trend toward requiring five years of training rather than four as a qualification for certification.

In the next decade there will be change in various facets of school organization, including consolidation of smaller school districts into larger units. At the same time there appears to be a movement toward decentralization of large city school systems in order to avoid the inefficiencies of large-scale bureaucratic organization. There is likely to be considerable variety in the way elementary and secondary education is divided into major segments. The K-8, 9-12 and K-6, 7-9, 10-12 patterns will be maintained in many areas, while other school districts introduce newer patterns such as K-4, 5-8, 9-12. Kindergartens will become an integral part of the total educational sequence, and in some areas a prekindergarten program will be added.

Financial Support

Virtually every item included in the educational forecast for the next decade will make the national educational enterprise more expensive. A United States Office of Education estimate places the total financial support required for all levels of public and private education at 83.4 billion dollars for 1975. This compares with an actual expenditure of 49.9 billion for 1965. The cost is presumed to be warranted because the program will benefit individuals and the nation. While there may be resistance to increasing local educational expenditures (the school-bond rejection rate was 11 percent in 1960 and 25.5 percent in 1966), the increasing role of the federal government in supporting education will help to make the necessary money available. Total federal support for all kinds of educational activities, which currently approximates 10 billion dollars, will rise. Geographical mobility of the population, the national stake in education, and the desire to extend equal educational opportunity are three major factors which assure continued federal interest in education and financial support of it.

These considerations will probably lead also to more extensive public support of private and parochial schools. Resistance to such a policy is lessening while pressures for such aid are maintained. The National Defense Education Act and the Elementary and Secondary Education Act extend substantial "indirect" aid to private and parochial schools. More extensive support is likely unless it is prohibited by Supreme Court rulings. In this respect American education seems to be moving toward the type of policy which exists in some of the provinces of Canada.

Expansion of industries oriented toward the education market is one of the significant recent phenomena which may be the outcome of increased interest in and financial support of education. Textbook publishers have long served the school market. The flurry of interest in programmed instruction which occurred in the early sixties gave birth to new companies and new divisions of established corporations. More recently large corporations such as RCA, GE, CBS, IBM, Xerox, Raytheon, and Litton Industries have acquired textbook and test publishers or created education divisions, and have allocated substantial resources to developing products for the education market. This probably is the result of expectations of continuing increases in expenditures for education and confidence in their ability to utilize existing technical skills in the production of educational systems and equipment. The consequence may be that these large corporate suppliers of educational equipment will exert an even more substantial influence on the form and content of education than textbook publishers did in earlier generations.

II. THE CHANGING CURRICULM

Needs of society, potentials and needs of students, and society's accumulated store of knowledge are the three basic ingredients out of which curriculum is made. The proportions of each ingredient included in the curriculum recipe for any given time depends largely on the current mood of the nation, particularly on the values espoused by opinion leaders. In the 1920's the emphasis in progressive education was on the needs and potentials of the learner. In the late 1930's and in the forties, education was viewed as a significant means for advancing social goals. In the late fifties and early sixties the emphasis was on mastering available human knowledge organized into various subject fields. Much current thought on curriculum gives serious consideration to the contribution which each emphasis can make to a total educational program. Jerome Bruner, for example, advocates an approach to curriculum which combines a psychological theory of learning (with emphasis on the learner) with a profound respect for the integrity of the structure of subject matter (emphasis on organized knowledge). Some of the new approaches to curriculum organization seem to promise a way of coping constructively with the knowledge explosion.

An emphasis which undoubtedly will influence the curriculum in the next decade is the structure of the discipline approach. The structure of this approach to curriculum attempts to identify the concepts, operations, and skills which are fundamental to a given discipline or body of knowledge and then to organize instruction so as to help the pupil master these fundamentals. This approach was used in the earliest of the "new" curriculum projects—mathematics curriculum projects and the Physical Science Study Committee project started in the late fifties. Since then the assumptions of the structure of the discipline approach have come to be used in a great variety of federally-financed projects developing curriculum on virtually every school subject at virtually every age level. The approach has proved to be more difficult to apply in subjects such as English and social studies than in science and math.

Most of the current curriculum projects attempt to follow the pattern developed in the early projects. It involves curriculum development by teams of scholars and teachers, field testing and revision of material, eventual release of a complete and coordinated set of instructional materials for a given subject. Products of the early mathematics and science projects received wide use when they became generally available. Because of the multiplicity of projects under way now, it is less likely that the product of any single project will become a recognized standard. Projects range from science and humanities for high school to economics and behavioral science for the elementary grades. They are funded on a generous scale: the School Mathematics Study Group project received grants amounting to eight million dollars.

Several characteristics of material which emerge from these curriculum projects are outgrowths of the initial assumption that the structure of the discipline provides the key to the organization of instruction. Content is selected for inclusion in a course on the basis of its ability to assist pupils to understand fundamental concepts. The amount or variety of content included in a course is less important than the function it serves. Since the total knowledge content of any field is too vast to include in the curriculum of the elementary and secondary school, understanding basic concepts of a discipline is far more important than memorizing a conglomeration of factual material.

Operations and skills characteristic of a discipline are important also. For example, elementary school science courses are designed to help pupils develop thought processes that are similar to those used by highly trained scientists. The process of making observations, formulating hypotheses, devising and conducting experiments to test the hypotheses is a significant part of the course. Virtually all the newer curriculum projects attempt to make extensive use of the discovery or inquiry method as a means of promoting an understanding of the material rather than the accumulation of factual knowledge.

In some recent curriculum projects specific attention has been given to the need for developing an articulated sequence of courses in a particular subject, starting with kindergarten and continuing through grade twelve. Another recent emphasis is the desire to coordinate courses within broad subject-matter fields, thereby producing various high school science and mathematics courses that have a planned relationship to each other. This is reminiscent of earlier broad-field approaches to curriculum construction. Most current curriculum projects concern themselves with careful specification of objectives and include techniques for evaluating student achievement. The package of instructional materials provided by many projects includes pupils' texts and resources, detailed teachers' guides, audio-visuals, and laboratory materials.

Changes in Curriculum Content

Curriculum materials produced by various projects have resulted in some changes of course content by dropping some topics and adding others. This has occurred in the high school mathematics program, for example, with the addition of material on probability and statistical inference and the omission of material on solid geometry. New fields of study such as foreign languages for the elementary school (long a practice in bilingual Canada) and world cultures or international relations have been added in some school districts. Major new topics currently under consideration for inclusion are the explicit study of values, the objective study of religion, the development of critical thinking, more extensive sex education, and materials from the disciplines of economics, psychology, sociology, and cultural anthropology. Some curriculum change is introduced in locations where shared time or dual enrollment plans are used. There appears to be a tendency to introduce given material at a lower grade level than previously was the case, to give more attention to cognitive content in preschool education, and to provide advanced placement courses for able high school students who want to get a running start on college work. The result is the inclusion of more material in the precollege years and consequently a greater challenge to pupils and greater demands on them.

Development of curriculum for various population subgroups is under way. The last few years have witnessed the preparation of curriculum materials which take into account the distinctive character of the experiences and culture of inner-city pupils. Projects become as specific as developing a science curriculum for students of Spanish-speaking background. The New York City schools and the Educational Testing Service are cooperating in a project designed to develop curriculum for first grade based on careful observation and analysis of experiences and abilities of New York City first-graders.

Much curriculum-related research is being undertaken. The

relative merits of reading instruction through phonics versus the whole-word method are being investigated. The value of such devices as the simplified "initial teaching alphabet" in the lower grades is being tested. Title III of the Elementary and Secondary Education Act encourages curricular experimentation by providing funds for "projects to advance creativity in education." Interest is increasing in evaluating curricular outcomes. This is evidenced in the emerging program of national educational assessment and quality measurement projects conducted in New York, Pennsylvania, and other states.

A variety of approaches is being used for the youth who tend to drop out of high school. Federal support of vocational education goes back to the Smith-Hughes Act of 1917. Vocational courses offered by comprehensive high schools have perhaps been less successful in preparing youth for employment than those of separate vocational and technical schools. In many areas competitive admissions policies produce able students for the technical high schools and screen out low ability students. There is serious question as to whether vocational education is the most desirable solution to the educational problem of the slow learner and the disadvantaged. Programs which combine formal education with part-time work experience during the school year or during the summer seem to yield promising results. The entrance of industry into vocational education via the operation of Job Corps training centers has produced some encouraging successes as well as some disappointments. Other work-study programs sponsored by the U.S. Office of Economic Opportunity provide experience which will help to develop sound programs of vocational education. Other aspects of vocational education include union and industry operated apprentice programs and publicly operated post-high school technical institutes. Such programs, however, do not seem to meet the needs of all slow learners and disadvantaged students. Occupational training now available in various forms appears to meet the needs of able students whose life styles conform to the prevailing norms of society. Various programs now being introduced to provide similar opportunities for culturally deprived youth will provide evidence needed to develop reasonably effective training programs for them, and such programs may become somewhat standardized by 1980.

III. EDUCATIONAL THEORY AND PRACTICE

Since the time of Edward L. Thorndike, in the early 1900's, educators have looked to psychological studies of the learning process and human development for clues concerning how to organize the process of instruction and select content for the curriculum. Recent investigations have produced findings which call into question some of the psychological principles which had long been accepted as a basis for practice. These findings have been applied in designing new types of educational experiences.

One major area of new insights is the relation of experience to readiness and intellectual ability. Some educational efforts of the past were guided by a simplified concept of readiness as solely dependent on maturation. The current readiness concept does not discount the importance of physiological maturation, but it does emphasize the role of previous experience in creating readiness. Thus the school's responsibility comes to include providing experiences which can contribute to the development of a specified level of readiness as well as providing a sequence of instruction that is congruent with physiological maturation. Giving greater significance to the role of experience has led to greater emphasis on the development of cognitive skills in preschool programs, introduction of compensatory education for the culturally deprived, more cautious use and interpretation of intelligence tests, and introduction of some material at lower grade levels.

Individualizing Instruction

Limits placed on the intellectual development of a given individual by heredity are seen in a new light. The fact that few if any persons reach the upper limits imposed by their biological inheritance becomes more important than the limits themselves. It is felt that an individual's ability ceiling is determined by the interplay of genetic factors and stimuli and experiences to which the person is exposed. There is also a growing recognition that different individuals possess different cognitive styles, probably related to personality characteristics. For example, pupils with a high component of impulsiveness produce rapid proliferation of ideas, while more reflective pupils tend to function as critics and evaluators. Some students use a highly analytic approach to problem solving, some a trial-and-error approach, and some an intuitive approach. It may be more important to help a pupil make the best use of his own style than to attempt to lead all pupils to use a single cognitive style.

Given qualitatively and quantitatively sufficient experiences in situations conducive to learning, most individuals will progress much farther and faster than traditional measures of ability predict. Such progress is largely dependent on individualization of instruction. Schools are providing such individualization to a limited extent now through ability grouping and efforts of teachers to tailor work to the needs and interests of individual pupils. The use of a class group, however, as the basic instructional unit militates against extensive individualization. It can be provided by teaching strategies such as programmed instruction and by technology such as computer-assisted instruction. It is likely that efforts will be made to provide greater individualization of instruction in technology and re-education of teachers.

Creativity is another facet of current interest in the field of learning. Recognition is increasing that customary instructional procedures give greater weight to the value of convergent thinking than to the value of divergent thinking, with the result that divergent thinking and creativity are discouraged. While research is contributing to the clarification of the concept of creativity and conditions conducive to it, relatively little solid evidence is available to guide efforts to organize instruction in a way that will encourage creativity. Perhaps the most common approach at present is the use of the inquiry or discovery method in various subject-matter curriculums.

Increased interest in the education of the disadvantaged has led to an awareness of behavioral science analyses of differences between the culture of the middle class and the culture of the poor—differences in linguistic and behavior patterns, values, aspirations, and life styles. An awareness of such differences leads to a recognition that the usual educational pattern, appropriate for and effective with middle-class pupils, may be undesirable for disadvantaged pupils. The problem is further complicated by the fact that most teachers come from middle-class homes, either white or Negro, and understandably operate within that cultural framework. Creation of educational content and patterns appropriate for the disadvantaged is progressing, although slowly, on the basis of cultural analyses. Curriculum content is being reoriented on the basis of pupil experience, and teachers are being helped to develop less judgmental attitudes toward pupil behavior. Solutions should be identified by 1980 even though their full implementation will not occur until later.

The Nature of Instruction

The nature of the teaching act has become a subject for investigation. There have been many efforts to identify factors related to effective teaching—factors which can be measured and can be used for prediction, factors such as teachers' attitudes and behavior. The quest has produced criteria which for predictive purposes are only moderately superior to more subjective measures such as ratings by supervisors and principals.

Investigations of the effect of teaching style (usually "autocratic" versus "democratic") on learning tend to indicate that different styles are best with students possessing different learning styles. Studies of the effect of teacher personality on pupils also suggest considerable variability in effect, but indicate that characteristics associated with emotional health and maturity make a contribution to effective teaching. There is considerable current interest in analyzing classroom discourse as a possible clue to effective teaching. Various typologies are used. Some studies center on the logical or substantive content of teacher and pupil statements, some on the emotional content, some on constructs such as "teacher power" and "teacher responsiveness" expressed in statements by the teacher, some on the cognitive function of teacher and pupil statements. Progress in most of these investigations is not yet sufficient to provide clear guidance for organizing instruction.

Programmed instruction, or autoinstruction, has proved to be a manageable and productive approach to individualization of instruction and analysis of teaching. The most rudimentary programs allow each student to proceed at his own pace and assure a prescribed level of achievement for virtually all students. The more complex programs contain considerable internal flexibility which produces, in effect, a program tailored to each student's performance level. Differences in such matters as ability and cognitive style are taken into account in such programs insofar as they are reflected in the student's responses as he proceeds through the program. Principles used in programmed instruction provide guidance for organizing and presenting material in more conventional ways, thus clarifying criteria for aspects of teaching behavior which have to do with content, logic, and sequencing. One possible explanation for the progress that has been made in programmed instruction is its elimination of the complex variables involved in personal teacher-student-class interaction.

Educational Technology

More extensive use of educational technology, in all its variety, will occur in the future as part of the information storage and retrieval revolution. Data-processing equipment and computers offer the possibility of expediting many aspects of the educational enterprise. Record-keeping and clerical work of all varieties— finances, attendance, grades, schedules—can be done quickly and accurately for large numbers of students. Functions now performed by data-processing equipment in large school systems or on an experimental basis will be automated for larger numbers of schools in the future. The information storage and retrieval potential offered by electronic equipment and micropho- tography will gradually transform libraries into centers for stor- age and retrieval of information in forms other than books. The Toronto school system anticipated this by organizing a central library which accepts telephone requests for information and supplies the information by phone or mail. There will be more extensive use of complex equipment such as closed-circuit tele- vision, language laboratories, various forms of projected images and of simpler devices such as tape recorders and overhead projectors. Computer-assisted instruction will make possible com- plex autoinstructional programs and elaborate instructional sys- tems which incorporate personal presentations with recorded and projected material and instantaneous analysis of pupil re- sponse.

The U.S. Office of Education has made large research grants to schools for the design and implementation of comprehensive instructional systems which make maximum use of the most advanced technology available. The extent to which wide use is made of available and developing educational technology will depend on the funds available for this purpose and the devel- opment of a corps of persons skilled in the educational applica- tions of the technology. It seems certain that use of the simpler devices, from tape recordings and overhead projectors to lan- guage laboratories and educational television, will become quite widespread. Both commercial and non-profit producers of cur- riculum materials increasingly are preparing textbook-supporting material such as tapes and films. Courses offered by means of educational television are improving in quantity and quality.

Some psychologists speak of intellectual activity as information processing. The technology that gave rise to this concept provides a natural means of creating instructional systems which stem from the information-processing model of the intellect. Computer-assisted instruction, now in its infancy, will become more common. Even now some preschool children are being taught to read by means of computer-controlled typewriters. A computer is used for instructing first-graders in arithmetic and reading. Several colleges and universities have installed dial-access information-retrieval systems by means of which basic lectures and/or supplementary material are available to students at their convenience. Some of the systems utilize student responses for both diagnostic and evaluation purposes.

The consequences of wider use of advanced educational technology may include a more interesting, enjoyable, and efficient educational experience for most pupils. Material programmed for autoinstruction will allow each student to proceed as rapidly as he is able to do. Greater efficiency in learning should make more time available for the pursuit of individual special interests. Frequent use of the simpler devices should make class sessions more interesting. This is not to say that the millenium will have arrived—unless the technology is accompanied by an abundance of personnel able to use it creatively and effectively. Problems associated with securing funds for equipment and developing personnel will probably prevent the universal use of such devices much before 1980.

The Role of the Teacher

Developments described above suggest that a new role is emerging for teachers. It may be seen as a dual role. First, the teacher will become a designer of educational programs for each pupil in the class, choosing and making available to the pupil the learning resources required by his program. Ideally, teachers will work cooperatively with each student in designing his instructional program and will be aided by a data bank of information about the student's characteristics. The other facet of the teacher's role is the more familiar function of a tutor, giving each pupil personal help as required. This dual concept of the teacher's role is quite consistent with earlier ideas. It will be more attainable in the future because there will be a greater variety of resources available for individualizing instruction. The dual role of the teacher will also be more attainable as wider use is made of semiprofessional personnel as teachers' aides and for the clerical work currently performed by many teachers. Availability of counselors and other specialized personnel at all levels of schooling will further enable teachers to create programs which meet the particular needs of each pupil. Of course, the ideal will not be reached in all schools by 1980. But most schools will be moving toward the condition described.

Various forms of nongrading, which rose from 6 percent of elementary classrooms in 1955-56 to 26 percent in 1965-66, will become more widespread. This will encourage individualization of instruction. Many more schools will use some form of nongraded or continuous-progress plan through grade three. The concept of nongrading is likely to exert greater influence on the educational program of the upper elementary grades and secondary schools. The many varieties of team-teaching will continue to be useful ways of making the greatest use of special talents of various teachers.

The search for new educational practices will continue, spurred by schoolmen and scholars who want to improve the educational process, federal encouragement of innovation and creativity in education, and commercial concerns which stand to benefit from the sale of new products or procedures. Uncritical acceptance of new and untested practices may become as much of a danger as the inertia which resists any change from established patterns.

IV. HIGHER EDUCATION

Earlier social goals of universal elementary education and universal secondary education are being succeeded at present by the goal of post-high school education at public expense for all who can benefit by it. The goal is being implemented by increased financial support for state colleges and universities, financial grants to private institutions and the expansion of community colleges. The intent is to increase the enrollment capacity of higher-education institutions to the point where they will be able to accommodate virtually all high school graduates. Other policies are aimed at providing equality of educational opportunity. Publicly and privately supported scholarship and student-loan funds are designed to insure that able students with limited finances will be able to attend private as well as public institutions. Programs which provide special opportunities for talented students from disadvantaged homes contribute to the reduction of inequalities.

Enrollment Increase

Growth in college enrollments will be quite rapid, from 5,675,000 in 1965 to 7,424,000 in 1970 to approximately 10 million in 1980. A more rapid expansion will take place in Canada, as is evidenced by a 1960 college enrollment of 102,000 and an anticipated 1970 enrollment of 312,000. The spread of aspirations for college attendance no doubt stems from the upward social mobility that has characterized the population as a whole. A college education is becoming a prerequisite for both social and occupational success. The increase in college enrollment is created by both larger numbers of young people of college age and by an increase in the proportion of high school graduates who go on to college. In 1958, 35 percent of the total population of eighteen-year-olds attended college. It is anticipated that the comparable figure for 1968 will be 46 percent. Enrollment in graduate schools will increase at a faster rate than undergraduate enrollments. The number of doctoral degrees granted annually will more than double between 1965 and 1975, and the number of masters degrees will increase from 525,000 to about 900,000.

Increase in enrollment will be accompanied by an increase in the number of institutions of higher education and by an increase in the size of existing institutions. The concept of publicly supported community colleges has gained wide acceptance in recent years and may be expected to lead to the establishment of a greater number of such institutions. By 1975 community colleges are expected to account for approximately one-half of the total higher-education enrollment. Of students attending community colleges, about one-half may be in two-year terminal programs and about one-half in the first two years of a program leading to transfer to a four-year institution. Past experience may be an indication of what to expect in increase in size of institutions. In 1955, 43.2 percent of college students in public institutions were attending schools with enrollments of less than 5,000; the percentage declined to 24.9 by 1965. In 1955, 32.5 percent of students in public institutions attended schools with more than 10,000 enrollment; this percentage increased to 55.6 by 1965. The proportion of students in public institutions is expected to increase and the proportion in private schools to decrease. Even so, there is likely to be an increase in the *number* of students at private schools.

Faculty members have benefited from the increase in college enrollments. The consequent increase in demand for faculty and the simultaneous growth in demand for research personnel has produced stiff competition among schools for faculty. This situation is likely to continue for some time, since faculty requirements for higher education are expected to increase from 420,000 positions in 1965 to 695,000 in 1975.

One of the consequences of the increasing size of institutions of higher education is the multiplication of the problems of administering large universities. One difficulty is the matter of efficient and rational management of the organization as such. The serious state of university administration has stimulated such efforts as a Carnegie Corporation study of "the managerial revolution in higher education." Difficulties of introducing administrative procedures appropriate to a large organization are complicated by the traditional concept that the total faculty has a primary role in determining university policy. The problem is to preserve the values of the traditional procedure and at the same time to introduce administrative procedures which are more suitable for large organizations.

The College Generation

Increases in institutional size have had an effect on students. The more extreme forms of protest against school or government policies seem to occur at the larger universities, although smaller schools are by no means immune. One hypothesis is that a subculture rejecting adult values develops when students have little or no opportunity for personal contacts with adults. The anonymity which a large campus produces may stimulate assertion of individuality by some students and irresponsible behavior by others. In the effort to serve large numbers of students, universities have necessarily introduced procedures which routinize and depersonalize faculty and administration contact with students: large lecture sections in which students are identified by seat number, the use of data-processing equipment for handling registration and grades, test grading by anonymous graduate assistants or by machines, computer-assisted instruction which minimizes student contact with faculty. The irony is that such measures, which make possible the education of large numbers of students, produce quite understandable resentment on the part of students. Such phenomena as "free universities" express the need for personal attention. Students undoubtedly are affected by the competition for grades that continues after they successfully run the admissions race. Those who gain entrance to the prestige schools find that their new peers set an even faster pace than their secondary-school colleagues. The competition both stimulates effort and takes its toll on emotional stability.

There are many indications of a strong altruistic and humanistic sentiment among college students. The most obvious expression is in activities which benefit others: civil rights activity, tutoring disadvantaged children, Peace Corps and VISTA service. The humanistic sentiment may also account for relative declines of enrollment in business administration, science and engineering and relative increases in enrollment in the liberal arts. The decline in academic achievement of medical-school candidates may reflect the changing image the public has of physicians. There is an alternative explanation of an apparent preference for the liberal arts. It is possible that the present college generation, having grown up in an age of economic prosperity and security, does not have a strong drive toward economic success and the occupations which traditionally have been avenues for economic advancement.

Ministry to college students continues to reach a small proportion of even those who maintain a reasonably close relationship with their home congregation. The long-standing college-age characteristic of at least questioning and at most rejecting the religious heritage is perhaps becoming more pronounced. College students are probably more aware than the general population of such ideas as situational ethics and "God-is-dead" theology and more likely to give them a hearing. The present college generation has grown up in "the world come-of-age" and undoubtedly tends to regard religion as irrelevant. The desire to find life's meaning in authentic person-to-person relationships may be an expression of religious need as well as a reaction to the impersonality of large universities.

The College Curriculum

The knowledge explosion has affected the curriculum just as the enrollment explosion has affected the size and organization of the universities. It has intensified the long-standing tension between fragmentation and wholeness, between specialization and a liberal education. Faculties have attempted to deal with the problem in various ways: establishing a core of required subjects, introducing interdisciplinary courses, providing science courses more suitable for nonscience majors. Some departments of business administration, education, and even engineering have attempted to reduce the strictly professional preparation requirements in order to provide for a broader liberal education. In some cases this has resulted in a five-year program which awards the graduate both a bachelor's and a master's degree. Other curricular innovations include modifications to shorten the college-professional school sequence in the fields of medicine, dentistry, and law.

The level of academic accomplishment expected of students tends to rise. In the prestige schools this occurs both because of the demands the faculty makes on students and because of the high level of competence possessed by students. Higher academic standards are being set also by the smaller liberal arts colleges. It is anticipated that community colleges will attain a level of academic standards similar to that of the liberal arts colleges. In all colleges there will be more emphasis on skills of research work, even at the undergraduate level.

Computer-assisted instruction and other educational technology will be used to an increasing extent in colleges and universities. The President's Science Advisory Committee recently urged colleges to spend 400 million dollars a year on computer instruction by 1971 and suggested that the government provide subsidies for this purpose. Most universities possess computer facilities, but their use for instructional purposes is limited. The committee estimated that 75 percent of undergraduates are taking courses in which a computer would be useful, but that only 5 percent of the students have adequate access to computers. A recent survey indicated that more than one-half of the nation's colleges (as distinguished from universities) do not have any kind of computer facility. On the other hand, universities use computers to offer courses which include geography, economics, literature, engineering, business administration, political science, architecture, international relations, art and music. The increasing use of computer-assisted instruction and other educational technology will spread at the college level, as it will at the elementary and secondary school level, as adequate financing and trained personnel become available for use at all levels.

One of the curriculum developments of particular interest to the church is the increase in the number of departments of religion or schools of religion at both state universities and private institutions. Sizable numbers of students elect courses offered by these departments. Part of the appeal seems to be that the courses are academically-oriented rather than church-oriented and that they are not identified with sponsorship by a particular denomination. Some universities have enlarged religion departments which offer graduate programs and in a sense compete with theological seminaries for students. For the most part, graduate religion departments seem to appeal to students who are not interested in entering the ministry and who are attracted to the study of theology simply as an academic discipline.

Financial Support of Higher Education

Total financial resources required for the support of higher education are expected to increase from 11.9 billion dollars in 1965 to 22.5 billion in 1975. Probable public support for this expansion is indicated by the fact that in a recent Gallup Poll on national goals Americans listed education as having first priority. At the same time there are evidences of resistance to larger expenditures for education from some groups. The most publicized example of this in recent years was the attempt to reduce, at least temporarily, state financial support for the University of California. It is likely that federal support will increase in the form of funds for construction of new facilities, for establishment of community junior colleges, for scholarships and loans, research grants and contracts, and other specific programs.

Although the greatest part of the increase will come from public funds, costs to families with children attending college will also increase. In 1965 the average cost to families with students attending public institutions was $1,560 per year and $2,370 per year to families with students attending private institutions. By 1980 the cost of attending a public institution will exceed the 1965 cost of attending a private institution; it will amount to $2,400 per year. At the same time the cost of attending a private school will have increased to $3,640 per year.

The magnitude of federal support is indicated by the fact that more than 25 percent of higher education's total budget comes from this source. Nearly 50 percent of the total income of some schools, such as the University of California, comes from Washington. Federal support has increased dramatically in the past twenty years. At the University of Pennsylvania, for example, it increased from 1 million dollars in 1947 to 30 million dollars in 1967. In 1957 federal support accounted for 12.5 percent of that school's total budget; in 1967 it accounted for 29 percent. Increase in federal support raises the issue of governmental control or influence on the conduct of American higher education. It is felt that a system of unrestricted appropriations would be preferable to the present practice of supporting specific activities or programs. Colleges then could use funds on the basis of their own priorities rather than conforming to government programs.

Mushrooming federal support has intensified inequalities between the large public or private universities and the smaller liberal arts colleges. A large proportion of these federal funds is devoted to grants for research and training. There are over one thousand colleges and universities in the United States, but in the 1966-67 school year 29 institutions received more than 50 percent of federal research dollars. With a larger proportion of higher education's total support coming from the government and being distributed chiefly to the larger universities, liberal arts colleges are hard-pressed to compete for faculty. For the most part they are not in a position to offer salaries and facilities comparable to those in the large universities. Liberal arts colleges have more difficulty than the universities even when it comes to securing funds for expansion of their physical plant with additional dormitories, laboratories and classrooms.

It seems likely that there will be movement toward a more equitable level of public support for liberal arts colleges. In some cases formerly independent institutions are being transformed into public institutions. The trend toward greater public support of all types of higher education inevitably raises questions about the role of the church in higher education. Church funds now amount to a small proportion of the income of church-related institutions; the proportion is likely to become even smaller in the future. Many church colleges are becoming increasingly oriented toward their communities. It seems likely that these broad trends in higher education have contributed in some measure to recent developments which tend to reduce church control over some Roman Catholic institutions.

V. CONTINUING EDUCATION

Continuing economic growth and technological change are expected to lead to an increase in continuing education programs for adults. In the 1970's more persons will participate in such study than the thirty million reported by the National Opinion Research Center in the early 1960's. The increase will be due in part to more leisure time on the part of adults and in part to the need for occupational updating and retraining caused by technological advance. While opinions differ as to the extent to which leisure will be increased, there is near unanimity that there will be some increase in time which adults have available to use at their own discretion. If the experience of recent years can be used as a guide, many adults with more leisure time will devote at least part of that time to formal or informal study. In many circles it is felt that technological advances will produce occupational obsolescence requiring each person to be trained for three different jobs during his working life.

Programs of continuing education can be grouped into two categories: those which are occupation-oriented and those which are essentially leisure-time, personal-interest programs. The first category accounted for 39 percent and the second for 62 percent in the NORC study. The goals of continuing education on a broad scale can be identified as: (1) preparing persons for actual and expected change in jobs and professions, (2) providing continuing liberal education for a leisure society, (3) providing a new kind of counseling for lifelong learning, (4) overcoming social and cultural lags, (5) educating non-technologists about technology, and (6) exposing technologists to a humanist point of view.

The main features of future occupation-oriented continuing education are probably visible in present programs. Change is likely to produce expansion of existing programs. Personal motivation for participation in such programs stems on the one hand from the employer who provides such programs and encourages employees to participate, and on the other from the individual's desires for advancement and to possess a salable skill when his existing skills become obsolete.

Occupation-oriented programs take a wide variety of forms. They include courses and training programs conducted by the employer, programs conducted by educational institutions under contract with the employer, support by the employer of employee participation in programs conducted by educational institutions, study programs pursued by individuals on their own initiative, government-sponsored training programs of many kinds, programs sponsored by professional associations, private training schools operated for profit. Most occupation-oriented programs stress achievement of specified performance levels.

The relation of the programs to the individual's occupational future provides incentive for individual effort.

As in occupation-oriented programs of continuing education, existing leisure-time and personal-interest programs of continuing education probably indicate the main features of similar programs in the future. The chief change may be that in the future more persons will participate in such programs. The two major types of leisure-time programs are the traditional academic fields and avocational-recreational interests.

Continuing education in the academic fields includes a broad scope of programs, from adult literacy programs through evening and extension courses offered by universities. It includes evening high school courses and college courses offered to the public via television. It includes innovative programs such as that at the University of Kentucky which offers free tuition to all persons aged 65 and over. The National Opinion Research Center study showed that 38 percent of all adults engaged in continuing education made use of opportunities for academic study.

Avocational, recreational, and personal-interest programs of informal education enlisted 23 percent of the continuing education clientele of the early 1960's. The most popular subjects were "hobbies/recreation" and "personal development," followed by "public affairs" and "home and family life." "Religion" and "agriculture" were each represented by 1 percent of the total.

Wide use is likely to be made of the newer educational media in occupation-oriented programs and in formal adult education in the future. Corporate training programs were among the early users of programmed instruction and closed-circuit television and make extensive use of various audio-visual devices. The academic type of adult education will make wider use of educational television and of techniques which utilize the individual's home telephone. New and more efficient approaches to adult literacy training and basic adult education will utilize the newer technological resources.

VI. SUMMARY AND IMPLICATIONS

A. *Summary*

1. Efforts to insure equality of educational opportunity at all levels, preschool through graduate study, will intensify. Significant advances will be made by 1980, although progress is likely to be uneven.

2. Increases in elementary and secondary school enrollments are likely to be moderate in the 1970-1980 period. There will be a sharp rise in college enrollments, with the 1980 total estimated to be nearly double the 1965 total.

3. There will be continued increase in the average educational level of the population, with higher proportions completing high school and college. This, combined with widespread continuing education, will mean that persons will invest a larger portion of their lives in education. The proportion of the adult population engaged in various forms of continuing education will increase.

4. There will be continued progress toward excellence at all levels of education. In 1980 students will learn more in less time than they do in 1970. The chief factors contributing to improvement will be a better understanding of the learning process, improvements in the design of curriculum, procedures for individualizing instruction, and use of advanced educational technology. The result will be a more highly educated population possessing higher levels of intellectual and technical competence and ability to deal with ideas at higher levels of abstraction and sophistication. Although the overall educational level will rise, there will be numerous individuals who for various reasons will have limited educational achievement.

5. At most levels of education the role of the teacher will tend to shift from that of the leader of a class toward that of a tutor and resource person for individual students.

6. A larger quantity and perhaps a larger proportion of national resources will be devoted to the educational enterprise

in the form of time spent in school rather than productive work, the number of persons employed as teachers, investment in facilities and equipment. Availability of public funds will be facilitated by the high value the population attaches to education, but there will be some taxpayer resistance to the large increases required.

7. All forms of education will come to be regarded as contributing to the national welfare. There will be a tendency to develop formal national educational standards. Public funds will become increasingly available to educational institutions operated by churches and other private groups.

8. The increasing size of educational institutions, especially in higher education, will tend to produce routine and impersonal treatment of students. This in turn will create a negative reaction which students will express in a variety of forms.

9. The academic and social life of the school will occupy the major portion of the energies and interests of most young people. Because opportunities for significant personal contacts with adults will be limited, tension between generations will continue to be serious.

10. Life styles, aspiration levels and occupational plans of students will be influenced by their economic and social backgrounds. Many students from middle-class families may tend to prefer altruistic and humanistic avenues of expression. For others, the irrelevance of materialistic motivation in an affluent society may produce feelings of normlessness and alienation. Attitudes of less advantaged students will depend on the extent to which discrimination and poverty are reduced.

11. Interest in religion on the part of high school and college students may take the form of a quest for a personally satisfying religion and an intellectual interest in theological ideas. Prevailing thought-patterns may lead a sizable proportion of students to regard religion of any kind as irrelevant. In general, students are likely to be prejudiced against traditional institutional forms of religion.

B. Implications

Public controversy is likely to arise in connection with certain expected developments: efforts to provide equality of educational opportunity by eliminating segregation; increase in public financial support of all levels of education; public aid to church-related schools. The church may desire to continue the practice of adopting official policies concerning these issues and to devise ways of taking direct action or encouraging its members to take direct action to implement the policies.

The likelihood that public funds will become generally available to church-sponsored educational efforts suggests the desirability of rethinking the church's role in education. It is possible that the church might consciously accept responsibility for specific educational ventures and seek financial support for them from the government. On the other hand, the church may decide that its role is to stimulate public agencies to meet the educational requirements of the community and the nation. Any formulation of the church's role in education would have implications for church sponsorship of preschool and compensatory education projects, parochial schools at the elementary and secondary level, church-related colleges, and programs of continuing education for adults.

The dominant place which both the academic and social aspects of schooling will have for increasing numbers of young people suggests the need to re-evaluate the church's ministry to youth. As college enrollments increase, it may be well to anticipate the need for increasing provisions for campus ministries. A careful analysis of objectives for campus ministry and of student attitudes toward religion might lead to designing experimental strategies. The results of this experimentation could produce new forms of college and university work. Similar procedures already under way may produce effective new forms for the congregation's ministry to high school youth. If one of the major causes of the tension between generations and of alienation among youth is lack of personal contacts between youth and adults, strategies to remedy the lack may be devised. Such strategies might help youth to an appreciation of the more traditional expressions of Christian faith as well as helping adults to an appreciation of more contemporary expressions.

The advancing educational level of the total population suggests that the church should find ways of presenting the gospel meaningfully to persons with intellectual sophistication and specialized technical training and to do so within a context of secular thought-patterns. At the same time it should continue to minister in more conventional ways to persons to whom traditional forms effectively communicate the gospel. While every age group will include both types of individuals, it is likely that the traditional forms will continue to be meaningful chiefly for the older age groups. Unless congregations become highly homogeneous in membership, it will be desirable for each congregation to provide a variety of forms of ministry and to encourage members to recognize the legitimacy or value of forms which they do not find personally satisfying.

Developments in educational theory and practice have implications for the church's work in Christian education at all age levels. Instructional procedures and curriculum content at various grade levels in the public schools should be examined to determine their implications for Christian education curriculum. Potentials and limitations of the use of instructional technology in Christian education should be studied. Patterns of personal interest and leisure-time adult education should be investigated in the development of a program of adult Christian education.

9

Religious Institutions

I. HISTORICAL BACKGROUND

The colonists were predominantly Protestant and largely of British stock, plus a considerable number of Dutch, Swedish, and German nationals. In the first decades of the nineteenth century the United States was in the main an Anglo-Saxon Protestant nation. Then came the deluge: in a little more than a century, over 35,000,000 men, women, and children came from every ethnic and linguistic strain in Europe. As a result, the American people became linguistically and ethnically the most diverse people on earth. One hundred years later similar waves of immigration poured in upon Canada, previously a nation predominantly Anglo-Saxon, with the principal exception of French-speaking Quebec. The title of "the most diverse people on earth" must now be applied to Canada as well.

These immigrants came to North America because of profound disturbances at home: the industrial and agricultural revolutions, a population explosion a century ago, and, more recently, war and persecution. They were largely peasants whose life for generations had been that of the village. They came to strange countries to find not the familiar round of seedtime and harvest on the land but the bewildering crush of great port cities and the deadening routine of new occupations. Their chief concern was to make a living. After that—and almost equal in importance—was the preservation of old familiar ways of life. In Europe the village was the center of existence, and the village church was at its heart. The unity of the village had forever gone, but a new identity emerged—the oneness of language primarily expressed by and in the church.

For any human being the most pressing questions in his life as a social being are "Who am I?" and "What am I?" Unless these can be answered, the individual remains anonymous—a nobody. And that is an intolerable state. To live, one must belong. These questions, basic for anyone, were crucial for the immigrants who found themselves on strange shores in a frightening situation of social disintegration and personal crisis. The answers could be found as immigrants were drawn together by their common language, which meant church and culture and nationality.

So ethnic groups began to emerge, and ethnic churches. In these associations the first generation was content in the secure and the familiar. Their children, the second generation, found in their ethnic associations a source of perplexity and conflict. They were Americans or Canadians, but only partially so. English was their first language. In school and on a street or playground, their viewpoint was North American. At home they spoke the old language and shared the ethnicity of their forebears.

It was a dual existence—and an unhappy one. Especially in religious life were the problems most vexing. Some continued to give allegiance to their subculture, although not in so complete a fashion as did their parents, while others drew away. Some drifted toward non-ethnic churches; others totally lapsed; still others became bitterly non-religious. That second generation has largely disappeared from the United States scene. It is to be found everywhere today among the "new Canadians."

The third generation has no interest in the perpetuation of the ethnic community. They are American in nationality, in culture, in language. That is to be expected without question. However, the person of this third generation is not expected to change his religion. In the third generation religion has become the differentiating element, the context of self-identification and social location. There was emerging a new and unprecedented social structure, the "religious community."

II. RELIGIOUS COMMUNITIES TODAY

Three religious communities are to be found in America today: Protestant, Catholic, Jewish. They are complex structures with sociological and religious characteristics. Sociologically the community is a context of self-identification and social location in contemporary American life. Here is unity in multiplicity, pluralism in community. Catholicism, Protestantism, and Judaism, says Herberg, are now regarded as branches of "American religion." This is not to say they share the same theology—although to some extent they do—but rather that they are three different representations of "spiritual values." American democracy is presumed to incorporate such values as the fatherhood of God, the brotherhood of man, the dignity of the individual human being. No one is expected to change his religion in order to become an American. Each of the religions is regarded as equally American; the American is expected to express his religion in the form which has come to him with his family. Denominations within the Protestant and Jewish areas are not considered objectionable—they are simply secondary.

That this development holds great importance is patently evident. If these three communities are representations of those spiritual values for which America stands, the American individual is exposed to subtle pressures to ally himself, be it ever so imperceptibly, with one of the three. The pressures are both internal and external. Being a Protestant, a Catholic, or a Jew is understood as a specific way of being an American and locating oneself in American society. This is not to imply membership in a particular church or participation in religious activities or assent to a creedal statement of any kind. It simply intimates identification with a group and location in society.

As Herberg begins his study of American religious sociology, he points to a peculiar dichotomy which many other commentators have tried to probe: on the one hand, there is a general acceptance of religion in America and on the other, there exists a secularism which permeates social and individual life. Here there may be a partial answer. Acceptance of religion may not indicate fervor toward God and humanity toward fellow men. It may simply be the reflection of the social need for belonging which today more and more connotes a place in one of the three religious communities.

That there was an upswing in the 1950's, if not in religious devotion at least in religious interest, is evident from the high degree of identification with religious institutions among Americans. *The Yearbook of American Churches* (1960) reported total church and synagogue membership as 63 percent of the United States population—the highest in United States history. Herberg estimates that nearly three-fourths of the American people regard themselves as members of churches, and that most of the rest identify themselves with one or another religious community without a consciousness of actual church membership.

Church attendance, irregular though it may be, is considerable and is growing. Surveys conducted by Elmo Roper since 1942 have included the question: "Which one of these groups (religious, government, business leaders) do you feel is doing the most good for the country at the present time?" The position of religious leaders increased from 17.5 percent (1942) to 32.6 percent (1947) to 46 percent (1957). The position of the oft-berated clergyman seems to be improving in American estimation. As clergymen increase in repute, so does religion. Some observers feel that in the world of culture, there is at least a receptivity to the message of the historic faiths—a marked contrast to the indifference or hostility of an earlier generation. What factors have caused this situation? Herberg believes there are four.

1. America—the United States at the present time and Canada

in the future—has moved from a land of immigrants with their ethnic groups to the "triple melting pot" where identification is found and social location established in one of the three great religious communities—Protestant, Catholic, Jewish.

2. A fundamental shift in character structure seems to be occurring among certain segments of the American people, namely from inner-direction to other-direction. Riesman and others have strikingly analyzed the desire for conformity and adjustment, to be particularly found in the growing suburban middle class.

3. The present state of Western civilization has forcibly brought home a sense of total insecurity: the hydrogen bomb, the menace of Communist totalitarianism, etc. The old foundations of assurance have crumbled. Men desperately look for reassurance and safety, for peace of mind.

4. Faced with the depersonalizing forces of urbanized industrial life in our mass culture, man looks to religion to give him personal authenticity. The secular "truths" by which moderns have previously lived have proved illusory under the tension of the times. Any contemporary turn to religion will owe much of its force to the search for a new and more viable philosophy of existence amid the spiritual chaos of our age.

What do Americans believe? Citing several surveys, Herberg finds a high percentage who believe in God, in prayer, in life after death, in the Bible. Lenski makes the same discovery: more than 75 percent believe in God, in prayer, in Jesus as God's only Son; about 50 percent believe in future punishment. In large measure, the survey of Glock and Stark testifies to the prevalence of orthodox beliefs. Thomas also reports a high degree of assent among Roman Catholics, Protestants, and Jews to the existence of God, and among Roman Catholics and Protestants to belief in God as a loving Father, the Trinity, the divinity of Christ, the Bible as the Word of God, immortality, heaven, and hell.

How deeply such beliefs penetrate the individual's life is another matter. Some feel religion has no real effect upon the individual as he engages in politics and business. Lenski, however, takes a different view. He feels that because of lifelong exposure to a religious group and its subculture, church members have been influenced in their perception and assessment of political and economic institutions. They in turn exercise influence as they participate in the political and economic life of the nation.

Herberg is not an advocate of secularization of religion. Religion must always be scrutinized in the light of faith. There then appear uncertainties from the standpoint of Jewish-Christian teachings. For example, the religiousness of America today possesses little orientation of life to God—little genuine inner conviction or existential decision. Outer-direction smothers inner-direction. The modern "religious" American cannot understand the zeal of Elijah or Amos, of Paul or Peter. There is certainly little, if any, evidence of lives surrendered to death because of a cause thought to be of greater moral significance than life itself.

Again, the Americanness of American religion robs the three faiths of their uniqueness and universality. The mind of the public tends to regard each as an authentic variant form of being religious in the American way. So historic authenticity is abandoned. Furthermore, the "American Way of Life" is *ipso facto* a culture-religion—a validation of culture and society without any attempt to bring them under judgment. National self-righteousness and self-will are reinforced and authenticated. Religion tends to be used for economic and political purposes.

Most notably, contemporary religiosity in America often finds its center in man, not God. It is peace of mind that men and women look for in religion. There is a religious narcissism by which the church becomes a psychiatrist's couch to relieve the worshiper of his troubles. In this kind of religion there is no awareness of the transcendent, no sense of the limitations of man and his works before a holy God. It is not man who serves God but God who is expected to serve man and his purposes— whether these purposes be economic prosperity, free enterprise, social reform, democracy, happiness, security, or peace of mind.

III. RELIGION AND SOCIETY

Social change affects the religious institution. In the United States, Protestantism for many decades was geared to a frontier and later, a rural society with emphasis on individual piety. Given proper living by the individual, social justice would naturally ensue. Whatever may have been the degree of success in campaigns to improve personal morality, Protestantism did become dominant in rural and small-town society. All was well, institutionally speaking, until the country was changed by the new currents of immigration, industrialization and urbanization. Efforts have been made to recover the old dynamic for the new society without much success. On the frontier more than a century ago, pioneer spoke to pioneer of the beliefs of the church. In town and country farmer witnessed to farmer and small entrepreneur to his fellow businessman. In the city and the factory however, Protestantism was largely middle class and had no one to meet the city poor and the blue-collar worker on equal terms. The peripheral Protestant sects of the disadvantaged (Nazarenes, Assemblies of God, holiness groups) have therefore entered.

The Catholic church in the United States faced the need for "Americanization." While Catholicism is as indigenous as is Protestantism (e.g., Maryland's colonization before 1650), the United States was never "Catholic" as were all western European nations before 1517. American society has made the Catholic church far more activist than it is in Europe. Also there has been a basic revision of thought on church-state relations and reorientation of theology and action in the light of a religiously pluralistic society. Under pressure from the American environment, American Catholics learned to operate in two arenas: in the self-enclosed microcosmic community of their own church and its complex of Catholic institutions; and in a tripartite macrocosm in which Catholics, Protestants, and Jews were conceived as coexisting under the benevolent aegis of American democracy.

Judaism has been affected by American society to a far greater extent than have its sister religious communities. Jewish people, in the great immigration waves of the nineteenth century, were not only members of ethnic groups but also adherents of a religious association tightly joined through persecution but not so thoroughly fused that the tents of Jacob were unified. The passage of the years has seen a lessening of anti-Semitism, the disappearance of the ghetto, increasing acceptance of Jews in the managerial class of business and industry, a mobility which has taken Jewish families into cities and towns where few if any of their co-religionists are to be found. All of this has brought about much self-searching in the religious community, as those ties which once tightly bound Jews together become more and more tenuous.

The effect of religious commitment on everyday life has been most thoroughly analyzed by Gerhard Lenski in *The Religious Factor.* Data studied here were gained in the Detroit Area Study —a "probability" sample survey—where a representative cross section of 750 Detroiters was selected in 1958 for interviews. Interviews were completed in 87 percent of the cases. Since the fundamental purpose concerned "the effect of religious commitment on daily life," it was necessary to identify socio-religious groups and to determine commitment to a type of religious orientation. The four major socio-religious groups dealt with were white Protestants, white Catholics, Negro Protestants, and Jews. Religious orientations were limited to two: doctrinal orthodoxy and devotionalism.

An exhaustive précis of Lenski's project is not possible here. Suffice it to say that five general areas were examined in the survey: economics, politics, family life, education, and science. Briefly, these conclusions were reached:

1. *Economics.* Religion does influence men in their economic activity; there is a relationship between devotionalism and loyalty to the spirit of capitalism when social conditions of individuals are held constant. Commitment to capitalism differs with the degree of involvement in Protestant churches; there is great

similarity in economic values between Negro Protestant and white Catholic workers.

2. *Politics.* Devotionalism and political party preference are not related; but doctrinal orthodoxy is positively linked with a preference for the Republican party. Humanitarian interest is linked to devotionalism but seems unrelated to orthodoxy. Orthodoxy has no relevance for most aspects of secular life since it fosters a compartmentalized type of religious belief and experience; devotionalism seems to encourage its adherents to disregard the distinctions between the "religious" and the "secular."

3. *Family Life.* Doctrinal orthodoxy discourages personal autonomy. The more orthodox indicated a preference for association with relatives rather than friends. The family is basic as a source of those personality traits necessary for success on the job (e.g., motivation, values, beliefs, and abilities).

4. *Education.* Dropouts are more frequent among Catholics. The Catholic parochial school system seems to foster a negative attitude toward work, an increased preference for the Republican party, a disinclination to be interested in world affairs, the attitude that non-Catholic clergy should not be permitted to publicly preach subjects contrary to Catholic teachings, and greater respect for constitutional government.

5. *Science.* Very little relationship was found between devotionalism and views on the relationship between religion and science. Membership in the Catholic group was found to inhibit the development of scientific careers to some degree.

The Current Scene

Organized religion must reckon with phenomena such as atheistic secularity which embraces a concept of autonomous man left to his own resources. There is an ecclesiastical Gresham's Law: whenever God the Absolute is deposed, then false gods arrive. This is not only of theological concern, but there is also much impact on society and social change. Such existential atheists as Sartre, Camus, and Malraux, in their obsession with the supposed dreariness of life, infect society with pessimism, irresponsibility, and bewilderment.

A characteristic of our time is a rejection of traditional patterns and an openness to change. So there is a headlong rush for freedom—freedom from poverty, from prejudice, from any form of enslavement. But true freedom depends upon absolutes, and when the vertical is increasingly blurred, the quest for freedom becomes blindman's buff. This is a society enamored of deed and action. American religious institutions for many years were not interested in the development of technology, its impact on society, and its influence upon individuals. To the present technological revolution, the Industrial Revolution was merely prologue. A new materialism is accelerating its impact in the more highly developed areas of the world. Still in its first stages in the remaining areas, its influence will become momentous in the future. Technology sets forward the development of a universal secular civilization, presenting the options of global coexistence or global annihilation.

A mass pluralistic society is characterized by standardized goals, towering fears, loneliness, and depersonalization. The average worker lives longer, enjoys a shorter work week and more vacation days than did his father. The end is not yet; automation and cybernetics promise increasing freedom from routine and drudgery. The portents are profound. DeGrazia says that free time may be an entrance to freedom, an opening up of the individual to the delight of life. Free time can also be frightening in its cold emptiness. The recreating use of time is a social demand already of great importance and one which will become increasingly insistent in North American society. Free time needs to be regarded as honest, respectable, and socially significant—just as is work.

These constitute only a partial list of clamant social phenomena in this restless time. Religion and religious institutions are an integral part of every culture and society. They must exist in tension with society. Religion tends to sanctify the cultural present—to justify and support on cosmic terms the way things are. Religion also is a constant judgment on the way things are and a thoroughgoing critique of the cultural present, out of a deep-seated commitment to the way things ought to be.

IV. SUMMARY AND IMPLICATIONS

A. Summary

1. The value system associated with North American culture will continue to exercise influence on religious institutions. Shifts that occur in the dominant value system will stimulate some responses of reaction and some of accommodation among the churches. The churches will continue to be aware of their roles as contributors to and critics of society.

2. The various religious communities will develop consciousness and appreciation of their historic roots even as they participate in dialogue and cooperative ventures with other communions. The long-term trend toward closer relationships among Protestants will continue, even as obstacles to Protestant-Roman Catholic communication and cooperation are lessened.

3. Greatest strides toward interchurch and interfaith cooperation will be made in the area of social action.

4. The function of the congregation as a source of personal identity and social location first had as its locus the various immigrant cultural communities. There has been a shift toward a new locus, that of socio-economic status; it is likely that there will be a further shift, this time in the direction of consciously chosen interest in a given style or type of religious expression. Congregations, if not denominations, may develop distinctive characteristics.

5. Many uncertainties are involved in forecasting the future level of interest the population may have in religion. Interest level will be affected by developments on the world scene, trends in the domestic economy, and changes in cultural mores.

B. *Implications*

In considering its role among the churches and in society, the church should take account of its social-psychological function as well as the theological formulations of its nature and mission. Identification of the contemporary social-psychological function of Lutheran congregations may assist in the development of policies and programs through which the church intends to express its nature and mission. Traditional concepts of "evangelism" and "church membership" need to be defined in terms that are appropriate to the social setting in which the church lives.

Alertness to changes in relationships among religious communities should enable the Lutheran church to identify its distinctive role among the religious communities of North America. Present definitions of desirable forms of relationships (e.g., interchurch agencies, theological dialogue, cooperation for social justice) will undoubtedly be subject to continuing evaluation.

The American Family

According to Margaret Mead the family is the toughest institution we have. The oldest of social institutions, it has survived innumerable changes in rates of marriage and divorce, in standards and customs, in size and function, and in the roles and relationships of its members. On the American scene the Industrial Revolution of the mid-nineteenth century and the development of urban society forced the family to adapt itself in order to survive and to perform its basic functions. The acceleration of scientific and technological advances since 1900 has virtually revolutionized American family life. Yet anthropologist Ralph Linton, in depicting the world holocaust toward which he believes we are being led, insists that the last man will spend his last hours searching for his wife and child.

I. MARRIAGE AND DIVORCE

Americans have been marrying on an unprecedented scale. Not only is the number of marriages increasing, but also the proportion of persons marrying is rising. At the turn of the century, one person in seven remained unmarried. Now the prediction is that in the future one person out of fourteen will not marry.

Young people in the United States marry earlier than those of almost any other country in the world. The present median age in first marriages for brides is usually reported to be slightly under twenty, and for grooms slightly under twenty-three. In a study of marriage trends, reports demonstrate that during the decade from 1940 to 1950 a decline of more than one year occurred in the median age at first marriage. When seen in the perspective of many decades, the one-year decline is a large change for a single ten-year period. In the fifty years previous to the decade of the forties the decline in median age in first marriages for husbands was only two years. A fluctuating, but overall downward decline of about one-half year existed for wives.

Of particular significance in the trend toward earlier marriages is the fact that at the present time some forty percent of all brides are between the ages of fifteen and eighteen. According to predictions, half of these marriages will not survive five years.

The reading-listening public is bombarded continually with statistics, predictions, and analyses of causes and effects of the American divorce rate. According to one authority, the divorce rate for the United States in 1910 was 87 out of 1,000 marriages; by 1965 it had risen to an estimated figure of more than 300 out of 1,000 marriages. A significant rise in the divorce rate is predicted as the population becomes younger and as people marry at a younger age.

Although the divorce rate is generally on the increase, there has been a drop in the number of divorces after the first year following World War II. Using a different basis in computing, reports show that there were 4.3 divorces per 1,000 population in 1946. By 1962 the rate had fallen to 2.2 per 1,000 population.

Changing Attitudes Toward Marriage and Divorce

Concomitant with the mounting divorce rate are changing concepts of marriage and attitudes toward breaking up a marriage. No longer is there much validity in an emphasis on marriage as the only way to survive. The view of marriage in terms of adequate achievement of family functions, i.e., securing individual maintenance and group survival of the members, has been supplanted gradually by a view that measures the success of a marriage in terms of personal happiness and the individual development of both mates. A marriage is also weighed by the relationships of love and fulfillment which have been established between the spouses and between the parents and their children.

Values relating to endurance of the marriage, its fertility, its good repute, its yoking of the spouses in working harness have been discarded. In contrast to the belief that marriage is a lifelong arrangement, today's husbands and wives consider a marriage ready for dissolution when it no longer fulfills their expectations, or when its antagonisms outweigh its benefits.

Enmeshed in these changing views is the matter of preparation of young people within the family circle for marriage. In the farm home which produced most of its own necessities, young people, working alongside their parents in an apprentice role, learned methods and skills which prepared them for marriage. Today, preparation is less specific, and considerable emphasis is placed on human factors, values of personable qualities, and social aptitudes, all of which are much more difficult to transmit.

The attitude of the general public toward divorce and the divorced has gradually eased within the past twenty-five years. As more and more divorced people were observed living satisfactory lives and making their contributions to community life, the public attitude changed. Today divorced persons do not have to bear the brunt of the social ostracism or community scorn which existed previously. In a sense this attitude has contributed to the rising divorce rate. With the relaxation of the social condemnation of the divorced, more persons have been willing to try divorce as a solution to their problems.

Until the middle of the nineteenth century in most of the states, adultery or cruelty were the only grounds for divorce. Furthermore, divorce was granted by legislative enactment. Generally only persons with money or political influence were able to use the legislative process for this purpose. This limited divorce to members of the upper classes and, except in rare cases, specifically to upper-class men. Liberalized laws, which substituted judicial for legislative action and included desertion as legal grounds, made it possible for women to initiate divorce action, with the result that they were granted more and more divorces.

At the present time in the United States, societies within the legal profession and concerned citizens are exerting pressure for reform of existing divorce laws. Advocates for a current reform of these laws argue that the variation among state codes works an unfair advantage on the citizens, and that today's laws are an anachronism and examples of "cultural lag," since they vary so far from actual practice.

Current Remarriage Trends

A high remarriage rate accompanies the high divorce rate in the United States. It appears that six out of seven of those divorced in recent decades are remarrying. Studies show that in subsequent marriages, divorced persons, especially women, tend to make better adjustments than they did in their first marriages. Authorities claim that the high divorce rate, by itself, gives an incomplete picture of the stability of the American family. This opinion is supported by pointing out that despite the personal tragedy in these experiences for both parents and children, most of the individuals concerned move forward into new family units. Thus, the responsibility for maintenance, status placement, and socialization of the children is preserved. As a result, there is little evidence that our high divorce rate is undermining the larger social structure.

II. THE SEXUAL REVOLUTION

The freer, more open attitude toward sex has affected almost every facet of contemporary American society involving communication in general and contacts between individuals. Homes, classrooms, and churches permit a more honest discussion of sex. The opinion makers of the mass media utilize open attitudes about sex in manipulating their audiences to conform to whatever life-styles they suggest. The appeal of sex is the backbone of advertising: sex sells automobiles, food, toiletries, and farm equipment. The arts capitalize on sex appeal to get their message across to the public.

Although premarital and extramarital sexual experiences are as old as the history of mankind, significant changes have been taking place. There appears to be some increase in premarital and extramarital sexual experience on the part of both men and women.

In describing the sex standards of youth, the following are held to be factors which encourage experimentation with premarital sex: readily available contraceptive devices, high physical mobility, adult-mimicking social behavior, a consumer-oriented life-style with approval of self-indulgence, splintered value systems, the declining role of the family as a behavior-defining agency, emotional insecurities suffered by youth when jobs become scarce, alienation of some of the more privileged youth, and a turning to intense personal relationships as an answer.

It is postulated that these same factors will encourage sexual experimentation among more adults—especially among those envious of the freedom of youth. Adult behavior will reinforce similar behavior in youth.

One of the problems brought about by the sexual revolution is the ambiguity of standards. On a private level the tacit approval exists that "anything goes as long as one is not caught," while on the public level society still disapproves of premarital sexual experience. Another problem is the failure to develop new restraints when the social taboos which once presented formidable barriers to "going wrong" lost their sting. A related problem is the disappearance or complete transformation of the social rituals which once controlled the dating-mating cycle.

The old courtship pattern limited freedom of choice to local

eligibles. Girls had few opportunities to circulate. Formal introduction was usually followed by parental supervision during
the development of the relationship. Engagements were long,
and premarital discussions and agreements were restricted.

In contrast to these older patterns, reports illustrate these
current trends in dating, courtship, and lovemaking:

—Dating and courtship begin at an early age.

—More frequent single dating among very young pairs.

—Dating and courtship last until later at night.

—More privacy for dating pairs.

—More young sweethearts and love affairs.

—"Going steady" more generally accepted.

—Wider range of intimacy and sex play.

—Increased venereal disease and illegitimacy.

—Greater readiness for marriage and family life education.

—More young marriages prone to divorce, separation, and
annulment.

Dating partners generally want "no strings attached." In other
words, the pleasures and enjoyments of dating are enough in
themselves to justify the association. A further study of the
courtship pattern reveals a change in the direction of a single
common standard of behavior for men and women. Women
assume new roles in initiating dates, sharing expenses, and generally planning and arranging the date itself.

III. FAMILY SIZE, TYPE, AND FUNCTION

Fundamental changes in the size, types, and functions of the
family have been taking place as a natural and perhaps inevitable part of the adaptations which the family has made in
reaction to the Industrial Revolution. Most authorities believe
that these changes do not represent a "decline of the family."
Rather, the family still has important services to perform even
though it is no longer a self-sufficient economic unit.

Family Size

One of the major changes in the American family has been the decline in size. In 1790 the approximate size of the average household was 5.79 persons. In 1957 the average size was 3.34— a decline of almost two and one-half people in little more than a century and a half. During the decade following, the trend was toward an increase in size; however, recent evidence does not support the continuation of this trend. It appears that the family is still declining in size. One observer projects an average of 2.8 children for women born in the fifties.

The decline in family size affects the relationships and activities of the family members: (1) the husband-wife relationship improves, (2) activities are more likely to be adult-centered with more interests outside the home, and (3) parents tend to devote more time and give more attention to each child. The decrease in the number of children per family has also made it possible for more women to work outside the home.

Smaller family size can be only partially attributed to the invention and use of contraceptives. The effect of "the pill" on family size has not been as great as was predicted. The place of birth seems to be related to family size. For example, the birth rate is lower in cities than on farms partly because birth-control techniques are more easily transmitted in the city, and cities contain more adults-only and fragmented families. In addition, rural areas are popularly considered to be more favorable for rearing children than are city areas. Children are an economic asset in rural areas and a liability in urban areas.

Types of Families

Rural and urban have been the two outstanding types of families. Historically, the difference between them has been great. The household economy of the rural family, for example, is quite different from that of the apartment family in a metropolis. However, the gap is rapidly being bridged by transportation and communication inventions. School buses, joint schools, and higher rural incomes will tend to reduce this difference still further.

Other family types are related to geographical factors, age and number of children, and age of spouses. Housing patterns provide evidence of these types. Older persons with larger incomes prefer residential hotels, which have been limited in number. However, many new accommodations of this type are now being built, making it possible for low-income elders to select this type of housing. Families with one or two children can be satisfied in the compact modern apartment, while families with more children settle in single-family dwellings with play space. Very young couples, older couples without children, and families involved in migratory occupations choose trailers and develop trailer communities.

The burgeoning megalopolis will accent the difference between types of families. More children per unit of population now live on the fringes of large cities than within the cities. When the population is equal for central cities and the fringes, in areas over one million, 43 out of 100 children younger than 14 live in the central city, 57 of the 100 live in the fringe areas. More middle-aged families, more persons who have never married, and a large number of divorced or separated people live in the central city.

The suburban family or satellite-community family has characteristics of both the town family outside the metropolitan orbit and the city family. It has more children and fewer elders than the city family. There are also fewer divorced and widowed people.

Changes in Function

The home is often pictured as becoming little more than a place to eat and sleep. Family and business, family and leisure, family and society, family and school, family and church are all developing within different coexistent spheres. People are often caught in deep conflicts, especially in a time of rapid social change. They still think and react in terms of old family-community structures, when they must live here and now in the new industrial society. These tensions are bound to be reflected in the family, especially between young and old.

The family has become a more specialized agency than before, probably more so than in any previously-known society. This represents a decline of certain functions which traditionally have been associated with families. One of the major changes in function has been the shift from a producing to a consuming economic unit. Protection of the home, historically the responsibility of the family, has become a function of the state. Formal education has been transferred to the schools, and public educational services have been increased by the addition of nursery schools and adult programs. The recreational function entails both more and less family responsibility, as modern living allows more time for recreation. The growing popularity of television, games, and camping means more time spent together in family groups, although other recreational activities tend to draw individuals away from the home. Religious instruction as a family responsibility has been turned over to the Sunday school and youth programs of the church.

In spite of the loss of the traditional functions, it is necessary to recognize that the family has retained two of its basic functions: meeting affectional needs and serving as the primary culture agent. These functions are reflected in the criteria for a successful marriage discussed earlier. Family life is increasingly based on love, companionship, and common interests. There is little indication that meeting the affectional needs of the child will be transferred outside the family. Home atmosphere, that is, attitudes, behavior, and relationships of the family, are of vital importance. Also of great significance are family events and celebrations, family traditions and memories, and common interests and activities.

Fulfilling the affectional and cultural functions is more important in urban society than ever before. The high rate of mobility compounds the problems of family members being separated from each other and from the familiar surroundings and friends of the communities in which they grew up. Students of family life believe that the family which meets the affectional and cultural needs of its members makes a substantial contribution to preparing them for life in a complex society.

IV. THE CHANGING ROLE OF WOMEN

Who is unaware of the dramatic difference in life-styles which divide the family woman of today from her feminine ancestors? The change began when the economic role of the family shifted from producer to consumer and was aided by the invention of labor-saving devices for almost every manual chore of the home. Impetus was added by the demands of living in an affluent society in which desires were created for more and more goods, and one pay check per family was often not enough.

Employment of Women

The movement away from the home into paid employment by married women is one of the most startling social changes in American history. In March 1965 there were nearly 26 million women workers in the United States, and the forecast for 1970 is 30 million. One worker in three is a woman. In 1962 about 62 percent of working women were married. In addition to those in paid employment, an undetermined number spend hours away from the home in volunteer work for church and community.

Figures released by the United States Department of Labor in 1966 indicates that more than one-half of the married women workers with husbands in the home had children under eighteen years of age. Most worked because their families could not manage without their earnings. Forty-one percent with children under six years of age and 31 percent with children six to seventeen years of age had husbands whose incomes were less than $5,000 a year. In families headed by a woman, and in families whose husbands are unemployed or unable to work, most women were forced to work by economic necessity.

Although there seems to be fairly widespread acceptance of women working outside of the home, there is not so wide an acceptance of employment of mothers of small children, even by mothers who work. And there is a special resistance to mothers who work with no apparent need for doing so. One of the chief concerns of working mothers has to do with the effect of their working upon the children.

The questions concerning the effects of maternal employment on families remain unanswered. It is not possible to generalize that a mother's working is in sum good or bad for her children, because so many other factors are involved—such as the age of the children, the mother's motivation for working, the skill of the mother and that of her substitute, the composition of the family, the stability of the husband, and the absence or presence of tension between the husband and wife.

Part-time employment may be the answer for mothers of young children. From 1955 to 1975 the number of part-time workers is expected to increase by 75 percent. At the present time nearly one-third of the total number of working married women work part-time. There is a declining rate for part-time workers in the thirty-five and over age group and an increase for women in the twenty-five to thirty-four age group.

It is claimed to be socially advantageous to have more part-time jobs available, because mothers can be at home when needed. Family life is benefited when the mother's part-time work means a reduction in father's work-load, and when mother's and father's job schedules are arranged so that one parent is always available.

Education is an important correlate of paid employment for women. Studies show that the more education a woman has, the more likely she is to be in the labor force. In 1966, 34 percent of women with less than eight years of school were working, as compared with 58 percent of women who had at least four years of college.

In addition to economic necessity and the influence of education, other factors which draw women into the labor force are the contemporary social mores, improvements in health and a lengthened life span, ease of household work, and expansion of opportunities for employment. Forces which tend to restrain them are (1) the rising standards of child-rearing on mother-child relationships, (2) the difficulties which middle-class families face in attracting and keeping competent domestic help, and (3) the relocation of younger middle-class families from the central cities to the suburban areas, which presents the problem of transportation to and from work.

Education

At the turn of the century, women acquired approximately 20 percent of all the baccalaureate or first professional degrees that were granted. Three decades later they had considerably narrowed the gap between themselves and men. By 1960 women earned 40 percent of all baccalaureate degrees awarded, 30 percent of all master's degrees, and 10 percent of all doctor's degrees. These figures reflect the relative position of the number of women receiving degrees as compared to the number of men; however, these figures hide the fact that the actual number of women earning degrees in higher education has increased rapidly. About 55,000 received a bachelor's degree in 1930; the comparable figure for 1960 was 139,000. At the master's level the number increased from slightly below 6,000 to 24,000, and at the doctor's level from about 350 to 1,030.

The education of women tends to have these effects on the family: (1) There is generally a higher standard of living and the desire that daughters, as well as sons, be educated. (2) Women have greater opportunity to find high-salaried jobs and/-or jobs which bring the most satisfaction. (3) There is an increase in democratic principles in family life.

Soon women may be divided into two categories: the non-career women with too little education to break out of the domestic trap, and the growing group of career women—including college girls—who are interested in laying a foundation for future careers (i.e., after marriage and children).

Inequality and Limited Opportunities

Attention should be directed to the prejudice which closes technical and professional doors to women or, at best, opens them on a different basis than for men. Women, for example, are represented in the professions, in business and industry, and in government. However, their jobs are predominantly confined to the lower-paid job categories. As a nation we cannot politically, economically, or socially afford to continue this practice at a time when there is a desperate need for more technicians and professionals in science, mathematics, research, and the major professions.

If women are to develop interests and obtain the necessary training suited to the wide range of occupations available in the closing decades of the twentieth century, parents and counselors must accept and stimulate girls in the study of the physical sciences and mathematics. Traditional vocational guidance has emphasized careers in teaching, nursing, and secretarial work. Now, considerable efforts are being made to encourage girls to enter all fields.

Despite increased counseling efforts and the elimination of many subtle limitations imposed by custom, certain restrictions remain. Some discriminatory provisions are contained in common law, and others are written into statutes. Restrictive practices of labor, industrial, professional, or governmental organizations discriminate against women in apprenticeship, training, hiring, wages, and promotion.

Until women participate on an equal basis with men in politics, occupations, and the family, there will be no sex equality. Law and administrative regulations must permit such participation, but women must want and be able to participate. Since women have had and probably will continue to have primary responsibility for child-rearing, their participation in politics, the professions, or the arts cannot be equal to that of men unless ways are devised to ease the combination of home and work responsibilities.

V. THE CHANGING ROLE OF MEN

The patriarchal family in which the husband came first and his wife and children occupied roles of lesser status, except for a few pockets of isolated cultures, is about as up-to-date as buttonhooks. A new family characterized by democratic ideals of equality for men and women, husbands and wives, is taking its place. In the earning and spending of money, in governing the children, in matters of religion, and in social and recreational activities, decisions are made by both husband and wife as a team. In fact, the whole family makes up the team. The husband is among equals as the family plans and works cooperatively toward certain goals. No increase in male authority over the family is foreseen. A greater separation of the place of work and home and the growth of traveling occupations may further decrease male authority.

Although the husband/father role of the man is changing in the modern family, he is still made to feel responsible for satisfying the physical, mental, emotional, and spiritual needs of the family. In addition to fulfilling these responsibilities, a man is expected to possess certain manipulative skills termed charm and tact, which were once deemed to be characteristic of women. As a husband, he is responsible as lover for both his own and his wife's sexual satisfaction. As a father he bears most of the legal responsibility for his children even though his authority over them has lessened. Finally, as a husband/father he has to succeed as breadwinner if he is to assert masculinity.

The effect of shifting from a patriarchal family to one characterized by democratic ideals has resulted in the blurring of the sexual roles of men and women. Formerly, women stayed close at home tending the children and household responsibilities, and the men dealt with matters in the larger world. Today, men are cooking and caring for the children, and women are searching for a part in family decision, working outside the home, and engaging in business management.

The husband's role as a parent is diminishing. Too exclusive feminine upbringing is becoming detrimental to the children, especially the boys. A noted sociologist further believes that the standardization of marriage roles (men as husbands and wage-earners, women as wives and homemakers) is necessary for societal survival. However, he pinpoints the conflict between his viewpoint and the opposite tendency toward greater freedom and variety in personal behavior now widespread in society.

VI. THE ROLE AND STATUS OF CHILDREN

The role and status of children in family life are closely intertwined with all the changes which the family has been encountering. Some of the effects of the decline in family size, the employment of both mother and father, increased education for the mother, and the emerging democratic style of family life have already been mentioned. One of the most profound changes in the upbringing of children, however, has been the value placed upon them as persons rather than as workers. This alteration in a basic value came about as the family changed from a producing to a consuming economic unit.

The value placed upon children as persons has manifested itself in a growing regard for their needs. More health and medical services, education, recreation, and protection are provided than ever before. The medical, biological, and psychological sciences have all contributed to this accentuation of childhood. The medical sciences, for example, have made great strides in nutrition and in coping with infections and contagious diseases. Rapid social change has also benefited children because they are the recipients of the new knowledge brought about by the scientific and technical revolutions. Rapid social change also affords increased social mobility, thus affecting the opportunities open to them.

The appreciation of children as persons has greatly enhanced their status. There is a new concern for their rights, evident in the changing parent-child relationship. Few parents today would say that children should be seen and not heard. Modern parents, in abandoning stern discipline, spend time trying to help children reach proper decisions by themselves. There is also a recognition of individual differences and potentialities in children. This change is consistent with the developing criteria for a successful marriage, in that the individual development of family members and their happiness is paramount. It also reflects the emerging democratic style of family life, which encourages participation and self-expression.

The recognition of individual differences and potentialities in children is not without its pitfalls, however. Children at an early age are encouraged to seek personal satisfaction outside the home. The result is a loosening of family ties. Time spent by both children and parents outside the family circle also affects the family's responsibility for developing character. Parents and children no longer spend enough time together to make such training possible—not that parents don't want to spend time with their children, but simply because conditions of life have changed.

Children and the Family Life Cycle

Using the concept of family life cycle, certain authorities state that it is possible to predict what lies ahead for families in the upbringing of children. Eight stages of the family life cycle have been postulated, each characterized by promises and problems for the family members. The stages follow one another in predictable sequence. While the challenges and crises of husband-wife-children relationships shift from stage to stage of the family's life cycle, they cannot be completely unexpected.

Despite the predictability of family life stages, parent-child relationships within these stages are changing. For example, parental control of young people during courtship years has virtually disappeared. The urbanization of America has multiplied the opportunities for contacts between young people. Parents frequently have never met the young man who is dating their daughter. Parental consent for marriage of children is required only for children under a specified age.

The breakdown in communication between adolescents and parents and its manifestations in our society are documented daily by the mass media. As seen by adults, the tension results from disrespect on the part of teen-agers. The young people see it as a conspiracy by adults to be dictatorial, distrusting, and arbitrary in maintaining control of them. Both age groups feel misunderstood and under-appreciated.

The increasing family rift between generations is traced to the attrition suffered by the kinship system: the effective family group has narrowed down to immediate members of families linked by blood and marriage through no more than three generations—grandparents, parents, and children. Seen in the lives of children today is a lack of experiences with relatives and adults, which tends to leave them less prepared to understand the older generation or be influenced by them.

VII. SUMMARY AND IMPLICATIONS

A. *Summary*

1. Both the number and proportion of persons marrying is rising, with a trend toward earlier marriage.

2. An upward trend in the number of divorces is accompanied

by an increased number of divorced persons remarrying. A more acceptable attitude toward divorce and the divorced continues to develop.

3. The criteria for a successful marriage will continue to be based on personal happiness and individual development of both mates and their children.

4. Sexual standards are becoming more ambiguous. The discussion of sex continues to be frank and free. An increased number of persons are engaging in premarital and extramarital relationships.

5. The size of the family has decreased, with "the pill" being less of a factor than predicted. Place of birth tends to affect family size.

6. The differences between the traditional rural and urban types of families will continue to decrease. More children per unit of population will live on the fringes of large cities rather than within the cities. More middle-aged, single, and divorced or separated persons will live in the central city.

7. Many of the traditional functions of the family have been transferred to other institutions. There is no indication that the affectional and cultural functions will be transferred.

8. More women are seeking paid employment, although the rate of participation in the labor force is influenced by economic status of the family, the extent of the woman's formal education, and the size of her family.

9. More women are receiving bachelor's, master's, and doctor's degrees than previously. The proportion of all degrees awarded continues to be smaller for women than for men.

10. Employment opportunities for women have increased, but discrimination in apprenticeship, training, hiring, wages, and promotion continues.

11. No increase in male authority over his family is foreseen. The place of work and types of occupations may even decrease male authority.

12. The blurring of sex roles continues as husband and wife

work together as a team in developing a democratic style of family life.

13. An increased value of children as persons is accompanied by an increased concern for their rights and a recognition of their individual differences and potentialities.

14. Knowledge of the family's life cycle makes it possible to predict what lies ahead in the upbringing of children, but parent-child relationships are changing within these stages.

15. The rift between generations persists. The narrowing of the kinship group tends to promote this rift and ill prepares children for being influenced by or understanding the older generation.

B. Implications

The increasing number of persons marrying, the earlier age of marriage, the rising divorce rate, and the changing criteria for a successful marriage suggest the need for the church to intensify its efforts in helping to develop persons who understand and are capable of assuming marital responsibilities. Careful attention needs to be given to interpreting the values of living which are integral to the affectional function of the family: the need to love and be loved, the sense of security, life purpose, and an awareness of the presence of God. When marriage fails, the church needs to learn how to deal more constructively with persons who are separated or divorced. Equally important is the role of the church in acting as an agent in changing social factors which contribute to the rising divorce rate. The church needs to consider employing professionally-trained persons to counsel in marriage and family life. Pastoral preparation should include a more adequate training for dealing with marital and family problems.

The ambiguity of standards of sexual behavior implies that the church needs to help young people, in particular, to discover the basic moral principles applicable to boy-girl relationships; to help them understand themselves and the problems they face; to prod them to question popular practices and attitudes; and to decide the morality of specific conduct. Adults also need to be confronted with their own attitudes toward sexual behavior and the influence of undesirable behavior upon younger persons.

In recognition of the fact that families spend little time together, the church needs to re-examine its own program and determine what it can do to enable families to be together. This examination should include an analysis of the ways in which the church helps the family to fulfill its cultural function. While emphasis is placed on Christian heritage and tradition, the church could perhaps contribute more meaningfully than it has in the past to developing family activities and transmitting family traditions.

Continued attention should be given to a growing variety of families of varying composition, needs, and geographical locations. The prevalent assumption that the husband, wife, children constitute the only type of family needs to be re-examined. Church programs must meet the needs of all family types and create an atmosphere in which single and married, divorced and widowed, couples with or without children, can all feel that they are a part of congregational life.

The roles of men and women have been changing within the family and society as a whole. In light of these changes the church needs to explore the ways in which the fullest potentialities of both men and women can be developed and used in the life and work of the church.

Art, Literature, Mass Communication

I. INTRODUCTION

Life consists of more than the expressly practical aspects of experience. Beyond the adaptations imposed by self-preservation lies man's need to frame and express certain hopes and ideals through the various available art forms. In part, the art world is the very fabric of culture. Culture reflects the facets of civilization and education within a particular society. Human forms of self-expression are affected by the social order and express changing attitudes and values.

Geoffrey Barraclough feels that changes consequential upon acceptance of the social implications of science and technology may be a sign of renewal. Barraclough traces development from an emphasis on isolated individual experience to the individual in society. The emphasis does not seem to be didactic or message-conveying, but rather a depiction of the manifestations of today's society. The theater of the absurd, the music of random sounds and silences, mobiles, and junk sculpture illustrate disordered and layered sights and sounds of the second half of the twentieth century.

McLuhan defines art as an anti-environment or a means of perceiving environment—that which trains perception and judgment, anticipates the future, and helps maintain a stable course toward permanent goals. The artist can be regarded as not only reflecting but influencing society. The artist perceives the cultural and technological challenge before its transforming impact occurs.

II. THE VISUAL ARTS

Architecture

The essential elements of architecture are considered to be *commodity* (i.e., utility), *firmness* (structural adequacy), and *delight* (design and expression). In these terms, architects in America today can point to many examples of magnificent achievement. Among these are Frank Lloyd Wright (Johnson Wax Building, Racine, Wisconsin), Eero Saarinen (David S. Ingalls rink at Yale and TWA at Kennedy Airport, New York), Minoru Yamasaki (Conference Center, Wayne State University, Detroit), Edward Stone (U.S. Embassy, New Delhi, and Center for Continuing Education, Chicago), Paul Rudolph (Yale).

The preservation of worthwhile architecture of the past, initiated by the Rockefeller reconstruction of Williamsburg, Virginia, has markedly influenced finer architectural standards. Even in the megalopolis the principles of commodity and firmness have been well achieved, but the artful expression and design have often given way to profit-motivated space utilization. Of special interest are the developing planned cities or "new towns" such as Columbia, Maryland, and Reston, Virginia. They aspire to functional beauty by the use of an increasing number of new structural and decorative materials accompanied by careful city planning. As North American megalopolises grow, such communities present tangible hope for the increase of better architecture, provided that care be continually taken that "old town" problems do not enter. And such one-concept community development in areas adjacent to heavily populated and excruciatingly ugly urban centers may be an incentive to an increasing number of well-designed, functionally planned redevelopment projects.

The general standard of all visual art in all parts of the world is rather low, as it has always been, for the simple reason that there are relatively few gifted artists who submit to adequate training and who are able to practice as they should. Yet, within this context, American architecture is generally held to occupy a relatively high level. The highest architectural standards have usually existed in the wealthiest countries. Quite clearly the United States falls in that category today. The financial ability to attract first-rank architects, the immense quantity of construction and money, and the general acceptance of new forms have all played their part in creating conditions which support high standards.

Provision for a much higher degree of population mobility is inherent in the new architectural projections. Enterprising locations will be tested by permanent-appearing mobile or movable unitized buildings. Banks are particularly ready to diversify their facilities for broader involvement in the new "instant communities." New designs and materials in church buildings can combine adequate architecture and flexibility of location with community parking and recreation facilities.

E. A. Sovik, A.I.A., has recently considered the way architecture should reflect religious concepts and attitudes. Religion is a search for reality. We must assume that religious architecture will express concern for and commitment to what is real. This rules out deceits, illusions, imitations, superficial prettiness, propagandizing. Therefore we must demand commitment to what is real, honest, and absolutely forthright. When architecture, in its abstract forms and explicit symbols, is able to establish a foothold for men in the world and the cosmos, it may be appropriately called religious architecture. Architecture can simultaneously express lucidity and mystery, strength and grace, humility and elegance, the ordinary and the unique.

Painting

Within recent decades painting has pursued ways of strange and fascinating exuberance. For centuries painting was representational. The last decade of the nineteenth century saw the genesis of a trend away from that concept. One factor was the improvement of photography, the results of which are more accurate than those produced by any human hand. Other deeper reasons, however, were changes in technology, industry, communication, transportation.

Painting in the twentieth century has been marked by wide diversity in style, movement, and concept. Representation was at first blurred, then distorted, then fractured with fragments, until it finally dissolved in abstractionism. Realism, cubism, expressionism, surrealism, and automatism can be identified. The prevailing theory (to hazard a guess) is that of "reality" which views every object encountered in life as potential art—objects such as soup dishes, mirrors, Coke bottles or cans, etc.

The grand international prize of the 1966 Venice Biennale went to Julio Le Parc of Argentina for a motorized "op-skip-and-jump" where ping-pong balls bobble and bounce behind plexiglas. A less complicated example, closer to the traditional view that painting is representation on a flat surface, is Walter de Maria's series of six large, identically white pictures, whose only difference is in the titles given by the artist (e.g., "Sky" on one, "River" on another, "Mountain" on a third). Here one may believe that de Maria is giving the spectator the freedom to decide for himself what sky or river or mountain he would like to have.

The concern for the individual is to be seen in the "art game" of Oivind Fahlstrom. Believing that the world has so many facets and mutations that no usual picture can convey a message of reality, and conscious of the threat to personality in social pressures, this artist makes a series of magnetized cutouts to be attached to a background at the owner's will.

There have been drastic changes in painting and a resultant conspicuous transformation in public interest. An increasing artistic interest and awarness has come about, whether traditional or modern painting is in view. The opening of the new Whitney Museum of American Art in September 1966 was a news event of first importance. The Andrew Wyeth retrospective exhibition drew record-breaking crowds in every city where it was shown. There is a marked revival of interest in the French Impressionists (Seurat, Manet, Monet, etc.), probably related to the popularity of Wyeth. Mass-merchandising now makes possible the purchase of oils and watercolors by masses of people. This "cultural explosion" has also brought in its train an increase in art frauds. Spurious paintings are sold to unsuspecting and gullible persons.

The role of physically viewing art is changing. Paintings are off the wall and out of the frames. Some advantaged homes already provide for art paintings viewed by rear projection on full walls. Parallel to such trends one must place Marcel Duchamp's concept of art as a mental act.

Contemporary painting is, as such art has always been, the record of man's response to his existence. If today the beholder feels confused and puzzled, the reason to be sought is not in the object he views so much as in the society it attempts to portray.

Sculpture

No less dynamic is the art-impulse pressed, carved, or shaped into solid-form materials. The restlessness of recent work in sculpture is one of the reasons for a resurgence of interest in this area. Another is the appeal of modern technology, with its creation of new materials: plastic, foam, metal, glass. It shows also the forms suggested by the space age—the nose cone, the missile housing, the smooth, lacquered, antiseptic finish. The union of technology and sculpture in the 1960's is phenomenal. For example, the chain saw has revolutionized working with wood. Donald Judd has gone even further in the use of technology— he has no studio. Creation and design are his métier and the actual physical work is done in a factory.

Kinetic sculpture goes back through mobiles to weather vanes and even farther, but it has become a definite trend, particularly in the hands of Jean Tinguely, a Swiss artist. Believing that art should be play, movement, change expressed by an art of chance, he constructs "meta-matics." These are unpredictable motor machines built out of hardware, springs, and electric motors. Once started, the machine goes through a series of changing motions calculated to puzzle, stimulate, and delight beholders. The kinetic appeal is heightened by clattering noise and dizzying light. Kinetic sculpture reflects a society always in flux and in some of its more extreme forms, self-destroying.

An obvious blending of sculpture with painting is ushering in an entirely new art form: "combines," in which "pop" and "op" art are tuned to momentary reality, expressing the dynamics of adjustment and adaptation required in a pluralistic world.

Freed from dependence only upon the physical materials of the past, sculpture is more and more able to portray the kaleidoscopic phenomena of modern life. That it will in the future increasingly express the wide variations of the day in which its practitioners live is more fact than prophecy.

III. THE PERFORMING ARTS

Music

The growth of interest in serious music has been phenomenal. High-fidelity recordings are now available for almost the entire range from classical to modern. Increased support for symphony orchestras, opera, music festivals, new centers for the performing arts, is growing. In 1966 the Ford Foundation initiated grants of $80.2 million to 61 American symphony orchestras for a ten-year period. Since much of this is given on a matching-grant basis, there is the prospect of a total of $140 million over the coming ten years. The National Council on the Arts is moving to establish a master chamber orchestra. The development of Lincoln Center and particularly the location of the Julliard School there in 1968 is noteworthy. Summer festivals increase—the Boston Symphony's Berkshire Festival has been joined by the Philadelphia Orchestra at Saratoga Springs, New York, the Cleveland Orchestra in a nearby Ohio rural setting, and the National Orchestra at Columbia, Maryland.

Serious music in the accepted sense of the term has greatly changed. Seventy years ago Debussy and Wagner, among others, led in a flight from that tonality of the seven-tone scale which had been the dominant language of western music for centuries. Consciously avoiding tonics and dominants, they developed a music of freer tonal possibilities. Musical sounds that were characterized as "dissonance" in the tonal system were accepted. Nearly all modern music-makers from Bartok to the Beatles have exploited the expanded aural possibilities, creating a music hugely different, and have extended man's sense of what music can be. It therefore appears that the morphology of music in the next twenty years will reflect both freedom of composition and a widened base of acceptance.

Experimentation in the search for new art forms has decisively become a part of serious music. The "Poème Electrique" of Edgar Varèse astonished and even angered those who heard it at the Brussels World's Fair in 1958. The same reactions are evident today upon hearing electronic music, which cannot be shrugged off as insignificant or as frivolous. The maturation of electronic music began at Columbia and Princeton. Electronic music centers are now to be found across the country in major universities. Protagonists such as Milton Babbitt and Usecheusky have been instrumental in alerting people to the amazing possibilities in this field.

Some proponents claim that avant-garde music is the contemporary edge of conventional classical music, occupying the relation to the classical that pure scientific research occupies in relation to applied science. It discovers new devices and practices, some of which will later be absorbed into the mainstream. In December 1967, Columbia Records released seventeen albums of avant-garde music, which they advertise as representing "the feelings and techniques of the twentieth century." Many of these are electronic.

The farthest "left" school gives its allegiance to chance music or aleatory music. A typical example is the combination or juxtaposition of an amplified violin, a piano played with fists and elbows, six radios each emitting the music of a different station at top volume. While this may seem to be a hit-or-miss concentration of sounds, some music critics recognize positive implications for the future.

A contemporary German tormentive sensationalist utilizes sound far beyond the twelve-tone system of the recent past. Steps are now possible by electronic means to eliminate instrumental limitations (e.g., the bassoon's inability to go beyond a tenth above middle c). The Columbia-Princeton Center for Electronic Music produces synthetic sounds which are edited by tape manipulation techniques. Naturally such recordings find limited acceptance, but the willingness to listen is increasing.

Within conventional instrumentation the American composer John Cage, whose aim is to avoid self-expression, produces what he calls "chance tonal operations." Compositions are designed so that for a given number of minutes the performer plays any notes he chooses within a specific range. This is called "indeterminacy"—music sounds which cannot be anticipated tonally. He also composes "variations" for "any number of players, any sound-producing means," interspersed with silences. At the other extreme of avant-garde music is Babbitt with his complicated revolutionary reordering of tonal possibilities produced by computer.

The morphology of music in the next two decades will reflect both the freedom of composition without regard to public expectation and a widened base of acceptance for synthetic sounds. Churches will find options to explore in both directions with the added potential for a new surge of hymnody developing from the stimulus of theology and music of the 1970's. The kinds of music listened to and participated in will reflect a new freedom of expression. Church musicians are already experimenting with contemporary forms of worship utilizing jazz, serial composition, and electronic music. Although in most congregations attention is wholly given to music of the distant past, developments in new creative music expression are evident. The Lutheran Society for Worship, Music, and the Arts is giving leadership and encouragement to new art forms. If the church is to meet the challenge of secular music, experimentations in creative music for worship must be pursued.

Drama

The theater perhaps more than other art forms has been subject to diagnoses, consultations, prescriptions, surgery, even post-mortems. It is, as Louis Kronenberger has said, "a fabulous invalid." Although the seats of Broadway's thirty theaters are well filled, there are those who would make the distinction between theater and serious drama. They claim that the stage is full of adaptations, forms of human journalism devoid of either content or invention. Lack of an adequate audience for serious theater is deplored. Walter Kerr confesses that the theater is still an unpopular art form in America. Yet there are outstanding playwrights: Arthur Miller, Tennessee Williams, Edward Albee, Robert Anderson, Frank Gilroy. These are established names, while "in the wings" a vital group of off-Broadway writers gather strength: Paul Foster, Sam Shepherd, Adrienne Kennedy, Lanford Wilson, and Rochelle Owens. The continuing appearance on the American stage of European plays strengthens the theater here. Recent seasons have seen Robert Bolt's *A Man for All Seasons*, Brecht's *Galileo*, Weiss's *Marat/Sade*, and Pinter's *The Homecoming*, among others. The particular contribution of the American stage to the theater has been the musical comedy, which continues strongly with *Cabaret, Mame, Hello Dolly*, and especially *Man of La Mancha*.

Broadway's financial complications are perennial, and its completely commercial context acknowledged. But, important as Broadway has been and is, the off-Broadway and community and college theaters in every major (and some small) United States and Canadian centers have proliferated in the last decade. It appears that growth in drama in the United States must take place away from the complete commercial control of Broadway. The power trilogy of playwright, producer, and performers subject to critic's evaluations and publicity promotion seems to be losing strength as distance from Manhattan increases.

The "west-of-the-Hudson" theater, strengthened by the growing interest of many colleges and universities in establishing departments and schools for promising actors, hopeful playwrights, and producers, may proceed in new and exciting directions. The theater of the absurd, often marked by black humor, with the motifs of isolation, savage despair, violence, man waiting in a time which may end in apocalyptic destruction, may find less interest.

The theater, as other art areas, is now confronted with a new dimension: subsidization by government. While initial legislation now provides only minimal support, beginnings have been made. Larger funds may provide for permanent repertory companies producing notable drama and giving opportunity for long development of excellence by actors. But the mere provision of funds will not automatically insure healthy theater. Witness the unhappy history to date of the New York State Theater at Lincoln Center.

Drama traces its genesis in western culture to the church. There it began and for centuries flourished. There is so much similarity between the plight of theater and that of the church today that objective description of "potential giant" suggests the increasingly definitive relationship. What the church may no longer be able to say effectively from the monologic pulpit could find a medium in dialogical drama, once again linking the church and dramatic arts in a new partnership. The scattered chancel plays of today's churches may become the patterns of the church's medium of proclamation tomorrow.

The Dance

The dance, as is music, is feeling the ferment of the present age. John Cage teaches that any sound can be music. Twenty years ago Merce Cunningham insisted that any movement however natural or ungainly could be dance. His concern was purity. The ballet should slough off the ancient trappings and become purely physical, with no symptomatic or subliminal overtones. He delighted in such movements as walking or standing still, and in anatomical parts of the posterior.

Of all the art forms ballet has experienced the most extraordinary popularity. In the summer of 1966 George Balanchine's New York City Ballet spent four weeks in Saratoga Springs presenting thirty-eight old and new ballets. The Ford Foundation and the National Council on the Arts have made substantial grants to dance groups. Tours of the Bolshoi, Royal Ballet, Covent Garden, and Royal Winnipeg—to name a few outstanding world dance ensembles—are standing room only. Anthony Dowell, Margot Fonteyn, Rudolf Nureyev are popular idols. Three academic ballet centers flourish in the United States: the Academy of the Washington (D.C.) School of Ballet, the National School of Ballet (New York), and the International Ballet School—West (Santa Monica).

The adaptation of the ballet to modern themes is a factor in the widening appeal of the dance. There is, for example, Eliot Feld's *Harbinger* presented by the American Ballet Theater in its 1966-67 season. *Harbinger* is a ballet about youth—uncertain, restless, reaching out. Youth walks alone, clings together, snaps its fingers at tradition, and also turns its many faces toward the sun. *Harbinger* mirrors both the pulse of an age and an attitude toward that age, commenting humorously and sadly on it.

The development of the ballet in the United States to its present high level is due particularly to Martha Graham, now in her seventies. Extraordinarily endowed with great talent, she has coupled that with an undaunted determination, a restless search for new material, and the development of a new technique based on simple body contractions and release. Graham's days as a dancer are over, but she still directs her dance company toward new, although not always popular successes—most recently

Cave of the Heart, Acrobats of God, Dancing Ground—new ways to portray old and eternal truths.

As in every form of art and literature, the new ranges of interest have undoubtedly stimulated the ballet, both in creative new directions and in the renovation of classic forms, to call forth the vast audience it enjoys today. The church has yet to avail itself of the dance. Only in isolated instances is it using dance forms from the culture of minority groups, the classic expressions, the novel tendencies of the present. Some of these have taken the form of interpretative chancel presentations.

IV. LITERATURE

The Novel

Today man no longer assumes he is "a little lower than the angels." He has largely abandoned belief in God and confidence in himself. The result, says Barbara Tuchman, is a sense of footloose purposelessness and self-disgust shown in literature. And just as naturally, it is the contemporary novel which portrays a contempt for the world.

The lines novelists follows today were laid down by D. H. Lawrence's *Sons and Lovers* (1913) and James Joyce's *Ulysses* (1922). Here there appeared the anti-hero, victim of all he surveys and of everything he does not behold. He is the symbol of a sick and dying society—a world deserving only of disdain. This is illustrated in the treatment of man's continual need for love which increasingly has turned toward erotic, blatant, often violent and bizarre sexuality. It appears that writers who dislike their fellowmen have taken over. The characters of current fiction are drifters and derelicts.

Many contemporary prominent writers of fiction come from two minority groups hitherto of less importance on the American literary scene: Jews and Negroes. Richard Wright led the way for Negroes. More notable successors are James Baldwin and Ralph Ellison. Among Jews, Bernard Malamud and Saul Bellow are outstanding. Such metropolitan writers are notable for their depiction of Jewish rural life in an urban setting. The small crises of daily existence form the warp and woof of engaging folk-tales. A sense of dislocation pervades Malamud particularly, which suggests the troubled relationship his characters feel about their Jewishness. Ralph Ellison said that if Negro and Jewish writers become the mainstay of American literature, it will be because they have learned their craft and used the intensity of their group experience to express a more significant picture of American experience than other writers.

In the field of the novel, the basic philosophy of many prominent novelists is a weary existentialism. Their humor, often symbolic and mythic, is strikingly illustrated in John Barth's *Giles Goat-Boy*. Walter Prescott Webb once summarized a writer's criteria as a belief that he has something to say, that it is worth saying, and that he can say it better than anyone else. That canon viewed in the present "eschatological despair of the world" (to use Van Wyck Brook's phrase) set forth in many novels could account for the paucity of commanding literary figures today. Hasty writing to obtain financial prosperity in a clamor of competition does not work to produce literature of high merit.

The violent currents which surge through the novel today are encountered in all areas of human expression. Poetry, drama, cinema, and the visual arts could well have their origin in the "death-of-God" philosophy. Man drifts along in existence, for this is a deserted world bereft of meaning. By the fundamental truths of his being, man must be concerned with love and death. Without God, he is an exiled alien responding to the demands of life in despair, disenchantment, and violence. New and exciting developments can and probably will develop. The church has a primary responsibility to assist in their materialization.

Poetry

Poetry today seems to possess a more vibrant and compelling message than does prose. While William Carlos Williams, Robert

Frost, Theodore Roethke, T. S. Eliot, Ezra Pound, and Wallace Stevens have entered the Valhalla of verse, there still remain such commanding figures as Marianne Moore, Robert Penn Warren, Robert Graves, Robert Lowell, Archibald McLeish, and W. H. Auden. In addition there are Richard Wilburg, James Dickey, Ann Sexton, Allen Ginsberg, Harold Nemerov, and Galway Kinnell —all important figures. Their poetry is a controlled and often deeply penetrating analysis of personal experience. By the imaginative transformation of such individual reactions, meaning is conferred—a meaning which is generally set in the framework of man's alienation from society.

The new poets tend to cluster in several locales. There is the "New American Poetry" in San Francisco, the "New Concrete Poetry" in the Middle West, the "Young Turks" who read regularly at St. Mark's-in-the-Bowery in New York, to name only a few. But wherever they gather, they fall most deeply under the influence of Richard Eberhardt, Stanley Kunitz, and Roethke.

These new poets are knights-errant tilting lances against artificial language, traditional meter, and ordinary subject matter. Theirs are non-symmetrical lines marked by frank language, taking the form and length which the writer desires, not what convention demands. W. H. Auden has said that the characteristic style of modern poetry is intimate, the words of one person addressing another. Its characteristic hero is not the great man, not the romantic rebel, but the man who manages to acquire and preserve a face of his own.

An elder poet who is one of the new school, Kenneth Rexroth sums it up when he says that poetry, the art most difficult to turn into a commodity, is the focus of life in this world. Contemporary disaffiliation is a religious challenge to universal hypocrisy. Poetry can give the most challenging expression to religious values. Most poetry of secession has been religious in spirit.

Trends of the Future

What are the forces with which the writer must contend? One

suggestion is offered by Storm Jameson, contemporary English novelist, who says that the electronic age is with us. The problem for the writer and for the man in the street is how he can be free in relation to the machine.

Technology has invaded the literary world. It not only provides subject matter, but it poses a threat as an overpowering influence, displacing the normative values of creative writing. The attendant phenomena of isolation and alienation loom large. Subsidization by government and educational institutions raises disturbing questions about the future of the writer. Regardless of what is written, the coming generation is already forming mental habits that are not based on dialogue through the printed word. The instantaneous nature of much present and future communication may well foreshadow trouble. The prediction of David Sarnoff in 1942 that television is the "ultimate form of communication" grows increasingly valid.

To admit to such change is even more compelling when the literary implications are spelled out. The media of mass communication perhaps cannot be used to transmit the imaginative vision of a new Proust, Kafka, or Tolstoi. For a mass audience, emotive language will always have to be thinned, robbed of its delicacy and subtlety.

Prediction of content can be an exercise in futility. It would, however, be possible to assume from the present attention given by authors to personal-level life involvements that the next two decades will more and more see the portrayal of the corporate life of man, his grapplings with group dominance, his rebellion against the individual's loss of freedom, and his sense of fatuity in a mass society of non-psychical proximity.

V. MASS COMMUNICATION

"Mass communication" refers to newspapers, magazines, television, radio, comic books, widely circulated paperbacks. Communication channeled through mass media presents ideas, sells products, and influences people. Spurred on by the information and education explosion, communications is part of a 200 billion dollar knowledge industry.

For most people mass communications provide continuing education for good or ill. The industry's choice of topics and emphases exerts a powerful influence on the population. It then follows that the industry's social responsibilities are those of the largest and probably the most influential educational system any society has known. Here is a responsibility which many observers feel is not being met. It appears to many that willingness to deal with significant social issues is overwhelmed by superficial entertainment. The Winnick report shows that often controversial topics on TV undergo deletions, softenings, or changes in order not to endanger profits.

Both Buckminster Fuller and Marshall McLuhan contend that the environment man creates becomes his medium for knowing it, as well as for defining himself and his role therein—that it serves an as extension of his central nervous system in order to receive and communicate information. The content of this information is at once about the environment and is directed or altered by it.

McLuhan declares that technological media are natural resources, just as coal and oil, and he stresses that mass media are moving into the electronic age. In place of the linear exactness of sequential print we are proceeding to configurations relayed electronically, which demand from the beholder a different level of involvement. The sheer bulk of information available today will move us toward the use of a series of complex symbols and combination of symbols. We are going from linear language toward more graphic ideograms which will provide an inclusive *Gestalt*. And this is much more natural to man, for consciousness is neither linear or sequential.

A new conceptual inventiveness is clearly called for to keep pace with promised technical developments. The time does seem not far off when huge quantities of information will be transmitted regionally or globally by the newer telecasting techniques. The progress made and promised for the future gives credence to David Sarnoff's statement that mankind is on the brink of a communication revolution that will change the patterns of life as profoundly as did the Industrial Revolution.

Newspapers, Periodicals, and Books

More than two thousand pages of printed materials are produced every minute. If one person tried to keep up with this deluge of ink and paper by full-time reading, he would fail by more than one billion pages every year. Electrostatic printing has made great progress in the brief span of five years and it will be even more widely used. By 1970 many composing rooms may be using a process for the electronic generation of character-images. There are more new processes than can be named here; the most important development is the employment of the digital computer in typesetting.

Unfortunately the "fourth estate" in the United States today is undergoing a decrease in metropolitan newspapers. Los Angeles, San Francisco, and Houston now have only two metropolitan newspapers. Chicago is down to two ownerships. New Yorkers, once able to read many papers, are now confined to three. There are only 45 cities with competitive newspapers. To some extent this void has been filled by the national newspapers, such as *The Wall Street Journal,* the *National Observer,* and the *Christian Science Monitor.*

A great increase, however, has occurred in the field of the suburban daily. As quickly as papers succumb in the great cities, new ones spring up in the suburbs. Here is a growth pattern contrary to that found in other industries, where larger firms increase in size and smaller businesses vanish. Statistics in the newspaper world reveal growth. In the last twenty years, employment has increased 33 percent, the average size in pages has almost doubled, total daily circulation is up by 19 percent, and advertising income has quadrupled. Nor has the end been reached. The American Newspaper Publishers Association estimates that by 1980 newspapers may look for 16,000,000 to 22,000,000 more potential readers, the majority of them in the suburbs.

The rosy glow of circulation and resultant fiscal health is tempered by other phenomena. The information explosion has exposed the deficiences of the press in handling subject matter. Irving Kristol pursues the subject as he declares that the profession of journalism and the business of newspaper publishing neither know nor begin to understand the critical state of their decay. Much American journalism is, on the surface, amateurish, naive, and nonintellectual. There still ferments the long-standing American populist-progressive idea which holds up "muckraking" as a goal, whose pursuit leaves newspapermen little time for the acquisition of that knowledge emphatically demanded by our complex society and robs journalism of the proper sense of proportion and clear perspective every newspaper should have.

Magazines proliferate in seemingly unending quantity, despite the demise in the last decade of a number of widely circulated favorites such as *Collier's*. By and large, the good stay good and the poor get poorer. In 1965 magazine publishers had in the neighborhood of a billion dollars in advertising revenue. To list the popular magazines—*Life, Look, Time, Reader's Digest, Mc-Call's, Saturday Evening Post,* and *Newsweek*—is to give evidence that there is entertainment and news, but not analytical knowledge nor inducement for individual reasoning on their pages.

The "pulp" magazines still retain their readers as evidenced by their continued popularity and display on the newsstands. At the other end of the spectrum is the substantial readership enjoyed through the years by *Harper's, The Atlantic,* and the *Saturday Review,* which provide intellectual stimulation for their readers.

Advertising is perhaps the most persuasive power in our society. In 1966 the dollar volume was in the neighborhood of

$16.3 billion. In the United States as many dollars are spent in commercial advertising as in the total major educational enterprises for children and youth. Even in a medium which is no longer in a position of prime influence—the newspapers—advertising revenue was close to $5 billion for 1967.

Research has shown the economically productive and psychologically powerful role played by advertising. Its manipulative aspects frighten many people, and with good reason. Jacques Ellul sums it up when he says that the primary purpose of advertising is the creation of a certain way of life. The object offered for sale is made to seem indispensable to the realization of this way of life. Advertising creates needs that conform to an ideal of life that man accepts.

What of the next several years? There will be increased public and governmental pressure to correct blatant abuses and to set up controls. Some feel that there is hope in the direction of what is called "idea" advertising. This will be built upon growing awareness that the interests of any one group will be best served by the mutual interests of all.

Television

Less than twenty years old, TV dominates mass media today. Commercial broadcasting began in 1946 with six stations and an audience of 8,000 families. As of January 1, 1966, there were 700 stations on the air with 124 more under construction and 179 applications on file with FCC. Of all family dwelling units in the United States about 95 percent are equipped with TV, and multiple-set ownership brings the total number of sets to 67 million. Viewers have invested nearly $30 billion in receiving sets; transmitting equipment represents a cost to the stations of over $800 billion. The dependency upon TV is illustrated by the fact that if the TV set breaks down, nearly half of the owners have it repaired or replaced within a day, and two-thirds within three days.

Educational television, long the poor stepchild of the industry financially while high in program quality, seems to stand on the threshold of better days. President Johnson's budget message for the 1968 fiscal year requested appropriation of $20 million. Possible use of Telestar income for National Educational Television may result in a high quality non-commercial network.

The ability of television to influence human behavior is beyond question. As evidence one need only consider the millions of dollars which are spent annually for television advertising. Indeed advertising is the tail which wags the TV dog, since the standards of television broadcasting are determined by the commercial value of its programming which in turn is determined by viewer ratings. The result has been not merely mediocre programming, but programming marked by violence, questionable ethics, and poor taste. We are only now beginning to study the effects of such programs on impressionable small children and on perhaps equally susceptible adults. It should be pointed out that Canada, which has set high government standards of TV programming, is far ahead of the United States in this respect. As we learn more about television's effects on human behavior, it should become possible to exert greater pressure and, if necessary, control over the levels of programming.

A recent encouraging development is a two-year experiment in public television financed by the Ford Foundation with a $10,-000,000 grant, called *Public Broadcast Laboratory,* a quasi-autonomous unit of National Educational Television, with its own board of directors. It premiered late in 1967 and plans a two-hour Sunday night culture and current events program. Under the direction of Fred W. Friendly, it is designed as "a practical demonstration of what public television could be."

Radio

It was once predicted that television would kill off radio. But radio has continued to show healthy signs of commercial growth. This is due in part to the greatly increased number of car radios now in use; yet even in the home, the radio still remains a primary source of information for many families. Aside from its news value, the principal function of radio appears to be the promotion of record sales among young people. Radio has concentrated on the youth market just as other media have. Hopes for raising the quality level of radio programming appear to be dim. An interesting new development is the telephone programs in which the listener is invited to talk with someone in the studio by telephone. The response to this type of program suggests that radio still offers one of the most immediate and intimate forms of mass communication, the possibilities for which have still to be fully tapped by the church.

Motion Pictures

It was once predicted that television would squeeze out the movie industry as it seemed about to do away with the radio industry, but after an initial slump, movies are back and better than ever. Since television has taken over the mass mind and is eagerly saturating it with mediocrity, movies have become more free to experiment and to try for higher standards of achievement. While many grade B movies are still being produced, and while old grade B movies are ever with us on the late night TV shows, the ratio of good pictures to bad ones is higher than it has ever been in movie history. A movie must compete for its audience and must therefore be able to improve its content and technique. A lowering of movie moral standards has resulted, but there has also been a raising of artistic standards, so that the overall effect has been a gain rather than a loss.

Perhaps the most interesting facet of the movie industry at the present moment is the so-called "underground" productions. With the cost of movie-making skyrocketing to the point where many American pictures are now filmed abroad to save money, new young directors are dispensing with the elaborate paraphernalia of more polished productions, and are working with simple equipment and great imagination to create movies which have opened up whole new frontiers.

The ability of movies to influence human behavior is not that of television. Thus movies are more likely to be symptoms than shapers of the times. Viewed as such, they indicate that these are times of change, of violence and of lowered moral standards.

VI. SUMMARY AND IMPLICATIONS

A. Summary

1. Artists of every kind will continue both to portray and to challenge society through the use of their creative abilities.

2. Architectural standards appear to improve as wealth increases. Rising affluence in North America may produce further improvement in architecture.

3. The rapid succession of various styles of painting and sculpture and experimentation with new materials and techniques is likely to continue. At the same time, more conventional forms will retain their appeal to wider publics even though the avant-garde subcultures will emphasize experimental styles.

4. In music, also, there will be a dichotomy between the experimentation lauded by the avant-garde and the more traditional forms preferred and supported by a wider public.

5. As the level of sophistication of the public rises, ballet may become a more popular art form than it has been in the past.

6. The split between Broadway commercial entertainment theater on the one hand and serious drama on the other is likely to continue. The growing popularity of off-Broadway productions seems to indicate an increase of interest in, if not appreciation of, drama that is more than entertainment.

7. Popular interest in all art forms seems to be increasing. Even so, it is nearly impossible for them to be self-supporting. It seems likely that there will be a trend toward governmental financial support of the performing arts at least.

8. Disillusionment and futility seem to be dominant motifs of contemporary literature, reflecting widespread disenchantment

with the frustrations of a complex technological society and man's loss of a sense of the transcendent.

9. The publishing industries appear to promise continued expansion. Even though there is a decline in the number of metropolitan newspapers, increases have occurred in total newspaper circulation, magazine circulation, and book sales. Such increases may be related to aggressive promotion campaigns and to higher educational levels which make more reading possible for more people.

10. Television is perhaps the most potent as well as the most persuasive of the mass media. It has become a dependable source of daily entertainment for millions and shows some promising signs of becoming a more sophisticated educational device.

11. Motion pictures continue to serve as popular entertainment, and at the same time are becoming an art form in their own right. There will be some continuation of the recent trend toward greater creativity of technique as well as a lessening of restrictions on subjects formerly considered beyond the pale.

12. Advertising will continue to exert powerful influences on the communications media which depend on it for financial support. Its influence, however, will be tempered by audience preferences.

B. Implications

In literature and other art forms the church may be able to perceive the emerging mood of the future. This will certainly be the case if the predictors are right in maintaining that the sensitivity of the artistic temperament expresses feelings that later come to be more widespread. The quest for novelty and the mood of disillusionment which can be observed in much of contemporary art may come to be more diffuse among the populace. The church will be challenged to find ways of expressing the gospel which will effectively communicate this possibly emerging mood. Perhaps, by creating channels of communication with contemporary artists, the church will be able to develop an understanding of their world of thought and to create ways of communicating the essential message of the gospel to it.

As more people become exposed to a rapid succession of forms and styles in art, a tendency toward relativism in all matters, including religion and morality, may accelerate. In the past, the church has tended to present its message in absolutist terms. This strategy may continue to become less appropriate and effective.

New art forms pose a direct challenge to the church in areas such as church architecture, music, liturgy, and symbolism. Traditional forms and symbols will continue to have highly significant meaning for many church members in the next decade. On the other hand, traditional forms and symbols may lose their meaning almost completely for increasingly large elements of the population. The challenge will be to develop new forms of artistic expression which are capable of expressing and communicating the content of the Christian faith. The most promising way of accomplishing this may be to establish continuing dialogue between the artists and the church.

Rising standards of living, educational levels, and levels of artistic sophistication among the total population will reinforce what many churchmen have said for years. In architecture, music, and other art forms used in the church, the goal should be high quality and impatience with mediocrity. At the same time there must be recognition of the limited artistic horizons of many church members and the need to improve their appreciation of good art; otherwise the church will tend to arouse their hostility and thus to alienate them.

Mass media will continue to perform their twofold function of entertainment and education, perhaps with increasing effectiveness. In doing so, they will be influenced by the desires of advertisers and demands of the public. The various media will continue to reflect the values that are dominant in the population and to exercise an influence on the shaping of those values and of American life-styles. The probability is that the media will continue to expose their audiences to aspects of life which were once considered inappropriate for public presentation. This may create greater tolerance for unconventional behavior or may create a reaction against it.

The church can profit by careful use of developing media techniques in the presentation of its message. Indications are that a subtle, soft-sell approach may be more effective than a more direct form of presentation. The church has not yet found fully satisfactory ways of influencing the content of mass media and should continue to search for them. It should be clear, however, that censorship or control is not the aim. Careful analysis of the values presented by media content and form may be a way of discovering less tangible characteristics of the population and finding methods of utilizing the media for the church's purposes.

12

Change and the Individual

I. DOMINANT THEMES

Perhaps the most obvious and noticeable effect of change on the individual will be that brought about by the population explosion. Stated simply, there are going to be vastly more individuals around in the coming decade. Already we are hearing complaints from people who feel that they are being swallowed up in the sheer size of the society in which they live. They see themselves less and less as separate individuals and more and more as part of a crowd. Names become less important—people become known by their bank-account numbers, their social security numbers, their zip codes.

This anonymity has both a positive and a negative side. In *The Secular City* Harvey Cox celebrates the freedom which such anonymity brings. Traditionally, people have escaped into the city in an effort to shake off the bondage of suffocating role-playing which the small society imposes on the individual. In the city of the future, he says, no such role will exist because human beings will be free to relate or not relate to one another according to their own needs and desires, and this is a positive gain.

It is also true, however, that people have escaped into the anonymous crowd as a way of evading and avoiding responsibility. A number of newspaper stories in recent years have recounted almost unbelievable examples of human unwillingness to become involved in the lives of those around them. Such uninvolvement is almost inevitable as society grows larger and thus more anonymous. Cox presupposes an individual of strength and character. The church's traditional ministry to the individual as a supplier of strength and builder of character would seem to be more rather than less necessary in the decade ahead.

An International Culture

Another feature of life in the next decade which will affect the individual is the emergence of what might be called an international culture. Rapid means of communication and an extremely mobile population will result in a growing similarity among people everywhere in their style of dress, their language, and their values. Already this sameness is apparent throughout much of the United States and Canada. Most metropolitan areas are indistinguishable from one another. Styles of architecture are freely borrowed and adapted from one part of the country to the next. Regional accents in speech are slowly disappearing. Styles of clothing tend to be more and more alike from one area to another.

This tendency toward sameness is now becoming apparent throughout the world, and the trend may be expected to continue and perhaps to accelerate in the next decade. Skyscrapers in Tokyo, motels in Beirut, discothèques in Stockholm, mini-skirts and cowboy hats in Bombay give evidence of a kind of world mass-culture which will become more and more unavoidable. This tendency can be expected to produce great pressures on the individual to conform, to lose his individuality in an imitation of a pattern set by a kind of international "Madison Avenue." Again, the church can provide a place in which the individual is truly free to be himself—in which he is transformed, not conformed, to the world.

In part, the problem is political and sociological. For all too many, certain aspects of present-day life have dimmed, if not destroyed, our sense of personal importance. The swift tempo of the times, the magnitude of scientific achievement, the threat of push-button thermonuclear warfare, the clash between free enterprise and big government, with the individual caught innocently but inextricably in the midst, and the distressing pockets of poverty, largely racial, in an economy of plenty, have all contributed to this loss of personal identity and worth.

But the problem is also moral and theological. Already, in some instances, automation makes men seen less important than the machines they tend. To magnify the dilemma, atheistic existentialism has robbed them of assurances that we once believed firmly fixed. Thus, many sincerely believe that they are completely alone, and that the only meaning life holds for them is what they themselves create.

Undoubtedly a major factor in this subtle disorganization of personality is the mass mobility of our people. To tear up roots and start over in the midst of different and often hostile cultures —not once in a lifetime, but again and again and again—does something to a family's standards and sense of stability. It may eventually prove fatal to our ideals to slough off the stabilizing restraints of familiar patterns and launch out into new environments peopled only by strangers for whose opinions we need not care because we will not know them long enough for their judgments to matter. To transport fathers to distant places for three, six, nine months—perhaps a year—to secure the foundations of new jobs while the mothers and children remain behind to face the old anxieties and battle alone the old problems of financing, schooling, and social functions can very easily lead to promiscuity, delinquency, and dull, deadening despair.

Another pressure which the individual is likely to feel increasingly in the next decade relates to human sexuality. Traditionally, the function of marriage in society has been procreation. But as the rate of population growth soars, children become less an asset and more a liability to society. Great pressures will be brought to bear upon married couples to control the number of births. But longer life spans and healthier individuals will increase the sexual urge, so that sexuality will replace procreation as the real purpose and function of marriage. The proportionate number of married people may increase, but the average size of families will remain constant or decrease slightly.

As sexuality replaces birth as the central function of marriage, sexual differentiation will decrease. One tendency in this direction may be seen in the growing number of young couples who dress alike, and in the increasing inability to distinguish between boys and girls. In this context, homosexuality may be expected to become more prevalent.

Expectations and Aspirations

A further factor of change which will affect the individual relates to his expectations and aspirations. As communication becomes easier and quicker, more and more people in every part of the world will become aware of the economic and cultural possibilities within their grasp. This wave of rising expectations across the world could have either a positive or a negative effect. It could help to lift hitherto morose and lethargic peoples out of their indifference and quiet despair and give them new incentive to work for the better future which they now see to be within their reach. Or it could set off another chain of revolutions, as the gap between rich and poor, have and have-not becomes greater and greater, and the possibility of closing the gap becomes less and less. Here again the role of the church seems clear as the conscience of society.

Another factor of change is the emergence of a world-planned economy in which the individual will be more and more locked in and less and less able to rock the boat. On several recent occasions, representatives of the major world banks have met in Switzerland to stave off impending financial disaster. They were not forced to come together, but did so out of mutual self-interest. The pattern of the future seems clear. By such cooperation between the countries of the world, major economic depressions may become a thing of the past. It may become possible by such cooperation to bring income levels up more quickly in some parts of the world, and thus bring about greater equality. Such financial cooperation may even lay the groundwork for a genuine world government in the political, legal, and military sense.

Thus the day of the rugged individualist and the self-made man appears to be over. The individual is more or less locked into a worldwide economy from which he cannot escape. For the same reason, the day when the strike was a useful economic weapon also appears to be going rapidly. It is likely that the next decade will see an economy which is more thoroughly planned and in which labor strife will diminish. This means that the church may once again have to serve as the spokesman for the voiceless masses.

Another factor in the coming decade which will affect the individual quite directly will be the necessity for continuous and life-long education. It is now said that young people graduating from high school should expect to change careers three times in their lifetime. This is a process which is easier for some people than for others. Those who find it difficult to make such sweeping life-adjustments will continue to need the support and understanding of the Christian community. In addition, the church itself will need to re-examine its own educational programs and practices so as to reflect this need for lifelong education. Adult education can be expected to loom larger and larger in importance in the next decade. A related factor of change is the expected increase in the amount of leisure time which will be available to more and more individuals. The church is already studying ways by which it may help people to make creative use of their leisure, and how such changing patterns of living may affect the corporate life of the Christian community.

We may note also the effect which space exploration is likely to have on the individual's understanding of himself and his world. Man has always needed a frontier, a horizon, a goal toward which to work. For most people, such frontiers are largely mythical, as witness the popularity of the cowboy western movie; but such mythology serves a very useful and important function in an individual's estimate of himself as a person. The myth of the frontier helps him to believe that he can break out of the confines of his world if he chooses, even though he seldom does.

The pioneer becomes the prototype—the vicarious hero who inspires a whole generation. The new frontier of escape toward which man can aspire, if only in fantasy, is outer space; and the heroes of the next decade will almost certainly be the space pioneers.

II. LEISURE

Some people in every civilization have always known what it meant to have leisure. The new factor, introduced to our American culture in the last one hundred years, is that a rapidly increasing number of Americans have more free time. Working hours are decreasing, financial income for the majority is increasing; more and more Americans are taking advantage of this affluence by touring the states and provinces, buying second homes, and occupying themselves with hobbies, recreation, and various other interests.

Sebastian de Grazia maintains that modern man doesn't know leisure as Aristotle and the Greeks defined it. Modern man is deeply committed to the use of free time—most of these uses being a far cry (perhaps the direct opposite) from the activities of music and contemplation.

Other have given various definitions: "A quality use of free time." "Leisure time is more like free time than leisure." "Free time is only potentially leisure time and leisure is the growing time of the human spirit." "Leisure is best identified with time rather than an attitude."

Webster defines leisure as free, unoccupied time during which a person may indulge in rest, recreation, and other optional activities. Since popular usage of the term makes no distinction between leisure and free time, these terms are used interchangeably here. When leisure is used in the classical sense, its meaning will be obvious from the context of its usage.

The "leisure revolution" is a revolution in work, time, money, property, the machine, mobility, and space. Less hours on the daily job, and the "economy of abundance" in America are the two keys which unlocked the door to so many changes in the American way of life. In 1850 the average work week in all industries was 69.7 hours. By 1900 it was 60.1; in 1940, 43.8; in 1948, 40.8; and in 1960, 38.5. Low levels of income have risen and the majority of Americans now enjoy the advantages which were once reserved for the few.

Three new factors of the twentieth century have made the leisure revolution what it is today: mass media of communication, geographic mobility, and the recreation establishment. The facts concerning mass media and geographic mobility need not be presented here. A few figures will serve to indicate the extent of the recreation establishment. There are 92 million tourists a year traveling over 40 billion miles—all due to longer weekends, paid vacations, higher income, increased life-span, improved highways, developing facilities, high levels of education, and changing attitudes. From 1951 to 1962 visitors to national and state parks have increased by 240 percent (from 86,000 to 432,000). Recreation is one of the top three income-producers in the economy of 29 states—some 30 billion dollars annually. More money is spent on vacations and recreation than on housing, and twice as much as on automobiles. People spend about 20 percent of their free time in outdoor activity.

A number of surveys and studies reveal what modern man is doing with his time. The Opinion Research Corporation of Princeton lists the ten most frequent activities in free time: television, reading books, pleasure driving, listening to records, going to meetings and organizational activities, visiting with friends, going out to dinner, special hobbies like woodworking and knitting, working around the yard and in the garden, reading magazines.

Not everyone agrees that we have that much free time in comparison to, say, the nineteenth century. De Grazia analyzes the situation, using a rather elaborate system of determining how many hours one works. The full-time worker of today is supposed to have nearly twenty-five hours of free time more than the full-time worker in 1850. Not so, says de Grazia. The factors which affect this hypothetical full-time worker are moonlighting, travel to and from work, do-it-yourself work, and women at work. De Grazia states that the net amount of free time which man gained from 1850 to 1950 is 8.5 hours at the most.

A study quoted by de Grazia indicates that on an average weekday men have 3.6 hours of leisure activities; women have 4.7. On Saturday men have 5.5 and women 5.3 hours. On Sundays the figures are 7.9 for men and 7.1 for women. Leisure activities include visiting at friend's or relative's home; games and sports, as a spectator or participant; other forms of leisure, where one is part of an audience; reading and any other activity at home that is not work (e.g., playing cards, listening to the radio, watching television, talking on the telephone, visiting with guests). A University of Michigan sociologist has stated that leisure time has not increased at all. American men today are spending more time on the job, a lot of it of the moonlighting variety, and their wives are spending even more time taking care of their children and homes. He claims that leisure accounts for about five hours a day, about the same as in the 1930's, and that television now consumes about a third of it.

Patterns of American living have changed significantly in the twentieth century, due primarily to an increase of production which has increased the individual's income; at the same time his working conditions and hours are much improved. Mass media, mobility, interest in recreation and outdoor living have developed tourism as a major industry. The trend indicates a continuing rise in affluence, tourism, and free time. Although free time may not be bountiful when all factors of modern man's living habits are brought into the picture, increased free time and affluence are still major factors to consider in understanding the changes which have taken place in the United States and, to some degree, in Canada. Times have changed—new patterns, new luxuries (for most), more travel, and more time which the individual is free to dispose of as he sees fit.

Let us now turn our attention to the implications such social factors have for the church. That there are implications for theology, and issues to which the church must address itself, is evident. The church is a social institution within society and cannot help but be affected by the current trends. The church has a message to proclaim, both to society and to individuals within society, and its message must be relevant. One writer suggests that the greatest mistake the church can make is to look upon leisure lightly.

Issues Related to Leisure

The ethic of work has been part of our American culture since the days of the Puritans. Work, from the Protestant view, is a vocation. It is the glory of man to labor—to toil on the farm or to contribute his talents and abilities to industry and production. It has been observed that a moral compulsion to work and to get ahead appears to be a characteristic of an efficient industrial system. The essence of this concept of work lingers in our ethics —it is, like most duties, unpleasant. Even today, many people feel guilty when they are not busy *doing* something.

Times are changing. Many feel no satisfaction or sense of vocation in their work. Factors which make work less enjoyable are the elimination of stepping-stone jobs, fragmentation of skills, growth in bureaucracy, and a growing isolation of rank-and-file employees from management.

The church must face this problem of the deterioration of the work-ethic and the rise of the new work-leisure rhythm of society. A balance must be created. If a man has a "calling" for his work he must have a "calling" for leisure. Equal to the creative use of work time is man's need for the creative use of free time.

Many of those who have written on the subject of leisure do not hesitate to give warnings of the danger ahead. "A frightening thing about leisure is that no civilization has ever survived its leisure revolution." "The most dangerous threat hanging over American society is the threat of leisure. Those who have the least preparation for leisure will have the most of it." Use of leisure time reveals the meaningfulness or the pointlessness of life. Leisure may be a challenge or a threat, a hazard or an opportunity. Whether it will be a boring nuisance or an unmatched opportunity will depend on the perspectives and resources we bring to the problem.

The church should have something to say in preparing man for the use of his free time—especially in helping man use some of this time, both in preparation for leisure and in using free time for leisure in the classical sense of the term.

III. CHANGING MORAL VALUES

Authoritarianism in ethics has largely disappeared. A *Time* essay, "Tradition or What Is Left of It" (April 22, 1966), describes the modern addiction to "new brooms" in many, if not all, human interests: work, sex, the lively and the graphic arts, fashion, family, and social customs. Certainty has given way to provisional proposals. In such kaleidoscopic times, codes of morals derived from an authoritarian ethical system have little force.

What has caused this restless panorama of modern life? Some factors are the emergence of an affluent society, a completely this-worldly orientation to life, the holocaust of twentieth-century wars and the threat of world destruction, the population explosion, that mobility of people which is destructive of human rootage, the weakening of family ties, technology with its denigration of the individual, increase of leisure.

This, however, does not preclude the development of an ethical system. There is still an intrinsic need for absolute assurance of values. The survival of organized society depends on the existence of widely-accepted moral standards. We need criteria of goodness by which the actions of individuals and groups can be guided. The ethics of the future will likely develop from an examination of empirical effects of actions and the consequent development of a code of primary values.

Responsibility, the sense of obligation, is a mark of the civilized moral person. The absence of a feeling of responsibility has been the concern of many perceptive critics of society in the recent past. Observation of the modern scene suggests that the lack of responsibility ("I couldn't care less") is disappearing, at least among young people. A corporation president was recently quoted as saying: ". . . business hasn't yet understood what youth is looking for—not higher salaries, fancier split-levels, but the feeling that they're contributing to something bigger . . . it's wonderful that they maintain as much normalcy as they do. They do silly things, sure, but often in connection with issues bigger than their own individual lives: war or peace, death or survival."

Appalled by life as they see it—its regimentation, spiritlessness, hypocrisy, confusion, brutality, materialism—young people move into the slums to help the hopeless, into distant lands to aid the unfortunate, into regions of intolerance to crusade for civil rights. The event which triggered this change in mood was the civil-rights campaign, which was and is a matter of conscience. This explains in large part the movement's impact on the campus generation. Civil rights has offered scope for individual initiative and effectiveness—something our society does not often provide for the young.

This sense of responsibility is evidenced in the clamor for "student power," i.e., freedom of students to express and advocate political and social issues, to play an important role in academic affairs, to redefine education. At a national student conference in November 1965, central importance was given to the definition of a good education. Three essential elements, it was agreed, were relevance to a world of rapid social change, commitment to the value of the individual in the educational process, and a readiness to explore new development opportunities. A significant segment of students are demanding a voice in the shaping of their own education because they believe that exercising this privilege is itself educative.

At the other end of the ethical scale, however, there is an

alarming breakdown in respect for the law, especially among the very young. While some young people give indication of a growing concern for the human situation, others tend to drift into anti-social and illegal attitudes and practices.

Ethics demands that human actions are to be doubly judged: they are to be determined as events in time, and they are to be evaluated for value and dignity. If ethics is to be evaluated by events in time, what is the promise of the future? The issue of *Look* for June 28, 1966, contains an article on "Where the California Game Is Taking Us." Using that state "as a window into the future," the author suggests what the future will be "in human terms." He makes three points: (1) Richness and variety of human behavior will be accepted as a positive value. (2) Relationships among persons will gain new depth and subtlety. (3) Developing the potentialities of each person will become a chief concern.

That viewpoint which saw life in terms of the conventional virtues, such as social respectability, is going, if it has not already disappeared. But other "greater" virtues—qualities of human moral wealth—are visible as possibilities of the future: firmness of individual principle, power of man's vision, involvement with others, and confident assurance. If the church is to challenge the validity of the indictment that the churches have failed to supply moral leadership, it must interpret these ethical values in the context of their relevance in today's changing society.

Problem Areas

Today throughout all of western society there is an emphasis on sex. The revolt against repression has carried the day. Rollo May has written that as sex becomes more machine-like we find a progression from an anesthetic attitude to an antiseptic one. Sexual contact then tends to be avoided. The sexual revolt comes finally back on itself and returns to an ascetic attitude. Homosexual conduct is becoming more common, or at least more overt. Into this freewheeling world has come "the new morality." Situation ethics does not deal only with sexual behavior. Some of its principal proponents, however, give major consideration to sexual morality. Sex mores appear to be cyclic. Since we are now passing through a period of great sexual freedom, the future may see a swing of the pendulum toward greater guidance.

Drug addiction is not a widespread or pervasive problem in western society as are delinquency, crime, and mental illness. Even in the United States, which has more addicts than all of Europe, probably fewer than 60,000 persons are addicted to drugs other than alcohol, as against an estimated five million alcoholics. In recent years there has been an increasing recognition on the part of the medical and legal professions that they have a responsibility to help achieve a more effective program to deal with it.

It is estimated that 85 percent of all known narcotics addicts are males. A study of addiction in New York City revealed that 83 percent of the adolescent users lived in 15 percent of the census tracts. These tracts constituted the poorest, most crowded, and most physically dilapidated areas of the city. Furthermore, within these tracts drug use was highest where income and education were lowest and where there was a greater breakdown of normal family living arrangements. The central feature of the social milieu which produces the typical drug addict is the support it gives to behavior which is generally inconsistent with social norms and hostile to many of its expectations. This orientation is expressed in a variety of ways, but is most clearly and dramatically manifested in delinquency and in the search for an exploitation of "kicks."

A related problem has to do with the growing use of LSD and similar substances. Little is known as yet about the long-term effects of this drug, and few laws exist in regard to its use. Unlike the addictive drugs, LSD appears more attractive to the middle-class dropout from society than to the lower-class rebel against society. The use of marijuana has also grown more widespread, and there is pressure in some circles to legalize its use. While there is little indication that either LSD or marijuana are habit-forming in nature, the case histories of drug addicts indicate that they are sometimes the first step toward addiction. The easy availability of LSD and marijuana greatly increases the difficulty of controlling their use. Further studies must be made to determine to what extent society should make the attempt.

More and more hippies are reported to be hooked on "speed" (Methedrine), an amphetamine so potent it scares even its users. Methedrine is one of several trade names for methamphetamine hydrochloride, one of the amphetamine "pep pills." The drug acts as a stimulant to the central nervous system and has legitimate medical uses—to suppress appetite in persons trying to lose weight, to relieve depression, and to raise blood pressure. But "speed demons" usually take the drug in massive doses, either sniffed or injected into a vein. The result is a "flash," an immediate sensation of overwhelming pleasure. Users talk incessantly and acquire an immense feeling of power. Their behavior often becomes violent and aggressive. After a few days the user begins to experience paranoid delusions. During such psychotic reactions a user may attack a friend. Eventually he becomes so exhausted that he falls into a deep twelve-hour sleep, from which he awakens in a depressed state which drives him to start another run. Deaths from "speed" are apparently rare, but users lose weight and suffer malnutrition. As with LSD and marijuana, one of the most urgent questions about "speed" is its effect on the brain and genetic material.

Various estimates have suggested that the number of alcoholics in the United States ranges between five million and seven million. Alcoholism is sometimes listed as the third most serious illness in the nation. No one can say how many problem drinkers, apart from alcoholics, there may be—those whose lives are seriously disturbed or changed adversely as a consequence of using beverage alcohol. Authorities have suggested, on the basis of specific research projects, that there are from one to four problem drinkers in the country for every alcoholic.

The impact of alcohol consumption on the population goes

much further. The drinker's problems inevitably become in some way those of his family, friends, or employer—or a doctor, a clergyman, a psychiatrist, a social worker, an A.A. member, or a law enforcement officer.

Progress in treatment and rehabilitation has been made through various hospitals, clinics, and community programs. It should be emphasized that, for the first time in United States history, the President dealt explicity with alcoholism in his health message to Congress in 1966. A National Center for Prevention and Control of Alcoholism was established within the National Institute of Mental Health. Alcoholics are persons in need of diagnosis, understanding, guidance, and treatment. The churches share a pastoral concern for alcoholics, problem drinkers, and their families. We recognize that once drinking has passed a certain point it becomes alcoholism, an affliction which cannot be met effectively by the unaided efforts of the victims.

The complex origins of alcoholism and excessive drinking lie in social pressures, emotional instability, bodily functioning, and the nature of alcohol itself. Alcoholism is an affliction which requires treatment. The ethical aspects of the use of alcoholic beverages should be of deep concern to the church and the community as they seek to help the victims of alcoholism.

Although opinions differ about the validity of crime statistics, there is reason to believe that a marked increase of crime is occurring among teen-agers and those in their early twenties. It has been estimated that 20 percent of the population will have been arrested for some crime other than traffic offenses. Such estimates suggest that a crisis in morality is in the making.

Every year in the past decade has seen a rise in the number of individual crimes at a rate faster than the rise in America's population. There has been an especially rapid rise in crimes against property. Two striking facts that the United States Crime Commission reports and every other examination of American crime discloses are that most crimes are committed in cities. The two trends are not separate. They are entangled in many ways, and both are related to another trend—increasing affluence, which is also intimately associated with crime. An abundance of material goods and a scarcity of income with which to buy them provide both motive and opportunity for stealing, and stealing is the fastest growing kind of crime.

What appears to be happening is that parental and social authority over young people is becoming weaker. A young man in the city tends to be invisible. He is not subjected to the same scrutiny as the young man in the country or small town, and therefore feels little restraint on his activities. The slums have always been breeders of crimes. What makes today's slums so menacing is their inescapability. It is with such young people and slum dwellers who have been embittered by painful social and economic pressures that justice must deal.

Critical factors in the war on crime, aside from the alleviation of the social conditions in which it breeds, are public apathy, organized crime, and undermanned, underpaid, undertrained police forces. Local police forces need more government help than they are getting. But public attitudes will determine whether the war on crime is won or lost. A related problem on which action is long overdue is the regulation and control of the sale and use of firearms. There are many indications of a relationship between the easy access to guns and crime rates, but effective legislation is still not forthcoming.

But perhaps the most disturbing aspect of crime in the United States is organized crime. That crime is a well-organized and highly-profitable business has been known at least since the 1930's. What is relatively new, however, is the infiltration of the criminal syndicates into established businesses, so that it is no longer possible to know where respectable business ends, and well-disguised criminal fronts begin. The remedy is greater public awareness of the many manifestations of the problem, more intensive investigatory efforts, and more effective approaches to apprehending and prosecuting those engaged in large-scale organized crime.

Problems of a Complex Society

While the power of large corporations can be described statistically, it cannot be understood readily. There are more employees of General Motors than the combined personnel of the state goverenments of New York, Pennsylvania, Ohio, Texas, California, and Illinois. The tax collections of these six states plus those of Wisconsin, Connecticut, and Massachuetts do not equal the annual sales of Standard Oil of New Jersey.

The enormous size of corporations poses ethical problems also of colossal size. Three propositions of general validity have been stated to be: (1) The degree of moral complexity is becoming greater all the time. (2) Public interest decisions are always made by a complex process of multilateral communication among executives. (3) The problem for the individual executive is almost never to decide what is right but to choose between good or evil solutions or both at the same time. While these problems occur in other sectors of society, the nature of the corporation perhaps intensifies them.

Thus it becomes necessary to give attention to the power of large business to direct life and, therefore, morals. Even while rates of saving were higher than normal in 1967, evidence points to a loss of influence among the young of the older "work-and-save" ethic. High-pressure promotion of installment buying and seductive advertising of nonessential items undoubtedly contribute to the trend.

The ethic of spend and waste not only affects the consumer in his personal life, but also in the destruction of natural resources. The pursuit of wasteful practices has brought ruin in many areas: the pollution of air and water, the deforestation of timber tracts, the erosion of arable land. The abuse of nature testifies not only to a lamentable lack of foresight and to a wanton gambling with irreplaceable values, but also to a staggering lack of morality.

Technology looms large in its effect on ethical values. It sometimes creates jobs with assembly-line meaninglessness. Technology threatens the security a worker once found in the mastery of a trade. It is a truism that no American can now hope to settle down to a lifetime occupation. Young people entering the job market can expect to change work two or three times during their lives. "Education and adaptability" are the keys to success. Technology has ushered in a time of rapidly-increasing leisure for which the individual has had little preparation in using his free time creatively. Perhaps most important is the threatened obsolescence of the individual. The "organization man" is possibly a picture too general for truth. Yet corporations mold their white-collar workers—a class rapidly becoming the largest part of American society—in habits and style of life, in determining values and aspirations.

It must be said that business leaders are moving toward a greater interest in social responsibility. In 1966 the *New York Times* asked fifty-two leading executives to express their ideas on the vast technological advances, the new economics, the expanding role of government, and the campus revolt. While comments differed widely, many expressed the opinion that social responsibility of a business organization is inseparable from its response to the kind of world in which we live. Today's institutions cannot exist without reacting constructively to the goals of society and to current economic, technological, social, and political forces.

The expansion of government brings to bear upon the individual the power and direction of the state in myriad ways. On the one hand impends the stifling of individual effort and a flight from personal responsibility. On the other, in so complex a world, government must carry on projects of social welfare. Some way must be found to balance governmental care and individual responsibility. A current issue is the right of public employees to strike. Calvin Coolidge's statement in 1919: "There is no right to strike against the public safety by anybody, anywhere, anytime," is still fondly remembered. Recent events, however, indicate a strong trend in the opposite direction. There have been strikes by transit workers, public-health doctors, dentists, clinic nurses, and teachers.

Change and the Individual

The first ten amendments to the United States Constitution emphasize the individual's right to privacy: no establishment of religion, no indiscriminate quartering of soldiers, no unreasonable search or seizure. The maintainance of a secret dossier on an individual was once considered to be an activity of absolutism. Today serious study is given to the establishment of a national data center consolidating computerized information on millions of Americans from information scattered through official files. While such a center would have duplication and wasted effort, there are suspicions that a potential "Big Brother" could make use of a dossier bank for his own purposes. In the invasion of privacy, government has also played a passive role. Electronic eavesdropping has become a multi-million dollar industry. Wiretapping and "bugging" overtly or covertly are used by governmental agencies on the grounds of law enforcement. The guilt lies largely in the fact that there is no legal protection for the individual from private snoopers—employers, suspicious spouses, union officials, business competitors.

This problem is also related to the current explosive debates about the ethics of social and psychological research. The methods requisite to such research involve inquiry that may infringe on individual privacy, and studies that manipulate the subject directly, deceiving him about the real consequences of what he is doing in the experiment. The dangers may be moderated by integrity of scientific purpose, provision for consent, and the handling of data in a way that preserves anonymity of the individual. We might consider the development of institutions designed to insure private moments, possibly similar to the religious retreat, in otherwise unprivate lives.

In two professions, moral questions loom particularly large: law and medicine. The lawyer is an advocate, not for himself but for others in their legal actions. He is a partisan, but his professional responsibility demands he go further. Lawyers would certainly subscribe without reservation to the statement that they individually and the legal profession collectively are especially charged with reworking and refining the content of the law in order that as human demands collide, the resolutions of conflict are morally defensible.

The American Bar Association in 1908 adopted "Canons of Ethics" which still is supposed to be regulative. Canon 5 requires a defense lawyer to use "all fair and honorable means." This raises ethical questions such as: Is it proper to cross-examine in order to discredit an adverse witness whom you know to be telling the truth? Is it proper to put a witness on the stand when you know he will commit perjury? Is it proper to give your client advice when you believe that the knowledge may tempt him to commit perjury? Since our government is one of laws, not of men, the ethics of the legal profession is of paramount concern to everyone.

The relationship of the individual with his doctor is likely to be more intimate than any outside of his family. Patients expect not only medical care, but comfort, sympathy, relief, reassurance, and solace. They get far better medical care than ever before; yet the patient often feels that the physician is not interested in him as a person. When there is no personal relationship, anxiety becomes a burden. The profession is more and more realizing this problem. The ethicist must give aid as well.

Has the physician the right to "play God"? That question can be asked particularly as human life begins and as it comes to a close. It seems possible that genes may soon be manipulated—"turning off" defective ones and replacing them with others. This could happily prevent a multitude of birth defects. A question of vast ethical import therefore arises: Has man a God-given duty—or right—to consciously direct man's evolution in correcting human genetic errors? Dr. Leroy Augenstein, chairman of the biophysics department at Michigan State University, has been instrumental in emphasizing the place of ethical decisions in the field of genetic manipulation. He insists there are two crucial questions we must face. Why is man here on earth? Should society establish rules to guide genetic manipulation?

At the other end of the span of life, the physician must answer the question "How long should life be prolonged?" Even after the electro-encephalogram has indicated there is no electric activity in the brain and therefore no real hope of recovery, life or the simulation of life can be continued as the patient lies in a deep coma. When should artificial aids be discontinued and the patient pronounced dead? To what extent should the survivors expend time and money on a hopeless case? Is it right that other patients with expectation of recovery be deprived of the machines which feed a semblance of life into the hopeless? Is it ethical to recognize the fact of death early enough so that vital organs may be removed from the cadaver for transplant?

IV. SUMMARY AND IMPLICATIONS

A. Summary

1. There will be a decrease in the sense of individuality and an increase in the sense of anonymity.

2. The emergence of mass culture will increase the pressures for conformity.

3. Sex differentiation will tend to decrease, and the incidence of homosexuality will increase.

4. The revolution of rising expectations will produce both great hopefulness and great despair among the underprivileged of the world.

5. Self-reliance and rugged individualism will tend to be seen less as virtues and more as obstacles to a world-planned society.

6. Continually expanding horizons will produce the need for continuous lifelong education and for vocational flexibility.

7. There is reason to believe that increases in free time and personal income will continue to contribute to a leisure revolution.

8. A major effect of current social change on the individual lies in shifts in moral values.

B. Implications

The church, by providing models for expression of Christian faith and life, has in almost every age assisted persons to develop a sense of the meaning and significance of their lives within the existing social context. Anticipated social changes, most of which have already begun, suggest that this function may become more crucial as the rate and extent of change in the social context increases. To fulfill this function may well require a high degree of creativity, because of both increased differentiation within the population and increasing consciousness of incongruities between the dominant worldview and traditional expressions of Christian faith and life. Within this framework, specific areas which might receive attention are: personal freedom and responsibility; preservation of individuality within highly complex political, economic, and social units; the nature and expression of human sexuality; tensions caused by discrepancies between aspirations and achievements; changing roles and values of work and education; the potential effect of space explorations and scientific accomplishments on man's understanding of himself and his world.

Participation of larger numbers of people in various leisure-time activities suggests that the church explore ways of ministering creatively to persons who spend leisure time at resorts and those who spend leisure time at home. Growth of free time and economic affluence points toward a need for re-examining the traditional North American work ethic. Increased leisure means increased scope for responsible decisions about how to use free time; the church should help its constituents become aware of the issue and its implications.

Patterns of behavior and moral values have been influenced and will continue to be influenced by myriad changes in the social environment. Opinions differ about the desirable and undesirable results of the changes that are taking place. The situation may account, at least in part, for the many attempts that have been made in recent years to develop new conceptual frameworks in the field of Christian ethics. It is likely that continuation of such efforts will be required. The church has become aware that many cases of antisocial behavior are dysfunctional and self-defeating efforts to cope with a difficult environment, rather than courses of action that have been consciously thought out and executed. This is not to deny the reality of evil nor to identify its ultimate source. Another dimension of the ethical problem which is likely to become increasingly significant is the magnitude and complexity of ethical problems in a complex society made up of large organizations.

Selected Bibliography

CHAPTER ONE. THE NATURE OF SOCIAL CHANGE

Allen, Francis R. *et al. Technology and Social Change.* New York: Appleton-Century-Crofts, 1957.

Allen, Frederick Lewis. *The Big Change. America Transforms Itself, 1900-1950.* New York: Harper & Row, 1952.

Barnett, H. G. *Innovation: The Basis of Cultural Change.* New York: McGraw-Hill, 1953.

Boulding, Kenneth E. *The Meaning of the Twentieth Century.* New York: Harper & Row, 1964.

Brooks, John. *The Great Leap. The Past Twenty-Five Years in America.* New York: Harper & Row, 1966.

Brown, Harrison. *The Challenge of Man's Future.* New York: Viking Press, 1954.

Commager, Henry Steele. *The American Mind.* New Haven: Yale University Press, 1950.

Drucker, Peter F. *Landmarks of Tomorrow.* New York: Harper & Row, 1959.

Eiseley, Loren. *The Firmament of Time.* New York: Atheneum Publishers, 1960.

Ginzberg, Eli (ed.). *Technology and Social Change.* New York: Columbia University Press, 1964.

Gross, Bertram M. (ed.) *Social Indicators and Goals for American Society.* Volumes I, II. *Annals of the American Academy of Political and Social Science,* May and September, 1967.

Harrington, Michael. *The Accidental Century.* New York: Macmillan, 1965.

Heilbroner, Robert L. *The Future as History.* New York: Harper & Row, 1960.

Helmer, Olaf. *Social Technology.* New York: Basic Books, 1967.

Holton, Gerald (ed.). *Science and Culture.* Boston: Houghton Mifflin, 1965.

Kahn, Herman. *The Next Thirty-Three Years.* New York: Mc-Graw-Hill, 1967.

Mack, Raymond W. *Transforming America: Patterns of Social Change.* New York: Random House, 1967.

McCleeland, David C. *The Achieving Society.* Princeton, New Jersey: Van Nostrand, 1961.

Mead, Margaret. *And Keep Your Powder Dry.* (paperback) New York: Morrow, 1965.

Michael, Donald L. *The Next Generation.* New York: Random House, 1965.

Munby, D. L. *The Idea of a Secular Society.* New York: Oxford University Press, 1963.

Platt, John R. *The Step to Man.* New York: Wiley, 1966.

Potter, David M. *People of Plenty: Economic Abundance and the American Character.* Chicago: University of Chicago Press, 1954.

Rockefeller Panel Reports. *Prospect for America.* New York: Doubleday, 1961.

Rose, Arnold M. *The Power Structure. Political Process in American Society.* New York: Oxford University Press, 1966.

Schlesinger, Arthur M. *Paths to the Present.* Boston: Houghton Mifflin, 1964.

Toynbee, Arnold J. *Change and Habit. Challenge to Our Time.* New York: Oxford University Press, 1966.

Warren, Roland L. *The Community in America.* Chicago: Rand-McNally, 1963.

Williams, Robin M. Jr. *American Society: A Sociological Interpretation.* (2nd ed.). Revised. New York: Knopf, 1960.

CHAPTER TWO. THE WORLD SETTING

Blum, Robert (ed.). *Cultural Affairs and Foreign Relations.* Englewood Cliffs, New Jersey: Prentice-Hall, 1963.

Hauser, Philip M. (ed.). *The Population Dilemma.* Englewood Cliffs, New Jersey: Prentice-Hall, 1963.

Hoffman, Paul G. *World Without Want*. New York: Harper & Row, 1962.

Population Reference Bureau, Inc. *Population Bulletin*. Published bimonthly.

Ross, Alf. *The United Nations: Peace and Progress*. Totowa, New Jersey: Bedminster Press, 1966.

Sellin, Thorsten (ed.). *American Civilization: Its Influence on Our Foreign Policy. Annals of the American Academy of Political and Social Science*. July, 1966.

Shulman, Marshall D. Beyond the Cold War. New Haven: Yale University Press, 1966.

Staley, Eugene. *The Future of the Underdeveloped Countries*. New York: Harper & Row, 1961.

Stebbins, Richard P. (ed.). *The United States in World Affairs*. New York: Harper & Row for the Council on Foreign Relations, 1966.

Tinbergen, Jan. *Shaping the World Economy: Suggestions for an International Economic Policy*. New York: Twentieth Century Fund, 1962.

CHAPTER THREE. THE NORTH AMERICAN SETTING

Bass, Sam Warner (ed.). *Planning for a Nation of Cities*. Cambridge, Mass.: M.I.T. Press, 1967

Copp, James H. (ed.). *Our Changing Rural Society: Perspectives and Trends*. Ames, Iowa: Iowa State University Press, 1964.

Darling, F. Fraser and Milton, John P. (eds.). *Future Environments of North America*. Garden City: Natural History Press, 1966.

Davis, Kingsley. *The Modern Urban Revolution*. New York: Random House, 1966.

Ewald, William R. (ed.). *Environment for Man: The Next Fifty Years*. Bloomington, Indiana: Indiana University Press, 1967.

Graubard, Stephen R. (ed.). *The Negro American. Daedalus*, Fall, 1965.

Holland, Lawrence B. (ed.). *Who Designs America?* New York: Anchor Books, 1966.

Lecht, Leonard. *Goals, Priorities and Dollars.* New York: Free Press, 1966.

Merton, Robert K. and Nisbet, Robert A. *Contemporary Social Problems.* (2nd ed.). New York: Harcourt, 1966.

Pell, Claiborne. *Megalopolis Unbound.* New York: Praeger, 1966.

Spreiregen, Paul D. (ed.). *The Modern Metropolis.* Cambridge, Mass.: M.I.T. Press, 1967.

Tunnard, Christopher and Pushkarev, Boris. *Man-Made America: Chaos or Control.* New Haven: Yale University Press, 1963.

United States Advisory Council on Public Welfare. *Having the Power, We Have the Duty.* Washington: U.S. Government Printing Office, 1966.

United States Bureau of Census. *Population Estimates* (Current Population Reports, Series P-25).

United States President's Commission on Law Enforcement and Administration of Justice. *The Challenge of Crime in a Free Society.* Washington: U.S. Government Printing Office, 1967.

United States President's Commission on National Goals. *Goals for Americans.* Englewood Cliffs, New Jersey: Prentice-Hall, 1960.

Wattenberg, Benjamin and Scammon, Richard M. *This U.S.A.* New York: Doubleday, 1965.

CHAPTER FOUR. GOVERNMENT AND POLITICS

Burns, James M. *The Deadlock of Democracy.* Englewood Cliffs, New Jersey: Prentice-Hall, 1963.

Cater, Douglas. *Power in Washington.* New York: Random House, 1964.

Katz, Wilbur G. *Religion and the American Constitution.* Evanston, Ill.: Northwestern University Press, 1963.

Myrdal, Gunnar. *Beyond the Welfare State.* New Haven: Yale University Press, 1960.

Rossiter, Clinton. *Parties and Politics in America.* New York: Signet Books, 1960.

Sellin, Thorsten (ed.). *Intergovernmental Relations in the United States. Annals of the American Academy of Political and Social Science,* May, 1965.

Truman, David B. (ed.). *The Congress and America's Future.* Englewood Cliffs, New Jersey: Prentice-Hall, 1965.

United States Department of Housing and Urban Development. *Metropolitan Americans: Challenge to Federalism.* Washington: U.S. Government Printing Office, 1967.

CHAPTER FIVE. ECONOMIC TRENDS

Almon, Clopper. *The American Economy to 1975.* New York: Harper, 1967.

Burns, Arthur F. *The Management of Prosperity.* New York: Columbia University Press, 1966.

Denison, Edward F. *The Sources of Economic Growth in the United States and the Alternatives Before Us.* New York: Committee for Economic Development, 1962.

Diebold, John. *Beyond Automation.* New York: McGraw-Hill, 1964.

Dunlop, John T. *Automation and Technological Change.* (paperback) Englewood Cliffs, New Jersey: Prentice-Hall, 1962.

Friedman, Milton. *Essays in Positive Economics.* Chicago: University of Chicago Press, 1966.

Heilbroner, Robert L. *The Limits of American Capitalism.* New York: Harper & Row, 1966.

National Industrial Conference Board. *Economic Potentials of the United States in the Next Decade.* New York: National Industrial Conference Board, 1965.

Silberman, Charles E. *The Myths of Automation.* New York: Harper & Row, 1966.

Simon, Herbert. *The Shape of Automation for Men and Management.* (paperback) New York: Harper, 1965.

Slichter, Sumner H. *Economic Growth in the United States.* New York: Collier, 1963.

Theobold, Robert (ed.). *The Guaranteed Income.* New York: Doubleday, 1966.

United States National Commission on Technology, Automation, and Economic Progress. *Technology and the American Economy.* Washington: U.S. Government Printing Office, 1966.

CHAPTER SIX. NATURAL SCIENCE

Asimov, Isaac. *The New Intelligent Man's Guide to Science.* New York: Basic Books, 1965.

Dubos, René J. *Man Adapting.* New Haven, Conn.: Yale University Press, 1965.

Eddington, Arthur. *The Nature of the Physical World.* (paperback) Ann Arbor, Mich.: University of Michigan Press, 1958.

Glass, Bentley. *Science and Ethical Values.* Chapel Hill: University of North Carolina, 1965.

Hoyle, Fred. *Astronomy.* New York: Doubleday, 1962.

Margenau, Henry. *Ethics and Science.* New York: Van Nostrand, 1964.

Piel, Gerard. *Science in the Cause of Man.* (2nd ed.). New York: Random House, 1961.

Shapley, Harlow. *View from a Distant Star.* New York: Basic Books, 1963.

————, *et al. The New Treasury of Science.* New York: Harper & Row, 1965.

Taylor, Gordon R. *The Science of Life.* New York: McGraw-Hill, 1963.

Whipple, Fred L. *Earth, Moon, and Planets.* Revised. Cambridge: Harvard University Press, 1963.

Wiesner, Jerome. *Where Science and Politics Meet.* New York: McGraw-Hill, 1965.

Social Change

CHAPTER SEVEN. HEALTH AND MEDICINE

Discussions of current developments in the field of health and medicine appear chiefly in either technical journals which are difficult for the reader to secure or in publications directed to the popular market, which provide less information than is given in the text of Chapter 7. There is little point in listing publications of either variety here.

CHAPTER EIGHT. EDUCATION

Beauchamp, George A. *The Curriculum of the Elementary School.* Boston: Allyn & Bacon, 1964.

Bower, E. M. and Hollister, W. G. *Behavioral Science Frontiers in Education.* New York: Wiley, 1966.

Brickman, William W. and Lehrer, Stanley (eds.). *Automation, Education and Human Values.* New York: School & Society Books, 1966.

Bruner, Jerome S. *The Process of Education.* Cambridge, Mass.: Harvard University Press, 1960.

Clark, L. H., Klein, Raymond L., and Burks, John E. *The American Secondary School Curriculum.* New York: Macmillan, 1965.

Dropkin, Stan, Full, Harold, and Schwartz, Ernest (eds.). *Contemporary American Education.* New York: Macmillan, 1965.

Eddy, Elizabeth. *Walk the White Line: A Profile of Urban Education.* New York: Doubleday, 1966.

Elam, Stanley (ed.). *Education and the Structure of Knowledge.* Chicago: Rand McNally, 1964.

Frazier, Alexander (ed.). *New Insights and the Curriculum. Yearbook 1963.* Washington, D.C.: Association for Supervision and Curriculum Development, 1963.

Goodlad, John I. (ed.). *The Changing American School. Sixty-fifth Yearbook of the National Society for the Study of Education, Part II.* Chicago: University of Chicago Press, 1966.

————. *The Changing School Curriculum.* New York: Fund for the Advancement of Education, 1966.

Henry, Nelson B. (ed.). *Social Forces Influencing American Education. Sixtieth Yearbook of the National Society for the Study of Education, Part II.* Chicago: University of Chicago Press, 1961.

Hilgard, Ernest R. (ed.). *Theories of Learning and Instruction. Sixty-third Yearbook of the National Society for the Study of Education, Part I.* Chicago: University of Chicago Press, 1964.

Inlow, Gail M. *The Emergent in Curriculum.* New York: Wiley, 1966.

Kimball, Solon T. and McClellan, James E., Jr. *Education and the New America.* New York: Random House, 1962.

Klotsche, J. M. *The Urban University and the Future of Our Cities.* New York: Harper & Row, 1966.

Mead, Margaret. *The School in American Culture.* Cambridge, Mass.: Harvard University Press, 1951.

Miller, Richard I. *Education in a Changing Society.* Washington, D.C.: National Education Association Project on Instruction, 1963.

Morison, Robert S. (ed.). *The Contemporary University: U.S.A.* Boston: Houghton Mifflin, 1966.

Riesman, David. *Constraint and Variety in American Education.* New York: Doubleday, 1958.

Tiedt, Sidney W. *The Role of the Federal Government in Education.* New York: Oxford University Press, 1966.

United States Bureau of the Census. *Population Estimates* (Series P-25, No. 365) "Revised Projections of School and College Enrollment in the United States to 1985" (May 5, 1967).

United States Office of Education. *Projections of Educational Statistics to 1974-75.* Washington, D.C.: U.S. Government Printing Office, 1965.

Unruh, Glenys G. (ed.). *New Curriculum Developments.* Washington, D.C.: Association for Supervision and Curriculum Development, 1965.

Wilson, Logan (ed.). *Emerging Patterns in American Higher Education.* Washington, D.C.: American Council on Education, 1965.

CHAPTER NINE. RELIGIOUS INSTITUTIONS

Berger, Peter. *The Noise of Solemn Assemblies.* New York: Doubleday, 1962.

Crysdale, Stewart. *The Changing Church in Canada.* Toronto: United Church of Canada, 1965.

Glock, Charles Y. and Stark, Rodney. *Religion and Society in Tension.* Chicago: Rand McNally, 1965.

Graubard, Stephen J. (ed.). *Religion in America, Daedalus,* Winter, 1967.

Gustafson, James. *Treasure in Earthen Vessels.* New York: Harper & Row, 1961.

Heberg, Will. *Protestant-Catholic-Jew.* New York: Doubleday, 1960.

Lenski, Gerhard. *The Religious Factor.* New York: Doubleday, 1961.

Marty, Martin E. and Lee, Robert (eds.). *Religion and Social Conflict.* New York: Oxford University Press, 1964.

Moberg, David. *The Church as a Social Institution.* Englewood Cliffs, New Jersey: Prentice-Hall, 1962.

Niebuhr, H. Richard. *The Social Sources of Denominationalism.* New York: Holt, 1929.

Nottingham, Elizabeth. *Religion and Society.* (paperback) New York: Random House, 1954.

Smith, James Ward and Jamison, A. Leland (eds.). *Religious Perspectives in American Culture.* Princeton, New Jersey: Princeton University Press, 1961.

Thomas, John L. *Religion and the American People.* Westminster, Maryland: Newman Press, 1963.

Winter, Gibson. *The Suburban Captivity of the Churches.* New York: Doubleday, 1961.

Yinger, J. Milton. *Sociology Looks at Religion*. New York: Macmillan, 1963.

CHAPTER TEN. THE AMERICAN FAMILY

Bell, Norman W. and Vogel, Ezra F. (eds.). *A Modern Introduction to the Family*. New York: Free Press, 1960.

Bossard, James H. S. and Boll, Eleanor S. *Sociology of Child Development*. Revised. New York: Harper & Row, 1960.

Coleman, James S. *The Adolescent Society*. New York: Free Press, 1961.

Coser, Rose L. (ed.). *The Family: Its Structure and Function*. (paperback) New York: St. Martins Press, 1964.

Cummings, Elaine and Williams, E. Henry. *Growing Old, the Process of Disengagement*. New York: Basic Books, 1961.

Denton, Wallace. *What's Happening to Our Families?* Philadelphia: Westminster, 1963.

Duvall, Evelyn. *Family Development*. Philadelphia: Lippincott, 1964.

Erickson, Erik (ed.). *Youth: Change and Challenge*. New York: Basic Books, 1963.

Ginzberg, Eli *et al. Life Styles of Educated Women*. New York: Columbia University Press, 1966.

Glick, Paul C. *American Families*. New York: Wiley, 1957.

Goode, William J. *The Family*. Englewood Cliffs, New Jersey: Prentice-Hall, 1964.

Keniston, Keith. *The Uncommitted: Alienated Youth in American Society*. New York: Harcourt, Brace & World, 1965.

Lifton, Robert J. (ed.). *The Woman in America*. Boston: Houghton Mifflin, 1965.

Ogburn, W. F. and Nimkoff, M. F. *Technology and the Changing Family*. Cambridge, Mass.: Riverside Press, 1955.

Tibbets, Clark and Donahue, Wilma. *Aging in Today's Society*. Englewood Cliffs, New Jersey: Prentice-Hall, 1960.

United States President's Commission on the Status of Women. *American Women.* Washington: U.S. Government Printing Office, 1963.

Wynn, John C. (ed.). *Sex, Family, and Society.* New York: Association Press, 1966.

CHAPTER ELEVEN.
ART, LITERATURE, MASS COMMUNICATION

Colby, Vineta (ed.). *American Culture in the Sixties.* New York: H. W. Wilson, 1964.

Emery, Edwin *et al. Introduction to Mass Communications.* New York: Mead Dodd, 1965.

Hall, S. and Whannel, P. *The Popular Arts.* New York: Pantheon Books, 1965.

Jacobs, Norman (ed.). *Culture for the Millions.* Princeton: Van Nostrand, 1961.

Kazin, Alfred. *Contemporaries.* Boston: Little, Brown, 1962.

Kepes, Gyorgy (ed.). *The Visual Arts Today.* Middletown, Conn.: Wesleyan University Press, 1960.

Kostelanetz, Richard (ed.). *The New American Arts.* New York: Horizon Press, 1965.

Kronenberg, Louis. *The American Theater.* New York: Doubleday, 1960.

Lowenthal, Leo. *Literature, Popular Culture, and Society.* Englewood Cliffs, New Jersey: Spectrum Books, 1961.

Neumeyer, Alfred. *The Search for Meaning in Modern Art.* Englewood Cliffs, New Jersey: Prentice-Hall, 1965.

Peckham, Morse. *Man's Rage for Chaos: Biology, Behavior and the Arts.* Philadelphia: Chilton, 1965.

Peterson, Theodore *et al. The Mass Media and Modern Society.* New York: Holt, Rinehart & Winston, 1965.

Roper Research Associates. *Emerging Profile of Television and Other Mass Media: Public Attitudes 1959-1967.* New York: Television Information Office, 1967.

Rosenberg, Bernard and White, David M. *Mass Culture, the Popular Arts in America*. New York: Free Press of Glencoe, 1957.

Skornia, Harry J. *Television and Society*. New York: McGraw-Hill, 1965.

Ulanov, B. *The Two Worlds of American Art*. New York: Macmillan, 1965.

CHAPTER TWELVE. CHANGE AND THE INDIVIDUAL

Angell, Robert C. *Free Society and Moral Crisis*. Ann Arbor: University of Michigan Press, 1965.

Charlesworth, James C. (ed.). *Leisure in America*. Monograph 4. American Academy of Political and Social Science, April, 1964.

Childs, Marquis and Cater, Douglas. *Ethics in a Business Society*. New York: Harper, 1954.

Cleveland, Harlan and Lasswell, Harold D. *Ethics and Bigness: Scientific, Academic, Religious, Political, and Military*. New York: Harper, 1962.

De Grazia, Sebastian. *Of Time, Work, and Leisure*. New York: Doubleday, 1964.

De Vries, Egbert. *Man in Rapid Social Change*. New York: Doubleday, 1961.

———— (ed.). *Man in Community*. New York: Association Press, 1966.

Faris, Robert E. L. and Dunham, H. Warren. *Mental Disorders in Urban Areas*. (paperback) Chicago: University of Chicago Press, 1965.

Gardner, John W. *Self-Renewal: The Individual and the Innovative Society*. New York: Harper & Row, 1963.

Johnston, Edgar G. (ed.). *Preserving Human Values in an Age of Technology*. Detroit: Wayne State University Press, 1961.

Larrabee, Eric and Meyersohn, Rolf (eds.). *Mass Leisure*. New York: Free Press, 1958.

Merton, Robert K. and Nisbet, Robert A. *Contemporary Social Problems*. New York: Harcourt, 1966.

Moskin, J. Robert. *Morality in America*. New York: Random House, 1966.

Newcourt, Theodore. *Personality and Social Change*. New York: Holt, Rinehart & Winston, 1957.

Rees, John R. and LeShan, Lawrence. *The Health of the Mind*. New York: Norton, 1951.

Sellin, Thorsten (ed.). *Ethics in America. Annals of the American Academy of Political and Social Science*. January, 1966.

Selye, Hans. *The Stress of Life*. New York: McGraw-Hill, 1956.

Stein, Maurice, Vidich, Arthur J., and White, David M. (eds.). *Identity and Anxiety*. New York: Free Press, 1960.

Tournier, Paul. *Whole Person in a Broken World*. New York: Harper & Row, 1964.